Laboratory Animals in Research and Teaching

Laboratory Animals in Research and Teaching

ETHICS, CARE, *and* METHODS

EDITED BY

Chana K. Akins
Sangeeta Panicker
Christopher L. Cunningham

American Psychological Association • Washington, DC

Published by
American Psychological Association
750 First Street, NE
Washington, DC 20002
www.apa.org

To order
APA Order Department
P.O. Box 92984
Washington, DC 20090-2984
Tel: (800) 374-2721; Direct: (202) 336-5510
Fax: (202) 336-5502; TDD/TTY: (202) 336-6123
Online: www.apa.org/books/
E-mail: order@apa.org

In the U.K., Europe, Africa, and the Middle East, copies may be ordered from
American Psychological Association
3 Henrietta Street
Covent Garden, London
WC2E 8LU England

Typeset in Goudy by Stephen McDougal, Mechanicsville, MD

Printer: United Book Press, Inc., Baltimore, MD
Cover Designer: Berg Design, Albany, NY
Technical/Production Editor: Tiffany Klaff

The opinions and statements published are the responsibility of the authors, and such opinions and statements do not necessarily represent the policies of the American Psychological Association.

Library of Congress Cataloging-in-Publication Data

Laboratory animals in research and teaching : ethics, care, and methods / edited by Chana K. Akins, Sangeeta Panicker, and Christopher L. Cunningham.—1st ed.
     p. cm.
  Includes bibliographical references and index.
  ISBN 1-59147-145-1
  1. Laboratory animals. 2. Laboratory animals—Behavior. 3. Animal welfare.
4. Animal experimentation. I. Akins, Chana K. II. Panicker, Sangeeta.
III. Cunningham, Christopher L.

  SF406.L36 2004
  636.088'5—dc22   2004003218

British Library Cataloguing-in-Publication Data
A CIP record is available from the British Library.

Printed in the United States of America
First Edition

CONTENTS

CONTRIBUTORS

Chana K. Akins, PhD, Department of Psychology, University of Kentucky, Lexington

Nancy A. Ator, PhD, Department of Behavioral Biology, Johns Hopkins University School of Medicine, Baltimore, MD

Christopher L. Cunningham, PhD, Department of Behavioral Neuroscience, School of Medicine, Oregon Health & Science University, Portland

Nancy K. Dess, PhD, Department of Psychology, Occidental College, Los Angeles, CA

David A. Eckerman, PhD, Department of Psychology, University of North Carolina at Chapel Hill

Richard W. Foltin, PhD, Department of Psychiatry, College of Physicians and Surgeons of Columbia University, New York, NY

Nelson Garnett, DVM, Office of Laboratory Animal Welfare, National Institutes of Health, Bethesda, MD

Craig W. Gruber, Walt Whitman High School, Bethesda, MD

Harold A. Herzog, PhD, Department of Psychology, Western Carolina University, Cullowhee, NC

Donald F. Kendrick, PhD, Department of Psychology, Middle Tennessee State University, Murfreesboro

Sangeeta Panicker, PhD, American Psychological Association, Science Directorate, Washington, DC

Christine M. Parks, DVM, PhD, Research Animal Resources Center, University of Wisconsin—Madison

Jesse E. Purdy, PhD, Department of Psychology, Southwestern University, Georgetown, TX

John D. Strandberg, DVM, PhD, Department of Comparative Medicine, Johns Hopkins University School of Medicine, Baltimore, MD

Laboratory Animals in Research and Teaching

INTRODUCTION

CHANA K. AKINS AND SANGEETA PANICKER

1975, U.S. Senator William Proxmire (D–WI) awarded his first Golden Fleece Award to the National Science Foundation (NSF) for its support of a study on why people fall in love. The Golden Fleece Award was bestowed upon federal agencies that supported "outrageous examples of federal waste" (Irion, 1988, p. 17). Some of the awards were given for animal research on, for example, the biological causes of aggression. Another award that was widely discussed during my (Chana K. Akins) early years as a graduate student was for research conducted by my mentor, Michael Domjan, on the sexual behavior of Japanese quail. In stark contrast to Senator Proxmire's actions, the National Institute of Mental Health later honored Dr. Domjan with a Method to Extend Research in Time (MERIT) Award in recognition of his outstanding research contributions in the area of sexual behavior and learning. This is but one of many examples in which basic behavioral research with animals has been regarded as frivolous and wasteful and as not contributing to societal problems. Although some basic research provides valuable contributions to science without directly contributing to societal problems, even basic research that makes a direct contribution to societal issues often goes unrecognized (see Carroll & Overmier, 2001).

Educating the public about the importance of behavioral research and justifying the use of animals are growing challenges that all animal research-

3

ers share. However, increased costs and regulations of conducting such research and increased pressure from antianimal research activists make the challenge of establishing and maintaining animal research programs even more difficult. The obstacles that impede the establishment and maintenance of animal research programs may vary depending on whether one is attempting to conduct research at a large or small institution or at a primary research or teaching institution, and on varying amounts of institutional support and resources. In addition to these obstacles, anyone conducting research with nonhuman animals needs to be well versed in laboratory animal welfare issues as well as the laws and regulations that are in place for the ethical conduct of research with animals. In this regard, this book is aimed primarily at faculty members who wish to start a laboratory animal research program or use animals in teaching at smaller institutions, such as four-year colleges, high schools, and so forth.

The book is arranged in four parts, with each part serving a specific purpose. Part I of the book lays out the ethical framework for the use of animals in research. The first chapter in this part provides a historical perspective about the ethical debate surrounding the conduct of research with animals and describes how researchers might deal with this issue. The next chapter is devoted to helping teachers raise student awareness and promote dialogue about animal research ethics in the classroom. Part II includes chapters that give practical advice on methodological and animal welfare concerns in conducting behavioral research with animals, and how such research can be conducted at small, primarily teaching institutions. In Part III, the chapters provide a variety of creative strategies on conducting animal research in institutions with limited resources, for using animals in teaching, and for conducting animal research in high school settings. Strategies include how to acquire resources, use those that are available, and where to turn for additional support. In addition, some chapters describe exercises that can be used to teach basic behavioral principles, to educate students about the value of animal research, and to encourage student appreciation for such research. Finally, because psychologists should conduct their teaching and research in a manner consonant with relevant laws and regulations, Part IV of the book provides an overview of the regulations involved in conducting animal research. This book includes references to oversight bodies and regulations, therefore some chapters are rife with acronyms. Although terms are defined at their first appearance, a list of acronyms is provided in Appendix A. Also included are sample Institutional Animal Care and Use Committee protocols for using animals in various high school and college level courses (Appendixes F, G, I, and J), information on the Association for Assessment and Accreditation of Laboratory Animal Care international accreditation program (Appendix D), and government principles for laboratory animal care and use (Appendix L).

Much of the information in this book is based on the personal experiences of the individual authors. Thus, readers might encounter seemingly contradictory information. For example, while Kendrick (chap. 6) believes that Sniffy™ The Rat is a good computer-based alternative to the use of live animals in classroom demonstration, Eckerman (chap. 7) thinks otherwise. Such apparently conflicting information should not be viewed as contradictory but rather as reflections of the personal opinions of the authors. Readers should also note the use of the term *animal* in this book. As Hodos and Campbell (1990) pointed out, evolution is not linear, with humans being the most perfectly evolved result, but instead is branching, with *Homo sapiens* being only one of the more recently evolved limbs. Referring to laboratory animals as *infrahuman* or tacitly removing humans from the category of animals (as in the phrase *humans and animals*) has struck many behavioral scientists as inappropriate (Dess & Chapman, 1998; Poling, 1984). Thus, we use the term *nonhuman animals* to recognize this logic. However, for ease in writing, and because the U.S. Department of Agriculture regulations define and use the term *animal*, we juxtapose the term *animal* against the term *people* in its dictionary-defined sense of referring to human beings as distinct from other animals (Ator, 1991).

It is indeed unfortunate that important contributions of animal research in psychology are often overlooked. One striking example of this is its conspicuous omission in introductory psychology textbooks (see Domjan & Purdy, 1995, for a review). As of 1995, top-rated introductory psychology textbooks included descriptions of research in various topics of psychology, but they failed to explicitly acknowledge that much of the research was conducted with laboratory animals. It seems critical for the advancement of the field of psychology that researchers not only continue to educate the public about the contributions of animal research but also continue to maintain their animal laboratories and to train future animal researchers. We hope that this book helps investigators to establish and maintain animal research programs and that it also proves of interest to those who want a refreshing perspective on teaching and conducting research with animals in psychology.

REFERENCES

Ator, N. A. (1991). Subjects and instrumentation. In I. H. Iversen & K. A. Lattal (Eds.), *Techniques in the behavioral and neural sciences: Vol. 6. Experimental analysis of behavior* (Part 1, pp. 1–62). Amsterdam: Elsevier Science.

Carroll, M. E., & Overmier, J. B. (2001). *Animal research and human health: Advancing human welfare through behavioral science.* Washington, DC: American Psychological Association.

Dess, N. K., & Chapman, C. D. (1998). "Humans and animals"?: On saying what we mean. *Psychological Science, 9,* 79–80.

Domjan, M., & Purdy, J. E. (1995). Animal research in psychology: More than meets the eye of the general psychology student. *American Psychologist, 50,* 496–503.

Hodos, W., & Campbell, C. G. G. (1990). Evolutionary scales and comparative studies of animal cognition. In R. P. Kesner & D. S. Olton (Eds.), *The neurobiology of comparative cognition* (pp. 1–20). Hillsdale, NJ: Erlbaum.

Irion, R. W. (1988). What Proxmire's Golden Fleece did for—and to—science. *The Scientist, 2*(23), 17. Retrieved June 28, 2002, from http://www.the-scientist.com/yr1988/dec/prof_881212.htm

Poling, A. (1984). Comparing humans to other species: We're animals and they're not infrahumans. *Behavior Analyst, 7,* 211–212.

I

AN ETHICAL FOUNDATION

1

DEALING WITH THE ANIMAL RESEARCH CONTROVERSY

HAROLD A. HERZOG

Whether at large universities, small liberal arts colleges, or high schools, psychologists who use animals in their teaching or research invariably will be affected by the debate over the use of animals in science. In the present chapter, I hope to help scientists and teachers better understand the philosophical and historical roots of the animal rights debate and the forces impelling the current animal protection movement. This chapter is an overview of the animal rights movement and its philosophical underpinnings. In addition, general guidelines are suggested to enhance the potential for communication among animal researchers, students, faculty members, and the public.

HISTORICAL PERSPECTIVES AND MODERN ATTITUDES

The roots of the animal protection movement date to the 19th century (Rudacille, 2001). In England, public sentiment over the treatment of animals began to change in the early 1800s and resulted in the establishment of the first humane organizations and the passage of the first antianimal cruelty legislation by Parliament. In the 1870s, a highly organized antianimal research movement emerged in Great Britain, which attracted the support of Victorian luminaries such as George Bernard Shaw (1856–1950) and Alfred Russell Wallace (1823–1913). The antivivisection movement was opposed by a coalition of prominent scientists including Charles Darwin (1809–1882), Thomas Henry Huxley (1825–1895), and George Romanes (1848–1894). Similar trends were evident in the United States, roughly coinciding with the emergence of animal research as an important component of the developing field of experimental psychology (Dewsbury, 1990). J. B. Watson (1878–1958) the architect of behaviorism, was particularly criticized for a series of studies in which he deprived rats of perceptual capacities to determine the role of sensory modalities in learning. Watson was pilloried in the media and was the object of hostile newspaper editorials in *The New York Times* and *The Nation* (Dewsbury, 1990). By 1920, however, antianimal research attitudes had largely subsided in England and the United States. (It is ironic that the European country in which a strong animal protection movement emerged between the wars was Germany, where Hitler and other high-ranking Nazis were vehement in their beliefs about the protection of animals; see Arluke & Sax, 1992, for a compelling interpretation of this paradox.)

The 1970s saw renewed interest in the moral status of animals, due in part to the 1975 publication of the book *Animal Liberation* by Peter Singer, an Australian philosopher. The first public protests in the United States against the use of animals in research soon followed in the form of widely publicized demonstrations directed at animal behavior studies being conducted on cats at the American Museum of Natural History. In 1980, Ingrid Newkirk and Alex Pacheco founded People for the Ethical Treatment of Animals (PETA), an organization whose tactics are controversial even within animal activists' circles. The People for the Ethical Treatment of Animal's early growth, fueled by publicity garnered through its involvement in the well-known Silver Spring Monkey Case was spectacular; the organization grew from 8,000 members in 1984 to 750,000 members worldwide in 2003 (see http://www.peta.org/about/index.html, retrieved August 12, 2003).

Public interest in the humane treatment of animals grew throughout the 1980s and 1990s. There are several hundred animal protection organizations active in the United States, claiming somewhere between 10 million and 20 million members. The vast majority of these individuals, however, are allied with more mainstream environmental or animal welfare oriented groups, such as local humane societies, rather than organizations devoted to the elimination of animal research. It is also likely that many contributors to organizations such as PETA are concerned about single issues such as the use of animals for fur or consumer product testing rather than the abolition of all human uses of animals.

There is little doubt that the animal protection movement has had a substantial effect on public attitudes. Some practices that were unquestioned

20 years ago such as trapping animals for their fur are now seen as distasteful or even immoral by a substantial portion of Americans. But, the extent to which fundamental modifications in beliefs about the ethics of using animals is unclear (Herzog, Rowan, & Kossow, 2001). Public attitudes toward the use of other species are often inconsistent. For example, 47% of a random sample of Americans questioned in a 1993 survey agreed with the statement, "animals are just like people in all important ways" (Balzar, 1993). Similarly, a 1990 survey reported that about 80% believe that animals have "rights" which should limit the ways that humans use them (Orlans, 1993). Conversely, the majority of Americans clearly appreciate modern advances in behavioral and medical technology and most support the use of animals in applied research. This was shown by a 1989 Gallup poll in which 75% of the respondents agreed that animal experimentation was necessary for continued medical progress. Sixty-four percent of the participants supported animal research, whereas about 30% opposed it (Orlans, 1993). And, although a majority of people may say that they believe that animals have rights in some sense, the per capita consumption of meat in the United States increased about 10% between 1980 and 1988 (Fraser, Mench, & Millman, 2001).

Recent surveys show that these trends are also characteristic of psychologists and of students who major in psychology at American colleges and universities. Plous (1996a) randomly surveyed 5,000 members of the American Psychological Association (APA). He found that about 80% of respondents supported psychological research with animals. As with the general public, their degree of support varied with the species used and the degree of suffering involved in the experiments. Although a substantial majority of the clinical psychologists surveyed supported animal research, surprisingly few (8%) indicated that they used the findings of animal research in their practices. This suggests that the support for behavioral research on animals among clinicians is based on factors other than its direct use in their personal clinical work. The majority of psychologists supported the use of animals in undergraduate training, although most felt that laboratory work with animals should not be a required part of undergraduate psychology courses. A parallel survey of psychology majors (Plous, 1996b) indicated that the attitudes of undergraduates closely corresponded with those of psychologists.

THE CONTEMPORARY ANIMAL PROTECTION MOVEMENT

Millions of Americans identify in some way with the animal protection movement when defined broadly to include humane organizations and environmental groups as well as animal rights organizations. The beliefs of these individuals are, however, highly varied, as are the goals and methods of different animal protection organizations. It is important that educators and researchers who interact with animal activists and the public understand differences in the ideology, goals, and tactics of individuals and organizations with these different orientations. Scientists can establish fruitful, sometimes cordial relationships with some individuals who do not share their views about the importance of animal research. However, it may be impossible to establish meaningful dialogues with activists who are dogmatic in their convictions (see Groves, 1997, for an in-depth case study of relationships between animal researchers and animal activists).

Understanding differences between animal advocacy perspectives can enhance the possibility of communication about controversies associated with the behavioral and biomedical use of animals. Several typologies have been developed to characterize differences among animal protectionists (e.g., Jasper & Nelkin, 1992; Orlans, 1993). The most basic distinction is between those holding the welfare orientation and those holding the animal rights orientation.

The Animal Welfare Perspective

Individuals who have a welfare perspective on animal treatment believe that researchers have an obligation to treat animals humanely. Nonetheless, they make a moral distinction between human and nonhuman animals and place more value on human lives and well-being. Local and national humane societies such as the American Society for the Prevention of Cruelty to Animals and the Humane Society of the United States have traditionally assumed a welfare stance. In recent years, some of these organizations, reflecting the influence of the animal rights movement, have been critical of the use of animals for scientific and educational purposes. Often the relationship between animal welfare organizations and animal rights groups is uneasy at best. Animal welfare groups are frequently involved in practices such as euthanasia of unwanted dogs and cats that put them into conflict with more radical organizations.

Although animal welfare advocates may oppose research—which they consider to be trivial, unnecessary, or painful—they usually believe that animal research is necessary if we are to experience medical progress. In this context, animal welfare advocates, including many scientists, often support the "3 Rs" originally proposed by Russell and Burch (1959): *refinement* of experimental techniques so that suffering of experimental animals is minimized; *reduction* in the numbers of animals used in experiments; and the *replacement* of animal models with alternatives such as computer models and *in vitro* techniques using tissues rather than whole organisms. These replacements have proven to be useful for some biological and product testing applications, but at this time their utility as alternatives for behavioral systems is limited.

Animal welfare advocates may or may not make the fundamental changes in lifestyle that characterizes animal rights activists (described in the next section). As moderates, they tend to be willing to engage researchers in dialogue. Animal welfare advocates can be valuable contributors as community representatives on university and college institutional animal care and use committees (IACUCs).

The Animal Rights Perspective

Animal rights proponents differ from animal welfare advocates in that the former usually believe that all sentient creatures are in some ways moral equals. (As discussed later, not all animal "rightists" believe that animals are or should be entitled to rights in a literal philosophical or legal sense. Thus, the term *animal rights movement* is actually a misnomer, although it has come to have common usage beyond its technical philosophical meaning.) Animal rights activists generally oppose all activities that they perceive to involve the exploitation of other species. These include eating animals, wearing fur, hunting, keeping animals as captives in zoos and circuses, product testing on animals, and research on nonhuman species. Behavioral research with animals has been singled out for particularly harsh criticism by animal rights activists. In particular, the studies of Harry Harlow and his associates on the effects of maternal deprivation in monkeys and Martin Seligman's research on learned helplessness in dogs are often singled out by antianimal research organizations (see Blum, 2002, for an overview of the controversy surrounding Harlow's work).

In some ways, individuals who assume an animal rights perspective take on a heavy personal moral burden. As part of a study of the psychological underpinnings of involvement in the animal rights movement, I interviewed several dozen grassroots activists (Herzog, 1993). As a group, the activists were trying to bring most aspects of their lives into synchrony with their moral beliefs. They had made significant changes in their diet and avoided wearing leather products and in some cases, even wool. Many defined practices that most of us take for granted as moral issues: killing poisonous snakes, taking medicine that had been tested on animals, keeping pets, and even driving automobiles (tires are reputed to contain chemicals derived from animal blood). For many activists, "the movement" had become a major, if not the major, focus of their lives, affecting their behavior, basic beliefs, and even interpersonal relationships.

Although many activists are not allied with traditional religious denominations, there are significant psychological parallels between involvement in animal rights and involvement in fundamentalist religions (Jasper & Nelkin, 1992; Sperling, 1988). Activists often have an evangelical mission to spread their message. In addition, they usually try to bring their lifestyles in line with their beliefs. Finally, many animal activists, like some religious converts, live in a moral universe in which their views are seen as profoundly correct. Those who do not agree are perceived as wrong and perhaps immoral. For example, Galvin and Herzog (1992a) found that animal rights demonstrators were more likely than nonactivist college students to take an absolutist approach to ethical decision making. This perspective is characterized by moral idealism coupled with a belief in universal moral principles.

The Animal Liberation Perspective

Animal liberators are the militant wing of the animal rights movement. Most animal activists eschew violence as a tactic, believing that it is inconsistent with the nonviolent roots of the movement and that it is a counterproductive means of influencing public opinion. Nevertheless, a minority of animal activists believe that extreme measures are justified by what they consider to be the torture of innocent creatures. In 1993 the U.S. Department of Justice (1993) conducted a study of illegal activities by animal activists in the United States. Twenty percent of the 313 incidents that the report documented were directed at university research facilities. The majority involved either vandalism with minor damage or the theft and release of animals. In five incidents, property damage to university facilities exceeded several hundred thousand dollars, including an arson attack on a laboratory building at the University of California at Davis, which resulted in 4.5 million dollars in damages.

The media attention devoted to groups espousing violence may be greater than is warranted by the actual number of animal activists who use terrorism as a political tool. The U.S. Department of Justice report estimated that the Animal Liberation Front, the group responsible for 60% of the documented incidents, actually had fewer than 100 members. The report indicated that attacks on research-related facilities by animal liberationists increased steadily from 1977 to 1987 but declined considerably between 1990 and 1993. Note, however, that it is likely that the U.S. Department of Justice report underestimated the number of incidents including the harassment of animal researchers.

In general, animal rights advocates have had an uneasy relationship with the environmental movement. However, in recent years, there has been the tendency for animal liberationists to join with radical environmentalists in their opposition to issues such as factory farming and genetic engineering. For example, the Animal Liberation Front recently issued a series of joint communiqués claiming credit for arson attacks on fur farms.

WHO ARE ANIMAL ACTIVISTS?

Stereotypes of animal activists range from the well-intentioned, but slightly loony, little old lady in tennis shoes to the bomb-throwing, masked terrorist. In reality, animal activists are a diverse group. That said, a fairly consistent profile has emerged of the typical activists from psychological and sociological investigations of the animal rights movement (e.g., Jamison & Lunch, 1992; Lowe & Ginsberg, 2002; Plous, 1991; Richards & Krannich, 1991). For example, Richards and Krannich surveyed subscribers to the *Animals Agenda*, a prominent animal rights magazine. The readers were predominantly women (87%), White (97%), urban (73%), well educated (82% had attended college and 33% had earned a graduate degree), and had higher than average household incomes. They also tended to have pets (89%) but not children (70% had no children, and only 16% had children living at home at the time of the survey). The *Agenda* subscribers tended to identify with the liberal left wing of the political spectrum. Although 70% identified themselves with both the environmental and the animal rights movements, as a group they were not involved in other political causes (e.g., civil rights or the women's movement). Richards and Krannich reported that the activists, by and large, were opposed to the antiabortion movement, a grass-roots social movement that has some significant parallels with the animal rights movement.

There have been changes in the attitudes of some animal activists in recent years. Several researchers compared attitudes of demonstrators at national animal rights demonstrations in 1990 and 1996. The majority of activists at the earlier march indicated that the most important priority of the animal rights movement should be the use of animals in research; however, activists at the 1996 march indicated that animals for food was the most important issue facing the movement (Plous, 1998). Galvin and Herzog (1998) found that demonstrators at the later march felt that education would be the most effective movement strategy in the future and that liberating laboratory animals and harassing researchers would be the least effective tactic.

PHILOSOPHICAL PERSPECTIVES ON THE MORAL STATUS OF ANIMALS

Psychologists who understand the philosophical grounds for opposing the use of animals in research and education are in a better position to discuss these issues with their students as well as the public. Scientists often assume that objections to the use of animals in science are based on sentiment and misplaced anthropomorphism. Although it is true that emotional reactions are important components of moral judgments, it is not the case that all animal activists are hyperemotional misanthropes who prefer kittens to children. Indeed, the philosophical arguments both for and against the use of animals by humans are sophisticated and complex. Although many contemporary ethicists have addressed the topic of animal protectionism, there are two primary lines of argument for making fundamental changes in the moral relationship with animals: one based on the application of utilitarian thought to nonhuman species, the other based on the supposition that animals have rights.

The Utilitarian Approach

The architect of the utilitarian approach to ethics was the 18th-century philosopher Jeremy Bentham (1748–1832), who argued that ethical decisions should be based on a moral calculus in which acts are judged by the degree to which they result in pleasure and pain. Bentham argued that it is the simple capacity for sentience (i.e., the ability to experience pleasure and pain) which entitles a creature to moral consideration, not its degree of intelligence. The most prominent contemporary proponent of this view is Peter Singer, whose book *Animal Liberation* (1975) is often called the bible of the animal rights movement. (This label is somewhat ironic in that Singer's ethical stance does not presume that animals [or humans] are entitled to rights per se.)

In *Animal Liberation*, Singer presented a coherent utilitarian-based argument for a revised ethic of human–animal interactions in an engaging and accessible style. The crux of Singer's philosophical stance lies in what he refers to as the *principle of equality*—all sentient creatures have an equal stake or interest in their own life. Singer argued that adherence to this principle implies that one should not elevate the interests of one species, *Homo sapiens*, above those of any other. Just as differences in race, gender, and sexual orientation should not be used to discriminate against groups of humans, to Singer, a creature's species is also morally irrelevant—"From an ethical point of view, we all stand on an equal footing—whether we stand on two feet, or four, or none at all" (Singer, 1975, p. 6). The only morally relevant criterion is the *capacity to suffer*. By definition, all sentient animals have the capacity to suffer and therefore deserve equal moral consideration. Singer originally drew the proverbial line between creatures that could suffer and those that cannot at the level of mollusks. Subsequently, however, he confessed to being uncomfortable with this demarcation (Singer, 1990). To Singer, elevating the human species above all others on the basis of criteria other than suffering is "speciesism," which he believes to be as illogical and morally repugnant as racism or sexism. Even so, Singer's stance would allow research with animals under limited circumstances—if the results were sufficiently important that researchers would also conduct the experiments using analogous human participants (e.g., orphans with mental retardation with similar intelligence to the animals).

The "Rights" Approach

Singer's utilitarian logic is not the only route to a revised perspective on how animals should be treated. An alternative is found in an ethical theory referred to as *deontology*. Deontological views are not based on the utilitarian belief that behaviors should be judged on the basis of their outcomes. Rather, deontologists hold that one should "do the right thing" on the basis of general ethical principles regardless of the consequences. Ethics theories based on the supposition that individuals are entitled to rights are a variation of deontological thinking. The rights argument as applied to animals is most forcefully argued by philosopher Tom Regan (1983) in his book, *The Case for Animal Rights*, which, unlike *Animal Liberation*, is dense and technical. Rights theorists hold that some creatures are entitled to certain fundamental rights such as the right to basic moral consideration. The animal rights position does not imply that all creatures should have the same rights. Animal rights advocates do not, for example, believe that chimpanzees should have the right to vote. But Regan's view does imply that they are entitled to the same level of moral concern as humans.

One question immediately raised by any rights-based approach to ethics is, what entitles an individual to hold rights? Traditional anthropocentric views restrict rights holders to beings that meet criteria that are uniquely human—the capacity for language, self-consciousness, the ability to enter into reciprocal contractual obligations, a sense of ethics, and so forth. Animal rights theorists such as Regan (1983) broaden the criteria so that some animal species are included. For Regan, the fundamental criterion for having rights is a nebulous concept called "inherent value." He argues that creatures with inherent value have it in equal measure. Thus, they are entitled to certain fundamental rights including the right to be treated with respect and the right not to be harmed. Regan's criteria for meriting moral consideration are considerably more restrictive than Singer's. Regan requires that a species possess more than sentience; they must also be capable of having beliefs and desires, emotion, memory, intentions, a sense of the future, and a psychological identity. He argues that mammals more than one year old possess these capacities. Consequently, they are the subjects of a life and have moral rights. (Regan departs from this criterion in the case of infant humans, who he says should be treated as if they had rights even though they do not strictly speaking meet the minimum age requirements.)

For Regan (1983), there are a number of reasons for abolishing many uses of animals, including scientific ones. Science treats animals as renewable resources rather than as subjects of a life. He also argues that the rights view does not permit the sacrifice of an innocent few for the benefit the many. In Regan's schema, there is no moral justification for animal research; even an experiment that might benefit hundreds of thousands of humans or animals for that matter would not be deemed ethical.

Regan (1983) argues that animals are entitled to rights in a moral sense. In recent years, there has been a growing movement to give some species legal rights, and issues related to the status of animals as property have entered the courtroom. Many law schools have established courses in animal law, and a number of books have been published recently that provide the intellectual grounds for animal law as a legal specialty area (e.g., Francione, 1995; Wise, 2000). Legislation that would give legal status to animals has been introduced into parliaments in Europe and Australia. It is likely that the courtrooms and statehouses will become an important focus of the animal rights debate in coming years.

Comparisons

There are significant differences between the utilitarian and rights approaches to the treatment of animals. Singer (1975) argued that there are logical problems with the rights argument, and Regan (1983) argued that the utilitarian route to animal liberation is flawed. There are, however, commonalties in the two views. Both Singer and Regan acknowledge that there are important differences between humans and animals but believe that the differences are not relevant to the issue of basic moral consideration. Conversely, both theorists hold that there are fundamental similarities between humans and other species that are ethically significant (i.e., all sentient creatures have interests). The logical extensions of both the rights and the utilitarian arguments are vegetarianism and the elimination of animal research as it is presently conducted. Finally, Regan and Singer believe that making ethical judgments on the basis of speciesism is wrong, and they view the animal liberation movement as the logical extension of other contemporary civil liberties movements.

GUIDELINES FOR DISCUSSING THE USE OF ANIMALS

It is unclear, given the many ways that humans use other species, why the animal rights debate has become so focused on scientific research. It is, however, almost inevitable that scientists who use animals in their courses or their laboratories will be called on to justify their enterprise. Psychologists, like other scientists, should be able to communicate the reasons for using animals to a variety of constituencies, including students, fellow faculty members, the public, and the media. Whatever the audience, scientists who argue the case for animal research should be informed about the issues including the arguments against the use of animals in research. The literature in this area is voluminous. Particularly useful sources for psychologists interested in understanding these issues include the *Encyclopedia of Animal Rights and Animal Welfare* (Bekoff, 1998), *Animal Models of Human Psychology* (Shapiro, 1998), *Responsible Conduct With Animals in Research* (Hart, 1998), *Animal Research and Human Health* (Carroll & Overmier, 2001), and *The Human Use of Animals* (Orlans, Beauchamp, Dresser, Morton, & Gluck, 1998).

Communicating With Students

One of the most important goals of a college education is the development of citizens who understand and can discuss critical social issues including those related to science and technology. Discoveries in many areas of psychology including developmental, abnormal, and social psychology have been facilitated by animal research. Thus, discussions of the role of animals in psychological research should not be limited to upper level experimental or biological psychology courses. Indeed, introductory psychology courses offered as part of general education curricula offer a particularly opportune forum for discussing the role of animals in scientific research and the ethical implications of their use. Unfortunately, in introductory psychology textbooks, the coverage of the ethical and social issues associated with the use of animals in science tends to be, at best, superficial (Gerbasi, Gerbasi, & Schultz, 2003).

Often, the first item on the syllabus of introductory psychology courses is the definition and scope of psychology as a science. This topic offers an excellent framework in which to address the reasons that behavioral studies are conducted on non-human species. Psychology is typically defined as the study of behavior and mental processes. In this context, animal studies are important for three reasons. First, animal research provides insights into behavioral processes common to many species, including our own. Second, some behavioral scientists, particularly those in comparative psychology and ethology, study the behavior of other species because animals are interesting and important in their own right. Finally, some animal research is directed toward developing solutions to pressing human behavioral and biomedical problems.

The last point touches on one of the most difficult aspects of science for many people to understand: the relationship between applied and basic research. Individuals are often willing to support experiments with animals that they think will have a direct effect on human well-being. Yet, they are less likely to approve of research that they do not think will directly benefit humans (Galvin & Herzog, 1992b). Many scientists also agree that potential benefit should be considered when evaluating the ethics of an experiment (e.g., Driscoll & Bateson, 1988). That said, it is critical that students understand that treatments for mental and physical illnesses come only after extensive research aimed at the uncovering of fundamental scientific principles. There would no open-heart surgery without an understanding of the basic dynamics of the vertebrate circulatory system, and no biofeedback treatment for the relief of chronic pain without studies of visceral learning in animals.

Another issue that students may misunderstand is the role of replication in research. Animal rights activists sometimes criticize the use of animals in science on the grounds that it often duplicates previous studies. In reality, few, if any, scientists are interested in mindlessly repeating experiments that have already been conducted, and funding agencies are not interested in supporting such research. Prior to securing approval for experiments, researchers must demonstrate to an IACUC that they have conducted a search of the literature to make sure that the research does not unnecessarily repeat previous studies. In some cases, there may be legitimate questions about aspects of a study that require an experiment to be replicated by other scientists. Further, the more important the research, then the more important it is that the results be verified. Replication is not the same as duplication.

The ethical issues associated with animal research should be confronted directly in psychology courses. Possible topics for classroom discussion include the ethical arguments for and against the use of animals by humans, the APA guidelines for animal research, and the system of oversight of animal research. One method of involving students in discussions of these and related issues is through exercises in which students assume the mantle of IACUC members. The class can be divided into groups, each of which is given a hypothetical research proposal to evaluate. After evaluating the proposals, the groups report their decisions and their reasoning to the rest of the class. (Sample proposals are described in Appendix B.)

Students Who Object to Using Animals

Both faculty and students should acknowledge the diversity of opinions that reasonable people can hold on the ethics of animal research. The question of exempting students who object to the use of animals is particularly thorny. My view is that faculty members who use animals in educational settings should respect the beliefs of students who do not wish to use animals in classroom projects. Alternatives can be made available to students who have objections to dissection or to the use of live animals in laboratory exercises. As described in chapters 6 and 7 of this volume, there are a number of substitutes available, including computer simulations and videotapes.

Students can also be encouraged to work with invertebrates. A student who objects to using mice or rats in a research project may have no such problems studying the behavior of fish or ants. Likewise, few students will have moral concerns about ethologically oriented studies such as naturalistic observations of birds at feeders, free-ranging campus dogs, fish in aquaria, or mice in a colony. Some students may object to learning the principles of conditioning by reinforcing food-deprived rats in an operant chamber. The same principles, however, can be just as powerfully illustrated by having students use bits of desired food treats to teach tricks to their pet dog or cat.

Finally, students should recognize that the obligation to respect differences of opinion cuts both ways. Laboratory exercises with animals can provide unique and valuable learning experiences. Students with personal qualms about these labs should be afforded the opportunity to pursue alternative methods of learning. But, although students who do not wish to work with animals should be offered options, they do not have the right to impose their beliefs on the educational experiences of others by denying their fellow students the right to study animals.

Not all faculty members will agree with my rather liberal exemption policy, and there are other options available to instructors in response to students who insist that they not be involved in educational experiences involving animals. For example, one teacher I know conducts a sometimes lengthy meeting with any student who requests an exemption from animal laboratory exercises. During the meeting, he expresses his reasons for having students undertake the exercise and stresses the general importance of animal research. He also carefully listens to the student's point of view. If after the conference, the student still asks for an exemption, and if he is convinced of the student's sincerity (admittedly a judgment call), he offers the student an alternative.

Some teachers may feel that a particular exercise is critical to the students' understanding of course material and that students should not be exempted from the exercise. In such cases, the students should be informed of the instructor's policy during the first class period so that they can decide at the outset whether to take the course. A statement of the policy should also be incorporated into the syllabus. The legal status of college students who refuse to take part in laboratory exercises involving animals is presently unclear, but incidents in the past involving students who have ethical objections to the use of animals have often ultimately been settled in the students' favor.

Working With Student Researchers

Faculty members who are actively engaged in animal research will often have students working in their laboratories in various capacities—undergraduates serving as research assistants, graduate students engaged in thesis projects, and work study students hired to assist with animal care. Working with students in research settings affords faculty special educational opportunities. Many scientists originally decided on their career after receiving their first taste of the excitement of the laboratory as an undergraduate research assistant. Hands-on experience provides students with a view of the scientific process that cannot be acquired from textbooks or journals. Indeed, one of the educational advantages of smaller institutions is that undergraduates are more likely to have the opportunity to work with researchers than are students at large universities in which faculty members' time is disproportionately bestowed on graduate students and postdoctoral fellows.

Faculty members who invite students to become their partners in research take on additional responsibilities. They are role models for students working in their laboratories. Faculty members should convey respect for animal subjects and make sure that the conditions in their labs are beyond reproach. Students who work with animals in research settings must be given adequate training. Obviously, the educational goals of working in an animal laboratory are best served if the students are familiar with the background of the research, its purpose, and some of the details of the experimental design. Researchers should know that the ultimate responsibility for the humane care and treatment of experimental animals as well as the integrity of any data collected by undergraduate research assistants rests on their shoulders. Faculty members who maintain laboratories must ensure that students are closely supervised.

WORKING WITH FACULTY MEMBERS AND ADMINISTRATORS

College communities consist of faculty colleagues and administrators as well as students. Many colleagues will be supportive of animal research, and some may use animals in their own work. However, some faculty members may oppose the use of animals in science. Psychologists who use animals may find that they have common interests with colleagues in zoology, ecology, and related biological disciplines. At smaller institutions, it may be feasible for the animal researchers at a college to pool laboratory resources into a common animal facility. Sometimes even animals can be shared. For example, a biochemist who has a breeding colony of mice or rats may be willing to share animals for use in learning labs or animal behavior classes. Sharing resources both reduces the number of animals used at the institution and cuts expenses.

Institutional animal care and use committees can provide a forum in which psychologists can meet other faculty members who use animals in their research. Serving on an IACUC can involve considerable commitment. It can also be an interesting and intellectually challenging experience. Members of IACUCs become familiar with the research paradigms and procedures in fields other than their own, and they can benefit from hearing different perspectives in sometimes thorny discussions over the relative costs and benefits of protocols. That is, there may be a values clarification benefit to IACUC members that transcends the particular projects under review.

Administrators have an impact on the campus environment for the use of animals in research and education at the departmental and university level. In recent years in part because of the emergence of cognitive psychology as a dominant paradigm in the field, perceived social concerns about the ethics of animal research, and the prohibitive costs of complying with animal care regulations—some psychology departments have either scaled down or eliminated animal laboratories (Plous, 1996b). Undergraduates are currently less likely to have educational experiences with behavioral research using animals than they were 10 or 20 years ago. Psychologists who work with animals need to impress on their colleagues and department heads, no less than their students, the valuable role that animal research plays and continues to play in the behavioral sciences (Vazire & Gosling, 2003).

Administrators at smaller institutions, like their counterparts at research universities, should be prepared to deal with campus controversies associated with animal rights activism. Ideally, this should be done in a proactive rather than a reactive fashion. Universities are often caught off guard when faculty members are targeted by animal activists. Serious incidents associated with antivivisectionism continue to occur, and small colleges are not immune from animal rights controversies. Lutherer and Simon (1992) analyzed an attack by the Animal Liberation Front on the sleep research laboratory of John Orem, an experimental psychologist at the Department of Physiology at Texas Tech Health Sciences Center. They make a number of recommendations that university administrators may find useful in dealing with animal rights controversies on campus. Lutherer and Simon suggested that a member of the university public relations office become familiar with the animal research debate. They recommended that the university develop a crisis management plan that can be implemented immediately if an incident occurs. The institution should also take steps to educate appropriate university personnel, the local press, and the general public about the importance of animal research.

Attacks by animal activists on laboratories, researchers, and their families often have devastating effects on the individuals who are targeted. Support by institutional administrators and their colleagues is particularly important in helping researchers cope with the stress that is the inevitable consequence of these types of incidents. Representatives of the media often want to talk to scientists after such attacks. Experience has shown that researchers who have been the subject of an attack should not address the media after these incidents. Instead, the university or college should designate a spokesperson who is well prepared to respond the media inquiries.

Administrators are also responsible for ensuring that the animal research oversight procedures (e.g., IACUC protocol review process, animal facility inspections, etc.) are in place and are effective (see chaps. 8 and 9, this volume). One way that administrators can ensure their institution is in compliance with the complex federal regulations related to animal research is by encouraging IACUC chairs to attend the "IACUC 101" seminar regularly given around the country by the Applied Research Ethics National Association or one of the symposiums on IACUC issues that offered by the Scientist Center for Animal Welfare.

Communicating With the Public and the Media

Scientists are frequently called on to discuss animal research in public forums. Researchers who find themselves in these situations should bear mind the words of the theologian C. S. Lewis (1947/1988), who once wrote, "It is the rarest thing in the world to hear a rational discussion on vivisection" (p. 160). Dialogue between scientists and animal protectionists is often hampered by the stereotypes the parties have of each other. Scientists perceive activists as unrealistic, hyperemotional misanthropes who prefer kittens to human children. To many activists, scientists are, at best, callused and, at worst, sadistic (e.g., Gluck & Kubacki, 1991; Herzog, Dinoff, & Page, 1997; Paul, 1995). Getting beyond these images is difficult. For dialogue to occur between individuals with differing perspectives on a highly charged social issue, the participants must be committed to a level of civility and avoid couching the debate in terms of inviolate moral principles ("god terms"; Sanders & Jasper, 1994).

There are several points to consider when discussing animal research with the public and representatives of the media. First, individuals who understand both sides of the issue will be more effective communicators. It is surprising that relatively few grassroots activists, let alone scientists, go much beyond rhetoric and seriously explore the ethical problems inherent in our use of other species. Indeed, researchers who have made a good faith effort to study both sides of the issue by reading books or articles by the animal rights philosophers and their critics are often afforded a certain grudging respect from many activists.

Discussions, however, are two-way interactions. It is important that scientists listen to the concerns of those who do not support research if they are to expect the same openness in return. Nevertheless, it is unfortunately the case that some animal activists are unwilling to engage in rational discussions. Trying to engage in debate or discussions with individuals who will not listen serves no purpose and is usually counterproductive. Thus, researchers should distinguish animal protectionists with whom they can communicate from activists who are intransigent in their views. Likewise, public debates between individuals who support animal research often produce more heat than light. Like staged debates between biologists and creationists, these events rarely change the minds of the true believers who tend to make up the audience. These forums often result in increased polarization of opinions on the issue.

College administrators may want to identify faculty members to serve as resources for media representatives and community groups interested in information or programs on the topic of animal research. Needless to say, some faculty members will be better spokespersons than others. Faculty members designated to serve on speakers' bureaus or public forums should be articulate, have an excellent grasp of issues, and be sensitive to differences of opinion.

POINTS OF DISCUSSION

Scientists who are spokespersons should consider the following points:

1. Animal research helps people. A statement from the Public Health Service of the U.S. Department of Health and Human Services (1994) summarizes this point succinctly:

> Virtually every medical achievement of the last century has depended directly or indirectly on research with animals. The knowledge gained from animal research has extended human life and made it healthier through many significant achievements, as illustrated by the following examples: vaccines to prevent poliomyelitis and other communicable diseases; surgical procedures to replace diseased heart valves; corneal transplants to restore normal vision; new medicines to control high blood pressure and reduce death from stroke, antipsychotic drugs to treat mental disorders; broad spectrum antibiotics to treat infections; and chemical agents to cure or slow childhood cancers. (p.13)

Carroll and Overmier (2001) and Miller (1985) have reviewed the contributions of behavioral research using animals toward the treatment of human afflictions. These include the development of behavioral therapies for the treatment of a wide variety of mental and behavioral dysfunctions: behavioral treatments for the alleviation of chronic pain; rehabilitation for neuromuscular disorders the treatment of enuresis; the development of behaviorally active therapeutic drugs; and biofeedback-based therapies.

2. Animal research helps animals. Like human medicine, new vaccines, chemical therapies, and surgical procedures used in veterinary medicine are developed and tested using animal models. Millions of dogs, for example, are now spared rabies, parvo, and distemper because of the existence of vaccines developed through animal research. It is ironic that some animal activists seem more willing to allow animals to be used in research if the object of the research is to benefit nonhuman rather than human animals.

3. The number of animals used in research is small relative to the number of animals used by humans for other purposes. Accurate data on the total numbers of animals used for research in the United States are difficult to obtain, in part, because rats and mice, which make up about 90% of laboratory animals, are excluded from the reporting requirements of the Animal Welfare Act. In 1997, research facilities used about 1 million animals from species that are covered under the Act (dogs, cats, primates, and other mammals except rats and mice; Rowan & Loew, 2001). It is likely that some-

where between 20 and 30 million animals are used annually for research and educational purposes (Orlans, 1993). These are big numbers. One can contrast them, however, with the number of animals killed annually for consumption—35 million cattle, 93 million pigs, 5 million sheep, 300 million turkeys, and 6 billion chickens. Further, for every dog used for biomedical and behavioral research, 40 are killed each year in animal shelters.

4. Animal research is subjected to oversight by IACUCs. Experiments using vertebrates in biomedical and behavioral research and in education is subjected to scrutiny by IACUCs, including the use of animals for educational purposes in colleges and universities. Although the Animal Welfare Act is interpreted to exclude rats, mice, and birds, Public Health Service regulations pertaining to animal research, however, do include these animals.

CONCLUSION

Psychologists at both small and large educational institutions confront the same types of problems in dealing with the animal rights controversy. The essential ethical questions do not vary with institutional size nor does the spectrum of points of view. The environment for animal research, however, is likely to be quite different at small and large institutions. Researchers at small colleges usually have fewer resources at their disposal. Institutional support for animal studies in terms of funding, laboratory space, and like-minded colleagues is typically limited in comparison with larger universities. Conversely, faculty members at small colleges have the advantage of working within a more tightly knit intellectual community. This may encourage the possibility of communication between individuals holding different perspectives on the ethical issues associated with the use of animals in research and education.

REFERENCES

Arluke, A., & Sax, B. (1992). Understanding Nazi animal protection and the holocaust. *Anthrozoos, 5,* 6–31.

Balzar, J. (1993, December 25). Creatures great—and equal? *Los Angeles Times,* p. A1.

Bekoff, M. (Ed.). (1998). *Encyclopedia of animal rights and animal welfare.* Westport, CT: Greenwood Press.

Blum, D. (2002). *Love at Goon Park: Harlow and the science of affection*. Cambridge, MA: Perseus Publishing.

Carroll, M. E., & Overmier, J. B. (Eds.) (2001). *Animal research and human health: Advancing human welfare through behavioral science*. Washington, DC: American Psychological Association.

Dewsbury, D. (1990). Early interactions between animal psychologists and animal activists and the founding of the APA Committee on Precautions in Animal Experimentation. *American Psychologist, 45*, 315–327.

Driscoll, J. W., & Bateson, P. (1988). Animals in behavioural research. *Animal Behaviour, 36*, 1569–1574.

Fentress, J. C. (1973). Development of grooming in mice with amputated forelimbs. *Science, 179*, 704–705.

Francione, G. L. (1995). *Animals, property, and the law*. Philadelphia: Temple University Press.

Fraser, V., Mench, J., & Millman, S. (2001). Farm animals and their welfare in 2000. In D. J. Salem & A. N. Rowan (Eds.), *The state of the animals 2001* (pp. 87–100). Washington, DC: Humane Society Press.

Galvin, S., & Herzog, H. A., Jr. (1992a). Ethical ideology, animal activism, and attitudes toward the treatment of animals. *Ethics & Behavior, 2*, 141–149.

Galvin, S., & Herzog, H. A., Jr. (1992b). The ethical judgment of animal research. *Ethics & Behavior, 2*, 263–286.

Galvin, S., & Herzog, H. A., Jr. (1998). Attitudes and dispositional optimism of animal rights demonstrators. *Society and Animals, 6*, 1–11.

Gerbasi, K. C., Gerbasi, M. E., & Schultz, K. L. (2003, August). *What do "top selling" introductory psychology texts say about ethics and issues in animal research and how do students interpret this information?* Paper presented at the 12th International Society for Anthrozoology Conference, Canton, OH.

Gluck, J. P., & Kubacki, S. R. (1991). Animals in biomedical research: The undermining effect of the rhetoric of the besieged. *Ethics & Behavior, 1*, 157–173.

Groves, J. M. (1997). *Hearts and minds: The controversy over laboratory animals*. Philadelphia: Temple University Press.

Hart, L. A. (Ed.). (1998). *Responsible conduct with animals in research*. New York: Oxford University Press.

Herzog, H. A., Jr. (1990). Discussing animal rights and animal research in the classroom. *Teaching of Psychology, 17*, 90–94.

Herzog, H. A., Jr. (1993). "The movement is my life": The psychology of animal rights activism. *Journal of Social Issues, 46*, 103–119.

Herzog, H. A., Jr., Dinoff, B., & Page, J. R. (1997). Animal rights talk: Moral debate over the information highway. *Qualitative Sociology, 20*, 399–418.

Herzog, H. A., Rowan, A. N., & Kossow, D. (2001). Social attitudes and animals. In D. J. Salem & A. N. Rowan (Eds.), *The state of the animals 2001* (pp. 55–69). Washington, DC: Humane Society Press.

Jamison, W., & Lunch, W. (1992). The rights of animals, science policy and political activism. *Science Technology and Human Values, 17,* 438–458.

Jasper, J. M., & Nelkin, D. (1992). *The animal rights crusade: The growth of a moral protest.* New York: Free Press.

Lewis, C. S. (1988). A case for abolition. In A. Linzey & T. Regan (Eds.), *Animals and Christianity: A book of readings.* New York: Crossroad. (Original work published 1947)

Lowe, B. M., & Ginsberg, C. F. (2002). Animal rights as a post-citizenship movement. *Society and Animals, 10,* 203–215.

Lutherer, L. O., & Simon, M. S. (1992). *Targeted: The anatomy of an animal rights attack.* Norman: University of Oklahoma.

Miller, N. E. (1985). The value of behavioral research on animals. *American Psychologist, 40,* 423–440.

Orlans, F. B. (1993). *In the name of science: Issues in responsible animal experimentation.* New York: Oxford University Press.

Orlans, F. B., Beauchamp, T. L., Dresser, R., Morton, M. B., & Gluck, J. P. (1998). *The human use of animals: Case studies in ethical choice.* New York: Oxford University Press.

Paul, E. (1995). Us and them: Scientists' and animal rights campaigners' views of the animal experimentation debate. *Society & Animals, 3,* 1–21.

Plous, S. (1991). An attitude survey of animal rights activists. *Psychological Science, 2,* 194–196.

Plous, S. (1996a). Attitudes toward the use of animals in psychological research and education: Results from a national survey of psychologists. *American Psychologist, 51,* 1167–1180.

Plous, S. (1996b). Attitudes toward the use of animals in psychological research and education: Results from a national survey of psychology majors. *Psychological Science, 7,* 352–358.

Plous, S. (1998). Signs of change within the animal rights movement: Results from a follow-up survey of activists. *Journal of Comparative Psychology, 112,* 48–54.

Plous, S., & Herzog, H. (2001). Reliability of protocol reviews for animal research. *Science, 293,* 608–609.

Regan, T. (1983). *The case for animal rights.* Berkeley: University of California Press.

Richards, R. T., & Krannich, R. S. (1991). The ideology of the animal rights movement and activists' attitudes towards wildlife. *Transactions of the 56th North American Wildlife and Natural Resources Conference,* 363–371.

Rowan, A. N., & Loew, F. M. (2001). Animal research: A review of developments. In D. J. Salem & A. N. Rowan (Eds.), *The state of the animals 2001* (pp. 111–120). Washington, DC: Humane Society Press.

Rudacille, D. (2001). *The scalpel and the butterfly: The conflict between animal research and animal protection.* Berkeley: University of California Press.

Russell, W. M. S, & Burch, R. L. (1959). *The principles of humane experimental technique.* London: Methuen.

Sanders, S., & Jasper, J. M. (1994). Civil politics in the animal rights conflict: God terms versus casuistry in Cambridge, Massachusetts. *Science, Technology, and Human Values, 19*, 169–188.

Shapiro, K. J. (1998). *Animal models of human psychology: A critique of science, ethics and policy.* Seattle, WA: Hogrefe & Huber.

Singer, P. (1975). *Animal liberation.* New York: New York Review of Books.

Singer, P. (1990). *Animal liberation.* New York: New York Review of Books.

Sperling, S. (1988). *Animal liberators: Research and morality.* Berkeley: University of California Press.

Sutherland, A., & Nash, J. E. (1994). Animal rights as a new environmental cosmology. *Qualitative Sociology, 17*, 171–186.

U.S. Department of Health and Human Services, Public Health Service. (1994). The importance of animals in biomedical and behavioral research. *Animal Welfare Information Center Newsletter, 5*(2), 13.

U.S. Department of Justice. (1993). *Report to Congress on the extent and effects of domestic and international terrorism on animal enterprises.* Washington, DC: Author.

Vazire, S., & Gosling, S. D. (2003). Bridging psychology and biology with animal research. *American Psychologist, 58*, 407–408.

Wise, S. M. (2000). *Rattling the cage: Toward legal rights for animals.* Cambridge, MA: Perseus Books.

2

THE ETHICS CASCADE

NANCY K. DESS AND RICHARD W. FOLTIN

Reactions to a report on the evening news about brain research with rats may range from "Wow! I think that's great. We need more of it," to "How awful! It is wrong to use poor little rats like that." As members of a society that supports scientific research with both human and nonhuman animals, researchers are morally obligated to engage in ongoing, thoughtful deliberation about the ethics of the research enterprise. Research ethics is a complicated matter, comprised not of one or two simple issues but of many interrelated ones. Consequently, discussions about research ethics will be circular and frustrating when participants lack a common framework for organizing their conversation. This chapter should help teachers promote civil dialog, student self-awareness, and learning about ethics by providing a framework for organizing lesson plans or moderating spontaneous discussions.

The framework presented below aims to facilitate discussion by helping participants to (a) identify the ethical issue(s) central to the discussion and (b) better understand the values they hold that contribute to their agreements and disagreements with others. The seven ethical questions (see Exhibit 2.1) form a V-shaped cascade, flowing from broad issues to far more specific ones. The first steps concern large-scale questions, such as who has moral authority and whether people should "monkey around" with nature by doing research at all. Although such questions do not explicitly address re-

EXHIBIT 2.1
Summary of Steps in the Ethics Cascade

I.   *Who should decide* what is morally justifiable in the conduct of research?
II. Are controlled research studies *ever* necessary or appropriate?
III. Should all research have a *foreseeable practical benefit*?
IV. *At whom* should research be directed?
V.   What *specific topics* are worthy of research?
VI. What particular research methodologies are *scientifically valid*, as well as ethically appropriate?
VII. Of the valid methods, *which* should be used?

search with nonhuman animals, they may well be the basis of agreement or disagreement over whether, for instance, a rhesus monkey experiment described in the morning newspaper is morally right. As the cascade proceeds from Step I toward Step VII and narrows its focus, distinctions regarding morally right and morally questionable research become finer. A debate at Step VII, for instance, may concern which of two procedures for studying eating behavior in laboratory rats is preferable on moral grounds.

The later in the ethics cascade a disagreement arises, the greater the common ground. Discussants who see eye to eye through Step VI are far more likely to agree with each other about the moral rightness of a research program with laboratory animals than are discussants who differ profoundly at Step II. Moreover, those who concur at many early stages of the cascade will have a different sort of conversation about differences of opinion they may have regarding particular research activities. Pinpointing the step in the cascade at which agreement ends and differences emerge should be helpful in setting realistic goals for respectful and productive exchange. The brief scenarios concluding each step are designed to illustrate a difference of opinion related directly to the core ethical issue at that step, thus enabling teachers to recognize similar sorts of reasoning among students. Teachers may also wish to use the scenarios as class discussion questions, either as they are presented or they may adapt them to make them more culturally and age appropriate to the student populations with whom they work.

For the purpose of this discussion, research is defined as activity that manipulates the internal or external circumstances of a human or nonhuman animal participant, with measurement of how the manipulation alters various dependent measures.

I. WHO SHOULD DECIDE WHAT IS MORALLY JUSTIFIABLE IN THE CONDUCT OF RESEARCH?

What people or institutions should be entrusted to decide moral questions, including what sort of research gets done and how? Which research gets done depends on moral judgments made by (a) institutional review boards (IRBs) that have the final authority at the local institutional level to approve or disapprove a research project; (b) private and public funding agencies; (c) elected officials who appropriate money for government agencies; (d) the voting public and community activists; and (e) individual researchers. The moral sensibilities of the individuals within each group may vary and are shaped by parents, peers, teachers, religious beliefs, personal experience, and other moral agents.

> **Scenario:** One discussant, as a Roman Catholic, adopts the official moral positions of the Pope; another discussant feels just as strongly that each individual should follow his or her own conscience. How will this difference in values shape the individuals' discussion of research on, for example, fetal tissue, stem cell research, or new contraceptive methods?

II. ARE CONTROLLED RESEARCH STUDIES EVER NECESSARY OR APPROPRIATE?

Once discussion participants agree that they have some responsibility for deciding the role of research in society, they must address the issue of whether research— with humans or other animals—should be done at all. Is research a valuable human enterprise, or should scientists let nature take its course? How people feel about their proper role in the world will shape their attitudes about science in general.

Both human and nonhuman primates are naturally curious such that learning about the environment and mastery of the environment are powerful motivators of behavior (e.g., children endlessly watching the same video over and over again so that they can predict what will happen next, or nonhuman primates manipulating any new or unusual object placed in their environment). Curiosity, exploration, and learning have been important adaptive forces in our evolution and, in a way, research functions as institutionalized curiosity. However, human and nonhuman primates are also suspicious of change and in some circumstances are cautious or risk averse; this conservative tendency also has had adaptive value. Thus, a balance must be struck between the desire to learn new things and the desire to keep things the same and avoid risk.

> **Scenario:** One discussant, whose brother was disabled in a motorcycle accident, believes that head trauma research should get more funding; another discussant believes that people play God too much. Do these discussants differ in how much they care about the plight of accident victims? Or do their value systems differ in a more general way?

III. SHOULD ALL RESEARCH HAVE A FORESEEABLE PRACTICAL BENEFIT?

Once discussion participants agree that scientific research may be appropriate, they must decide what general types of research objectives are morally sound. Should all efforts go into research that is aimed explicitly at problem solving? Or is knowing more about the world in which one lives a worthy goal, even if the implications of the knowledge are not clear?

Although some basic research may not have any obvious immediate benefit to humans or other animals, it is information that can be placed in the "bank of knowledge" and withdrawn later, when more information is available. Many scientific advances can be traced to the synthesis of previous pieces of information, that is, the whole is greater than the sum of its parts (gestalt). The history of science shows that the basic or applied distinction is a blurry one. Many invaluable social, technological, and medical tools (e.g., cognitive-behavioral therapy, the transistor, and antibiotics) arose from basic research conducted without these applications in mind. And research earnestly directed at a particular problem can fail to solve it. If predicting the future is a precarious basis for judging the moral value of research, what role ought it play in those judgments? Different people answer that question differently.

> **Scenario:** One discussant brims with enthusiasm for research comparing the language abilities of chimpanzees and human children; another discussant snaps, "And what good will that ever do for children OR chimpanzees?" What assumptions might these discussants be making about what one learns from research, and what value do they place on its practical utility?

IV. AT WHOM SHOULD RESEARCH BE DIRECTED?

If one accepts that important advancements may come from either basic or applied research, the next question is about whom the research should benefit. Is it sufficient for research to aim at helping and understanding oneself? One's family and friends? One's country? All people? All animals like oneself? All animals? All living things? People can have different ideas about whom researchers should be trying to help. Various cultural worldviews differ in the extent to which other people and the rest of the natural world matter. These views will shape the value people place on various research objectives. For example, research aimed at alleviating anxiety in dogs may seem appropriate in cultures that prize dogs as companions, but less so in cultures that prize dogs as the main course at a meal. Thus, it may seem obvious to one person that researchers are responsible only for themselves and those most like them, yet equally obvious to another person that researchers are stewards of all living things.

Dichotomizing research that benefits us versus them is often unwarranted. For example, focusing only on the benefits of research for humans ignores the fact that research with laboratory animals may also benefit nonhuman animals. For example, many painkillers and dermatology medications that were tested in laboratory animals as a requirement for approval for human use are now used by veterinarians.

> **Scenario:** One discussant advocates for the importance of research on the welfare of nonhuman primates living in captivity; another discussant counters that with all the human suffering in the world, the last thing scientists should be studying is monkey happiness. What do these positions suggest about the discussants' values?

V. WHAT SPECIFIC TOPICS ARE WORTHY OF RESEARCH?

Even people who agree up to this point in the cascade may place very different values on specific research topics. For instance, two people may agree that both basic and applied research have value for humans and other species but disagree about various specific topics' deservingness of study. What is important: Heart disease? Child abuse? Understanding math? Learning to share? People often do not agree about the meaning or importance of pain, deprivation, or happiness. Suffering for one person may mean dying of AIDS and for another may mean having to attend their second-choice college. Accordingly, research on a particular issue may be perceived by some as crucial and perceived by others as fussing over frosting on the cake of life. Even if people agree on the definitions of problem and luxury, they may disagree about whether scientists should focus their research efforts on solving particular problems. In addition, people may agree that a topic is worthy of study but disagree about whether the research is a moral imperative (really essential) or merely morally justifiable (acceptable but not a high priority).

Whether people judge topics as worthy of study is influenced by the way they make moral judgments. In particular, patterns of placing blame for a problem and responsibility for a solution will shape their attitudes toward a research area. For instance, a person who sympathizes with innocent victims of congenital heart disease but blames smokers for getting lung cancer may value research on congenital heart disease more than research on lung cancer. Beliefs about what is important in life also will be reflected in values placed on specific research topics. Furthermore, social values are reflected in the topics that are prioritized for funding by public agencies. This is demonstrated most clearly by the increase in social awareness and support for research in an area when a well-known person is afflicted with the disease or injury (e.g., Christopher Reeve and spinal cord injury). The influence of social norms and values in this context of discovery means that scientists will eventually understand more about topics many people care about and may understand little about some orphan topics that are extremely important to a small or powerless group.

Scenario: One discussant wants to go to graduate school so that she can study how to reduce HIV risk-taking behavior (e.g., avoiding unprotected sexual contact), whereas another discussant thinks such research is irrelevant because telling people the right thing to do should be sufficient. How could two reasonable people have such different views?

VI. WHAT PARTICULAR RESEARCH METHODOLOGIES ARE SCIENTIFICALLY VALID, AS WELL AS ETHICALLY APPROPRIATE?

Good research begins with a worthwhile question, is conducted using scientifically valid methods, and ends with an answer to the question as well as new questions. The methods chosen must be appropriate to answering the question. If a method is not valid, the research is ethically questionable because it wastes resources and may involve unnecessary inconvenience or distress to the research participants. People with different opinions about the validity of different research methodologies are likely to draw different conclusions about how ethical the research is.

Sometimes validity seems obvious. For example, if a researcher is interested in how dolphins communicate and records the sounds they make when other dolphins are around, the method has face validity (i.e., it makes obvious sense). However, determining validity can be more complicated. Imagine a researcher who is interested in compulsive exercise and anorexia and chooses to study rats in a running wheel. Is the method valid? The method may have less face validity, but it has a more important kind of validity, known as construct validity (i.e., method is empirically and theoretically relevant to the question, or construct, under investigation). Rats with access to a running wheel will, if given limited access to food, exercise excessively and eat too little food to maintain their body weight. This hyperactivity and exercise-induced anorexia is related to behavior observed in some humans. Thus, validity is not always obvious or simple.

Another controversy in the area of validity of research methods is on the utility, and thus ethics, of using laboratory animals to model the human condition. Some groups opposed to all research with nonhuman animals refer to such research as "scientific fraud." They claim that none of the methods are valid because humans are so different from other animals and, that, because the researchers know this, the researchers are committing fraud. Other people believe that humans are like other animals in some critical respects, such that many human problems can be modeled in laboratory animals. For example, many humans, when given the option, abuse drugs of abuse, and similarly, many laboratory animals, when given the option, self-administer drugs of abuse. Thus, data obtained in laboratory animals about both biological and behavioral mechanisms of action of drugs of abuse are directly relevant to understanding human drug abuse. The validity of specific methods for studying specific topics must be thought about in a careful, detailed manner. In this context of justification, one must also consider such factors as the qualifications of the researchers and the support for the methods in prior research.

> **Scenario:** One discussant excitedly reports on some vision research with hamsters that might provide information about perceptual influences on decision making and traffic accidents; another discussant challenges the ethics of the study, saying, "But hamsters don't drive!" What is the basis of their disagreement?

VII. OF THE VALID METHODS, WHICH SHOULD BE USED?

Interesting, complex research questions usually can be studied in a variety of valid ways. The choice of methods involves some practical factors, such as how affordable and time consuming they are. But the choice also involves ethics. A common means of choosing among methods is cost/benefit analysis: Is the cost of the research (money, time, inconvenience, discomfort, pain, etc.) justified by the potential benefit of the research (understanding, improved health, social harmony, etc.)? A related factor that is sometimes neglected is the cost of not doing the research: What will it cost society if scientists do not better understand or solve the problem?

Different people assign different values to the costs of particular research methods. For instance, some people believe that the cost to a laboratory animal of living in a laboratory rather than being free to roam is infinite and thus is not justifiable, regardless of the potential benefit to knowledge or well-being. Other people judge the cost of some discomfort to a laboratory animal to be lower than discomfort to a person, such that work with laboratory animals is justifiable. Cost/benefit analyses also involve the value placed on the benefit. If, for example, a person thinks a research question is important, then a higher cost is justifiable. Finally, the perceived validity of alternative methods will influence ethical judgment. A person who believes that a particular type of in vitro tissue culture is a valid alternative to research with a living mouse may judge the living-mouse project to be unethical.

Emotional assessments also play a legitimate role in ethics debates. People should be sensitive to others' suffering and well-being. If a disease is painful, then the benefit of a cure seems higher; if a research procedure involves pain, then its cost seems higher. However, emotional appeals also can be used to strengthen weak arguments or to promote misinformation; they often can be used to argue either side of an issue. Thus, in making ethical judgments, people need to both acknowledge their feelings and be vigilant to the use of emotional manipulation.

In both cost/benefit analyses and emotional assessments, many people make distinctions not just between humans and nonhuman species, but among other species. Sometimes these distinctions have to do with how much a species is liked or an intuitive sense of how similar it is to humans; the more an animal is liked or the more humanlike it seems, the less acceptable its use in research is. Other people make distinctions among species on the basis of sentience (or subjective awareness) and thus capacity to experience distress or joy. Either rationale may lead to greater moral concerns about experimentation with, for instance, monkeys than snakes, even if the same, and equally valid, procedures were used.

> **Scenario:** One discussant believes that operating on frogs to obtain muscle tissue for research on multiple sclerosis is justified; another discussant argues that computer simulations and virtual reality technology are far better methodologies. What are possible bases for each ethical judgment?

CONCLUSION

The ethics cascade reflects a conviction that everyone addressing research ethics should avoid simplistic conclusions and, rather, think deeply about the bases of her or his agreement or disagreement with others on particular issues. Identifying the roots of agreement and disagreement is important. It helps individual researchers make informed, sound ethical decisions. However, ethical decisions are not entirely up to individuals. Collectives—such as collaborative research groups, colleges and universities, and professional and governmental organizations—debate ethical issues, reach a consensus, and develop ethical guidelines. Formal principles exist for the humane treatment of human and nonhuman research participants. For example, the United States government staffs offices that monitor adherence to federal codes designed to ensure the well-being of all research participants (Office of Human Research Protections, and Office of Laboratory Animal Welfare). Within psychology, the American Psychological Association (2002) has published *Ethical Principles of Psychologists and Code of Conduct*, which all psychologists are expected to follow, whether they work with human or non-human animals. Ethics, then, is a social process, not just a matter of individual conscience.

Researchers are responsible for knowing the ethical principles by which their work will be judged by others. In addition, they should play an active role in the review and reformulation of ethical standards. Many ethical decisions are not made once and for all; they require ongoing evaluation in light of new information. For example, new methodologies in a particular area of research might suggest ways of reducing the number of laboratory animals needed to obtain reliable results while preserving the validity of the work. Being sensitive to such ongoing developments and engaging in informed debate about ethical issues are the responsibility of the entire research community.

Today's children are tomorrow's scientists, voters, and policymakers. Ensuring high moral standards in the research community tomorrow requires introducing children today, in their earliest moments of science education, to the wonder of research and to the awesome responsibilities that accompany it. To the extent that the ethics cascade assists teachers engaged in that process, it will have succeeded.

REFERENCE

American Psychological Association. (2002). Ethical principles of psychologists and code of conduct. *American Psychologist, 57,* 1060–1073.

II

PRACTICAL ADVICE

3

CONDUCTING BEHAVIORAL RESEARCH: METHODOLOGICAL AND LABORATORY ANIMAL WELFARE ISSUES

NANCY A. ATOR

This chapter discusses basic procedures in behavioral research with nonhuman animals. Psychologists trained in behavioral research likely have had first-hand experience with some or all of the procedures and issues addressed in this chapter. The context of the presentation is to highlight animal welfare issues, especially those covered by U.S. Department of Agriculture (USDA) regulations that are set forth to carry out the requirements of the Animal Welfare Act (AWA). Many of those same issues and more are covered by the *Guide to Care and Use of Laboratory Animals* (the *Guide*), which guides adherence to Public Health Service Policy on Humane Care and Use of Laboratory Animals (PHS Policy). For students, this chapter provides an overview of responsibilities and concerns in establishing a program of behavioral research with animals.

Support during preparation of this chapter was provided by Grant RO1 DA04133 from the National Institute on Drug Abuse.

ORIENTATION TO SPECIES COVERED BY THE
USDA REGULATIONS AND PHS POLICY

The species covered by the Animal Welfare Regulations (AWR) are identified in the definition of *"Animal"*.[1] They include warm-blooded animals, but the regulations specifically exclude "birds, rats of the genus *Rattus*, and mice of the genus *Mus* bred for use in research" as well as horses not used for research and other farm animals, "used or intended for use as food or fiber" or related uses (Animal Welfare Act, January, 2002). Note that rats *not* of the genus *Rattus* (e.g., kangaroo rats) as well as other rodents such as gerbils are included in the definition of animal. The definition of animal specifically includes dead as well as live members of the covered classes, because some regulations apply to handling dead animals. Creatures that are not warm blooded (e.g., fish, reptiles, and amphibians) are not mentioned. During routine unannounced site visits, the USDA does not inspect research facilities that use species that are not covered by the regulations.

Broadening the regulations to include one or more of the species not initially covered may occur, as can other changes. Researchers need to keep abreast of such developments. Proposed changes must be published in the *Federal Register* for a period of public comment before any changes become final. Professional organizations and scientific societies typically disseminate information about proposed changes that might affect their members well in advance of the due date to encourage their participation in providing comments. Comments may be made by individuals as well as by organizations. The rationale for final versions of the regulations is published in the *Federal Register* along with the final rules and addresses the range of comments that were received. The requirements of the AWR quoted in the remaining sections of this chapter also appear, in the same or similar phrasing, in the *Guide*, which applies not only to animals covered by the AWR but also to all other vertebrate animals.

The PHS Policy applies to all institutions that receive federal funding or are performance sites where federally funded research is carried out. This policy covers all vertebrates, whether warm- or cold-blooded animals. The PHS Office of Laboratory Animal Welfare (OLAW) is entrusted with oversight of care and use of vertebrate animals at covered institutions. Such institutions are often termed *assured* institutions, because to receive federal funds for activities that involve animals, an institution must have filed an "Animal Welfare Assurance" with OLAW, which states the ways in which it will

---

[1]Throughout this chapter, phrases in quotation marks indicate that the wording is as used in a section of the USDA regulations. The regulations themselves are contained in Title 9 of the Code of Federal Regulations (CFR), Parts 1 (*Definition of Terms*), 2 (*Licensing, Registration, Identification of animals, Records, Institutional animal care and use committees and adequate veterinary care, Miscellaneous*), and 3 (*Animal welfare, Humane animal handling, Pets, Transportation*). Specific citations are not given in the interest of readability. Most of the phrases cited in this chapter are from 9 CFR Part 2, Subpart C–Research Facilities.

carry out PHS Policy. See chapter 9 in this volume for more information about PHS Policy.

INSTITUTIONAL ANIMAL CARE AND USE COMMITTEE

Prominent in the USDA regulations is the requirement that a facility that carries out research with species covered by the regulations establish an Institutional Animal Care and Use Committee (IACUC) to provide oversight for the "animal program, facilities, and procedures." A major responsibility of the IACUC is to determine whether activities involving animals at the facility are in accordance with the regulations. This is accomplished by reviewing proposals (sometimes termed *protocols*) submitted to an IACUC by a member of the institution who plans to conduct an experiment or use animals in teaching. (See Appendix C for the structure of IACUCs and their specific responsibilities.)

The USDA regulations make clear that the IACUC is not to "prescribe methods or set standards for the design, performance, or conduct of research." However, the IACUC must request that the proposal include enough information to enable adequate evaluation of the proposed use of animals for compliance with the regulations. This inevitably involves providing scientific rationale for purpose, design, choice of species, and the necessity for procedures that restrict access to food or water or involve aversive stimuli. In providing this information when writing the protocol, researchers should keep in mind that although the scientific importance of the planned research should be communicated, the primary concern of the audience for which they are writing is that appropriate consideration is being given to animal welfare.

RATIONALE FOR THE STUDY

The IACUC must determine whether there is "a rationale for involving animals" in the proposed activity. Providing an adequate answer requires setting forth the purpose for the study. Although the IACUC may include members who are themselves scientists, they may not be familiar with the specific research area of the proposed activity. To make the rationale for using animals clear and compelling, scientists should formulate the purpose in nontechnical language and in the context of briefly stating the reason he or she believes it is important to do the study. This will prepare the reader to understand the rationale for the procedures to be described in the proposal. Practice in communicating about research in nontechnical terms can be beneficial beyond the IACUC when opportunities arise to communicate the importance of behavioral research to the broader community, whether neighbor, legislator, or reporter.

EXPERIMENTAL DESIGN

The IACUC must require specification of "the approximate number of animals to be used and the appropriateness" of that number. Judicious consideration of the number of animals needed for each experiment is also important for conservation of animals and associated resources. The number of animals will be determined in large part by the experimental design. Choose the experimental design that is best for answering the experimental question, given the nature of the independent variable or variables and the conditions under which the experiment is to be conducted. Then choose the number of subjects needed for a meaningful conclusion to be drawn from the results. Choice of too few subjects can be as counterproductive for conservation of animals as use of too many subjects.

Group designs assume a level of uncontrollable within- and between-subject variability. To separate the effect of the independent variable or variables from variance, subjects are randomly assigned to conditions (or conditions are randomly assigned to subjects). Estimated extraneous variability is factored out in the statistical analysis. For conditions in which the effects are not strong enough to overcome variance, the number of subjects may be increased. Use of power analysis can refine estimates of the number of subjects needed to reach planned levels of significance. An estimate of effect size is an essential part of such a calculation (Rosnow & Rosenthal, 1996; Wilcox, 1996; see also Loftus, 1996).

Classic group designs (whether between-group, within-group, or mixed) have been prevalent in psychological research and may be best when critical sources of variability cannot be controlled experimentally. Group designs clearly are best when the effect of the independent variable is not reversible, which means that the effect of the independent variable cannot be replicated with each subject. Such designs are not inevitably the best when between- and within-subject variability can be minimized by good control of environment, history, and sometimes even genetics. In much behavioral research with animals, single-subject designs should be considered.

Single-subject designs focus on demonstrating replicable effects in individual animals (Bordens & Abbott, 1996; Sidman, 1960; when used with people, the design is sometimes called a single-case design, Kazdin, 1984). The single-subject design has practical appeal over group designs because it requires fewer subjects. It has experimental appeal because it aims to control variability sufficiently to be able to demonstrate the effect of manipulation of the independent variable in every subject. Key to appropriate use of this design to obtain interpretable results, however, is an understanding of the elements that are necessary to demonstrate the reliability and generality of an effect. Failure to use a single-subject design appropriately can result in an unsatisfying hybrid single-subject/within-subject group design (Ator, 1999).

In single-subject designs, well-controlled behavioral baselines are established. Experimental conditions are not changed nor tests conducted until behavior meets a performance criterion. Reliability is established by repeating the observations in the same subject (e.g., ABAB designs, in which A is the control, or baseline, condition and B is the experimental condition). Levels of the independent variable are manipulated within subject (e.g., ABACAD etc., where B, C, and D refer to different values of the independent variable). Generality is determined by replication of the effect across subjects. If baseline performances differ across subjects, one decides whether to manipulate parameters of the maintaining conditions to produce similar baselines across subjects; or this could be done in a later experimental condition if it appears that the nature of a result is a function of the baseline. Visual inspection of the data should yield unequivocal conclusions as to the reality, reliability, and generality of the effect (Branch, 1999; Perone, 1999); some special statistical methods may be useful adjuncts to visual inspection (Fisch, 1998; Krishef, 1991). Statistical methods developed for use on single-case designs in clinical settings may be used in some studies with nonhuman animals if events prevent full use of an ABAB design (Bordens & Abbott, 1996; Kazdin, 1984; Krishef, 1991; see also Davidson, 1999, for use of nonparametric statistics).

SUBJECTS

What is the rationale for choice of a particular species for a given research program? The USDA regulations require that the proposal to the IACUC contain the rationale for the "appropriateness of the species" to be used. The research question itself may well dictate the class or species needed; or any one of a number of species may be suitable. Much research in psychology laboratories focuses on investigating general principles of behavior. Because basic behavioral processes show continuity across species, it makes sense to begin new research programs or to continue established lines of investigation with animals that are bred for research, relatively inexpensive, whose care is well understood, and for which laboratory apparatus is readily and inexpensively available. The generality of the findings and the extent to which species-related characteristics influence the expression of behavioral phenomena is established through systematic replication that includes other species.

The American Psychological Association's Committee on Animal Research and Ethics (CARE) conducted surveys of animal research in psychology departments in 1983, 1986, and 1996 (S. Panicker, personal communication, October 14, 1998). The results have indicated that about 50% of the animals used were invertebrates; and the rest—rodents, birds, amphibians and fish—made up approximately 49%. Only about 1% were other mammals. Nonhuman primates, and to a lesser extent cats and dogs, probably are more often used by psychologists who conduct behavioral research in schools of medicine. Psychologists also conduct behavioral research with nonhuman primates and other less-often-used species in governmental intramural research programs of the National Institutes of Health (NIH). This chapter presumes that most readers will be using birds or rodents as subjects, but the principles are the same regardless of the species used.

Beginning work with a species new to a laboratory inevitably requires a considerable investment of time and effort to learn the details not only of housing, feeding, care, and handling of the animal (see below) but also to learn or even develop the research methods for training and testing the animals. Experimental psychologists who work with animals learn a great deal about their care during their graduate training. Beyond graduate school, the best approach to beginning work with a new species is to arrange to spend sufficient time in a laboratory that is already well experienced with the species to obtain hands-on training and learn the laboratory lore that supplements the published literature.

Obtaining animals. Animals should be obtained from dealers licensed through the Animal and Plant Health Inspection Service (APHIS) of the USDA to sell animals for use in research. Transfer between research institutions is also possible and is an especially important route for sharing of novel strains of mice and rats and transgenic animals. Strict contingencies govern the acquisition and holding of dogs and cats (see 9 CFR Part 2 Subpart I § 2.132 & 2.133 for relevant sections of the AWA). Rats and mice are bred for research purposes by well-established commercial suppliers, but they can be bred relatively easily in academic facilities. Intensive efforts to develop inbred and other genetically defined rodent strains for biomedical and behavioral research have resulted in some strains that exhibit differential rates of particular types of behaviors (e.g., exploration, shock avoidance, drinking particular types of fluids), which make them interesting models for a variety of research questions (Graves & VandeBerg, 1998). Birds, too, are sold for research purposes by commercial suppliers. For basic behavioral research, White Carneaux or homing pigeons have been favored. See Ator (1991) for an overview of species used in behavioral research: their characteristics, care, and handling.

Behavioral scientists often use male subjects as one means of holding constant variables that are not the focus of the research. The choice of male over female rats, for example, can be related to the fact that activity levels of female rats vary predictably across the 5-day estrous cycle or to a concern about uncontrolled behavioral variability if males and females must be caged individually but in the same room. These traditional rationales for using only male subjects have been replaced by a new emphasis in biomedical research (encouraged by the NIH) on the importance of systematic study of both genders. Psychologists, too, are designing experiments to determine whether or not particular results actually will differ for male and female subjects and to follow up experimentally the basis of observed differences (e.g., Craft, Heideman, & Bartok, 1999).

Quarantine. Quarantine procedures appropriate to the species should be followed when new animals arrive in the laboratory to protect the animals already in the colony. This is true even when the animals may be obtained by transfer from another research institution. Given the lengthy training that is a hallmark of many areas of research, the illness of even one animal can threaten the success of an experiment. The effects of illness spreading throughout a colony can be devastating. Aside from monitoring the health of the new arrivals during the quarantine period, quarantine provides a period of acclimation to the laboratory and personnel, and for feeding to stabilize under free access to food. Many research settings are attempting to eliminate particular diseases within their colonies by bringing in only specific-pathogen-free (SPF) animals from suppliers or at least restricting the locations in which SPF and non-SPF animals can be housed and used. Although this policy typically applies only to rats and mice, the principle can be extended to other species. For example, a colony of macaques can be restricted to include only those that have been certified to be free of the Herpes B virus, which can be life threatening in people.

Another quarantine issue to consider is the return of animals that are used in classroom demonstrations to the colony. Although this may not pose a problem for birds or some other species, laboratory rats are particularly susceptible to viral disease that may be triggered by environmental changes. It is safest for the colony to quarantine those that have spent time outside the laboratory before returning them to a colony. A related issue is that pets, even if of the same species, should not be brought to the laboratory or animal housing area. This may jeopardize the health of the laboratory animals and risk introduction of pests (e.g., fleas) into the colony.

The general rule is not to house different species of laboratory animals in the same room, without careful consideration of health risks. For example, White Carneaux pigeons generate a great deal of dust from their feathers that would increase the likelihood of respiratory problems for laboratory rats. Some species carry pathogens that are deleterious to other species but not to themselves (e.g., the Herpes B virus is dangerous to baboons as well as to people but not to macaques). Other examples of incompatibility can include behavioral factors such as circadian rhythms (e.g., nocturnal species versus diurnal species).

Records. Keep standardized records of animals received and housed. Consider animal identification systems that can provide current and historical differentiation of individual animals. The USDA regulations include specific requirements for identification of dogs and cats and their offspring. Although the USDA may not require identification details and other detailed records for species that are not covered by the regulations such as laboratory rats, mice, and birds, there are many advantages to having them, such as maintaining continuity in the laboratory and tracking each animal's experimental history. Most psychological research differs from most biomedical research in that in behavioral research, the animals are not routinely euthanized to gather tissue as a necessary part of the study. Once animals are trained, they can serve in different studies across their life span, subject to regulatory cautions for particular types of studies. Building on the histories of individual animals is a strength of much long-term behavioral research.

A central laboratory animal record can keep the experimental history of each subject (e.g., that a particular color light was used as a cue for a particular contingency with a pigeon). When weight regulation is used, as it is in much behavioral research, an historic record of free-feeding weights can be kept in the central record. Health problems and their mode of treatment can also be recorded for future reference. Such a central laboratory animal record can be a useful resource for preparing annual progress reports that may be required by the IACUC about the numbers of animals that have served under a particular protocol, their health, and their disposition (see chaps. 8 and 9 and Appendix C for more details).

Care and feeding. Researchers should become as familiar as possible with the physiology, needs, and potential health problems of the species with which they are working. Fortunately, a great deal of information about most species used in research has been published. The literature on rats is particularly extensive (Toth & Gardiner, 2000). See Ator (1991) and Ellenberger (1993) for information on general laboratory procedures and handling of animals; both chapters also have extensive reference lists. Poling, Nickel, and Alling (1990) also discuss food restriction in pigeons. With the advent of Internet search capabilities, specialized Web sites, and electronic mailing lists for groups of people with common interests, gaining specialized information is easier than ever before (Van Sluyters, 1997). Commercial services that publish the tables of contents of journals, grouped by subject area, on a weekly basis also provide an excellent means to keep up with current literature relevant to laboratory animal care as well as relevant to research in general. The National Research Council's Institute of Laboratory Animal Resources (ILAR) compiles and disseminates information on a range of topics related to laboratory animals through the *ILAR Journal*. The National Institutes of Health also provide guidelines for diet control in behavioral studies at http://oacu.od.nih.gov/ARAC/dietctrl.htm.

Knowledge of feeding and growth patterns for different species, as well as nutrient requirements, is important to determine rational weight control regimens. Although a specific rationale for food restriction may be the needs of the experimental protocol (see below), it is important for researchers to remember that unrestricted access to food is not the norm and may promote obesity in captive animals. Research with rodents and monkeys has shown that they are healthier and live longer if they are not allowed to become obese (Lane, Ingram, Ball, & Roth, 1997; Masoro, 1985). As long as a nutritionally balanced diet is supplied, restriction of caloric intake is recognized in the National Research Council (NRC) *Guide for the Care and Use of Laboratory Animals* (1996) as an accepted practice in long-term housing of animals.

In the wild, most species have access to food and water only for limited periods each day. Effort (foraging) is required to obtain them. Research methods that require the expenditure of time and energy to obtain food for limited periods each day are compatible with the natural pattern. USDA regulations recommend "foraging or task-oriented feeding methods" as a way to provide mandated "environmental enrichment" for nonhuman primates.

Information on the daily caloric, nutrient, and water requirements of many species is published in the NRC series, *Nutrient Requirements of Domestic Animals*. Balanced animal diets based on these recommendations are available commercially as pellets for reinforcement for a variety of species. The diet is all that is needed to feed laboratory animals appropriately under free-feeding conditions as long as the expiration dates are heeded. Under restricted feeding conditions, however, vitamin supplements may be used, depending on the species and the degree of restriction. Supplements may also be appropriate when feeding is not particularly restricted but the amount consumed decreases as a function of experimental manipulations (e.g., drug self-administration).

PERSONNEL

In most psychology laboratories, undergraduate and graduate students are responsible for conducting the experimental sessions from day to day. Sometimes they are paid, sometimes they are volunteers, and sometimes they are doing it for academic credit. In any event, it is part of their training in psychology. The proportion of people in psychology department laboratories who are nonstudent research assistants is low.

Appropriately trained people must care for the animals every day of the year, regardless of whether they also run the experimental sessions. Some institutions are able to employ, train, and supervise special staff members to provide daily care for animals. In other institutions, investigators themselves must bear this responsibility, or they choose to do so because of the needs of the experiments. Even in the former case, however, investigators and their students are wise to keep in close contact with institutional employees and their supervisor. Because behavioral experiments usually involve daily or almost daily experimental sessions, they can require control of food or fluid intake or both, and also require constancy in routine care and housing conditions. Therefore, good communication among laboratory personnel is essential for good experimental control as well as for assuring the well-being of the animals.

Federal mandates require that people who work with animals in research facilities be informed about "the basic needs of each species of animal" and "proper handling and care for the various species of animal used by the facility." They require "the research facility to ensure that all scientists, research technicians, animal technicians, and other personnel involved in animal care, treatment, and use are qualified to perform their duties."

Laboratory directors should carefully assess the qualifications of individuals assigned to work independently with laboratory animals, whether experimentally or in caring for them, or both. Individuals differ in the speed with which they acquire the skills needed to handle animals appropriately. If a person is apprehensive, pushing him or her to independent handling too quickly can result in poor handling practices and unnecessary risk to the animal and the handler.

The USDA regulations list several topics in which training and instruction must be provided and in which the qualifications of personnel must be reviewed. The USDA regulations are largely consistent with those in the *Guide for the Care and Use of Laboratory Animals* (National Research Council, 1996). Making copies of the *Guide* available to everyone in the laboratory is a good starting place for training. If species of animals in a laboratory do fall under the USDA regulations, however, firsthand knowledge of the legal requirements can be helpful when debate about particular issues arises. Preparing and updating, as needed, an easy-to-read Standard Operating Procedures (SOP) manual specific to one's own laboratory can be a way to provide members of the laboratory a general overview and guide. Such a manual can be useful to minimize miscommunications or failures to communicate information to new members of the laboratory. Some IACUCs require that a copy of the SOP manual be maintained in a readily accessible location in the laboratory.

Veterinarians. Establishing a relationship with a local veterinarian, if the institution does not employ one, is important to provide clinical backup for treatment of illnesses (see Parks, chap. 4, this volume). Not all veterinarians are as familiar with the idiosyncrasies of certain laboratory species as the behavioral scientist may be, but they are trained in many areas in which the psychologist is not (e.g., clinical diagnosis, surgical technique, the use of antibiotics). A strong partnership with a veterinarian in assessing and treating illness is a valuable asset for the welfare of the animals and ultimately a successful program of research. For regulated facilities, USDA regulations require that "medical care for animals . . . be available and provided as necessary by a qualified veterinarian" and that an attending veterinarian be employed under "formal arrangements." If the attending veterinarian is part-time, "the formal arrangements shall include a written program of veterinary care and regularly scheduled visits to the research facility."

APPARATUS

Most behavioral experiments use specially constructed apparatus, such as some version of an operant chamber (e.g., Skinner box). Behavioral experiments with rodents may use various kinds of mazes, running wheels, or open field areas (chambers and other apparatus are reviewed in Ator, 1991; see also chaps. in Sahgal, 1993a). The apparatus usually is automated to be able to present stimuli (e.g., lights, sounds, food pellets) and to record behavior (e.g., lever operation, licking a spout, locomotor activity) although some procedures do involve direct observation and recording of the animal's behavior by the experimenter. The apparatus into which the animal is placed may be situated inside a larger chamber designed to attenuate extraneous visual or auditory stimuli during the experimental session. Good chamber ventilation is important and most such systems require some regular maintenance.

Whatever specialized chamber is used, the animal typically remains in it for the duration of the experimental session. Experimental sessions can be very short (e.g., 10 minutes) or long (e.g., 3 hours); some studies conduct sessions intermittently or continuously over 24 hours (e.g., time course of drug effects). If the experiment requires the animal to remain in the experimental chamber 24 hours a day, then provision for access to water, regular timing of feeding, cleaning the chamber, and so forth must be arranged as a part of the experimental protocol.

Animals in behavioral experiments typically become habituated quickly to being weighed, transferred to the experimental apparatus or chair, and other routine procedures. The fact that, for good experimental control, it usually is the same individual (or a familiar substitute) who is handling the animal from day to day contributes to the habituation process.

Some form of restraint is used in experiments in which it is important to ensure a consistent orientation toward and precise distance from sensory stimuli. Experiments with squirrel monkeys or rhesus monkeys that involve drug delivery into a chronically indwelling cannula may require that the monkey be restrained during the experimental session to protect the connection to the cannula. A common form of restraint with small monkeys is to train them to sit in a specially designed chair during experimental sessions. As opposed to research that uses restraint as a stressor, the restraint in this context is a practical consideration for proper positioning of an animal or protection of an implanted device. The goal is to introduce the animal to the procedure in such a way that it is minimally stressful and so that the animal is well habituated by the time the experiment itself begins.

The duration of restraint and the particular procedures for inducing and monitoring it must be well justified and consistent with current scientific, legal, and ethical standards. Restraint of nonhuman primates for research purposes (whether as described previously or in studies of stress) must be specifically approved by the IACUC and "must be for the shortest period possible." If "long-term (more than 12 hours) restraint is required, nonhuman primates must be provided the opportunity daily for unrestrained activity for at least one continuous hour during the period of restraint" unless otherwise approved by the IACUC for that research proposal. The need for lengthy restraint is unusual in protocols in psychology research.

EXPERIMENTAL PROCEDURES

Some research does not involve training an animal to do something. The experimental question might be addressed primarily or exclusively by observation of an animal's spontaneous behavioral repertoire in a particular context (e.g., activity in an open field, running wheel, or elevated platform; social interaction with familiar or unfamiliar conspecifics of the same or a different sex; vocalization; maternal behavior such as pup retrieval; eating or drinking. See reviews in Sahgal, 1993a; van Haaren, 1993).

The majority of psychological research that uses animals involves training behaviors motivated by delivery of food, water, or a sweetened substance (e.g., fruit juice, saccharin flavored water, sweetened condensed milk) to study learning and memory, problem-solving, choice, perception, sensory processes, and more. The percentage of research that involves aversive stimuli (such as electric shock), aversive situations (such as social stress), implantation of devices (such as brain electrodes or cannulae), or administering psychoactive drugs (such as cocaine or alcohol) is smaller. Some experiments involve measuring both spontaneous behaviors as well as a trained behavior (e.g., study of adjunctive behavior, Falk, 1977).

The experimental question can involve studying how long it takes the animal to acquire the new behavior under particular circumstances or training the new response by a standard method to use that behavior as part of a well-controlled baseline. In most cases, methods for training that have been well developed and refined to take species differences into account are adapted for use within each laboratory and often adapted for each individual subject (cf., Ator, 1991; Gleeson, 1991; McNaughton, 1993).

Just as it is helpful to learn to work with new species by working in the laboratory of someone familiar with the species, it is labor- and timesaving to learn new procedures in laboratories where they are in regular use. For humane, scientific, and practical reasons, this is especially important for procedures that involve restraint, aversive stimuli, drugs, or surgical procedures (Morrison, Evans, Ator, & Nakamura, 2002). This is not to say that individuals new to a procedure cannot learn a great deal from reading materials and discussions with colleagues at scientific meetings. The Internet also provides the means by which researchers may be able to share details of methodologies from a distance better than ever before. Often, however, there is no substitute for firsthand observation and hands-on guidance. For the laboratory doing the training, there is the added benefit that someone fresh to a procedure may ask questions that prompt insights into ways that it can be improved.

Students or research assistants who conduct daily experimental sessions need to be trained to consider and address a range of behavioral, environmental, or equipment-related variables that might hinder training or disrupt food- or fluid-maintained performance. Inexperienced personnel may presume that the source of a problem in training a food- or fluid-motivated behavior is that the food restriction regimen is not strict enough (or in some cases that it is too strict). Poor performance in the task calls for a comprehensive assessment of all the likely variables rather than a presumption that greater food or fluid control is necessary. Other variables can include task criteria that are too high or were raised too quickly for the animal's level of training, equipment malfunctions, illness, and inadvertent water deprivation when food is the reinforcer.

USE OF APPETITIVE STIMULI IN BEHAVIORAL RESEARCH

Species as diverse as rat, pigeon, porpoise, goat, pig, sheep, cow, turtle, fish, octopus, crab, mouse, and monkey have been trained to perform simple to complex tasks under training procedures in which small amounts of a food or fluid (technically termed *reinforcers*) maintain performance. The use of consumable reinforcers predominates because of their well-studied ability to motivate the development of a new behavior and to maintain stable responding for extended periods.

Preferred food items (e.g., sweetened condensed milk, fruit juice) or "treats" (e.g., sugar pellets) can be used to maintain stable responding, but use of food pellets that provide a balanced diet as reinforcers has some advantages. The nutritional status of the animal may be better if the majority of calories are obtained from a balanced diet rather than from treats. Animals may eat a less balanced diet, even if freely available, if they receive a significant number of calories from treats. For some species that serve in the experiments for months or years, the possibility of dental cavities with frequent consumption of sugared food is a disadvantage.

Food restriction. When any caloric reinforcer is used, including treats, access to food typically must be controlled. The foremost reason is to ensure that the item will reliably maintain performance in the experimental sessions. Control of access to food and of body weights within a constant range can be important for reasons other than those specifically related to using food as a reinforcer. When animals have free access to food, the amount eaten in the hours just before experimental testing may vary within and across subjects, which may increase variability in performance in the experimental session both within and across animals. Weight regulation per se may be important to minimize other sources of variability for experimental results. In studies with drugs, for example, control of the animal's weight for the duration of an experiment assures uniform dosing throughout the study (i.e., that total amount of drug received per mg/kg dose, its absorption, and distribution remain relatively constant).

The USDA regulations state that "Deprivation of food or water shall not be used to train, work, or otherwise handle animals; *Provided, however*: That the short-term withholding of food or water from animals, when specified in an IACUC-approved activity that includes a description of monitoring procedures, is allowed by these regulations." Short-term food and water restriction thus is permitted under the regulations but the rationale and methods must be IACUC-approved and procedures for monitoring animals under food or water restriction must be specified.

The issue to be considered for purposes of the experimental protocol is the degree of food restriction. Researchers must determine the least restrictive regimen that will provide for stable performance from day to day. The reduced weight often viewed as a standard is 80% to 85% of a free-feeding weight. However, the species, the age of the subject at the time the free-feeding weight is calculated, and the duration of free-feeding before the weight is determined are critical determinants of whether the 80% rule is a reasonable one for a particular species. Weight regulation for a number of species used in behavioral research is reviewed in Ator (1991).

The goal of food restriction for research purposes is to select a weight range that permits the reinforcer to maintain responding during the experimental session and maintains the animal's well-being. A lower weight range may be necessary early in training than after performance has been established. The manner in which initial food restriction is accomplished and any target weight selected must be considered in the context of special requirements of the species.

Food-restricted animals are weighed frequently, usually before experimental sessions. Any animals on food restriction must have their body weight checked and recorded on a regular schedule, whether they are serving in an experiment in a particular period of time or not, to be able to detect any unexpected decline in body weight. USDA regulations specifically state that nonhuman primates, dogs, and cats "must be fed at least once each day" unless veterinary care (not research) considerations require an exception. Unless specific protocols require exemption, allowing most laboratory animal species to feed at least once per day is consistent with standards of humane care.

Feeding often may not occur until 15 to 60 minutes after a session to prevent the phenomenon of within-session response rate decreases that can develop when animals are fed immediately on return to the home cage (Bacotti, 1976). Feeding time usually is kept relatively constant from day to day, even on weekends and holidays, so that the animals do not have to go for unusually long periods between daily feedings. In all circumstances, good coverage of animals under food control is necessary 365 days a year to avoid additional, unprogrammed, food restriction.

Constant access to water typically is provided under food control regimens. The exception is when sessions are relatively short (e.g., less than a couple of hours) and water is not available until the animal is back in the home cage. There is an interdependency between food and water intake (e.g., food-restricted animals may drink less water), but species differ in their patterns of drinking during the day and in their response to food restriction.

When feeding is restricted for experimental purposes, consider whether breaks between studies or experimental conditions are long enough to warrant increasing the food ration for the period of the interruption or redetermining the new restricted weight altogether by returning the animal to free feeding for a 2-week period or longer. Practices vary, and there are several considerations, which include (a) the percentage by which weight was restricted for the study, (b) the age of the animal at the time of the original determination of ad libitum weight, and (c) whether there are problems created by abrupt shifts between restricted and unrestricted feeding (e.g., abrupt return to free feeding can produce life-threatening bloat in some monkeys).

Water restriction. Fluids may be more useful than solid food reinforcers for behavioral procedures that require the animal's head to be in a particular position (e.g., psychophysical studies or studies that monitor brain activity in behaving organisms), because a fluid can be delivered through a solenoid-operated sipper tube positioned at the animal's mouth. Another practical consideration in choosing to use water rather than food reinforcers is the low cost.

When water is used to maintain responding, access to water outside the experimental session needs to be controlled. Some other liquid reinforcers (e.g., fruit juice with monkeys) under certain conditions (e.g., procedures that require multihour sessions with many reinforcer deliveries) also may maintain performance most reliably when access to water is controlled.

Some studies require the animal to earn its entire daily fluid requirement during the experimental session, and these sessions typically are multiple hours in length. Others use shorter sessions but provide a period of supplemental access to water shortly after the session. On days that sessions are not conducted, animals should receive a period of access to water. Nonhuman primates, dogs, and cats "must be offered water no less than twice daily for at least 1 hour each time." Provision for specific exemption for all three species for "veterinary care" reasons is made in the USDA regulations but exemption by the IACUC-approved research protocol is provided only for nonhuman primates.

Animals remain healthy longer without food than without water, and some species are particularly susceptible to effects of deprivation (e.g., mice and guinea pigs). Determining the parameters of water restriction that do not produce dehydration requires careful consideration (Hughes, Amyx, Howard, Nanry, & Pollard, 1994). Information on fluid requirements can be obtained from the ILAR volume entitled *Nutrient Requirements of Laboratory Animals* (NRC, 1995). Animals under water control may lose weight because of reduced food consumption. To prevent this, feed the animals in close proximity to their access to water or moisten the animal's chow.

A good system of monitoring daily fluid intake is important. Keep records of the volume of fluid earned in the task as well as amounts of supplements consumed. Careful observation of the animal's behavior, together with regular clinical monitoring of the animal's weight and health are critical to successful use of fluid reinforcers.

USE OF AVERSIVE STIMULI IN BEHAVIORAL RESEARCH

Aversive stimuli are, by definition, those that an organism will avoid. In technical terms, they are called negative reinforcers when responses that remove them or prevent their occurrence become more probable. Behavioral studies that use aversive stimuli fall into several broad categories. Some studies examine aversively motivated behavior (e.g., avoidance, escape, and punishment). Other studies use aversive stimuli to study the immediate or long-term effects of stressors themselves on behavior or physiology. Some areas of behavioral pharmacology research rely on aversively motivated behavior to compare drugs from different pharmacological classes or with different mechanisms of action. Some studies focus on the neurobiology of aversively motivated behavior compared to appetitively motivated behavior.

The use of aversive stimuli in behavioral research probably provides some of the knottiest issues for researchers. Procedures that cause "more than momentary or slight pain or distress" call for special consideration in experimental design. They are particularly singled out by the USDA regulations for consideration by IACUCs. The USDA regulations define *painful procedure* as "any procedure that would reasonably be expected to cause more than slight or momentary pain or distress in a human being to which that procedure was applied."

The IACUC is required to determine whether procedures involving animals avoid or minimize discomfort, distress, and pain. Procedures that are considered to cause more than momentary or slight pain or distress are a focus of special consideration. The definition of painful procedure specifically says that the pain would be "in excess of that caused by injections or other minor procedures" (Institute of Laboratory Animal Resources, Committee on Pain and Distress in Laboratory Animals, National Research Council, 1992).

The USDA regulations require that the IACUC ascertain that "Procedures that may cause more than momentary or slight pain or distress to the animals will: (A) Be performed with appropriate sedatives, analgesics or anesthetics, unless withholding such agents is justified for scientific reasons . . . and will continue for only the necessary period of time; (B) Involve, in their planning, consultation with the attending veterinarian or his or her designee; (C) Not include the use of paralytics without anesthesia. . . ."

In a protocol, researchers must explicitly state why any procedure that may cause more than momentary or slight pain or distress is being used and why a particular method is being used. In the absence of contrary evidence, the scientific community recognizes that if the procedure would cause pain to a human, then it can be expected that it could do so for a nonhuman animal too. They should relate the use of such procedures to the published literature. For species covered by the USDA regulations, IACUCs must require that investigators provide "a written narrative description of the methods and sources" by which the investigator determined that "alternatives to procedures that cause more than momentary or slight pain or distress to the animals" were not available. The regulations specifically mention the U.S. Government Animal Welfare Information Center (AWIC) as an example of a resource that could be used to determine whether alternatives are available (see chap. 10).

Because of the extensive research on avoidance, escape, punishment, conditioned suppression, and the study of the phenomenon of stress in recent decades, there is considerable information on the behavioral processes that operate under such conditions (Azrin & Holz, 1966; Baron, 1991; Hineline, 1977; Morse, McKearney, & Kelleher, 1977; Paré & Glavin, 1993). In addition, a great deal is known about which stimuli will function most effectively to produce particular behavioral baselines. By careful study of the existing literature, trial and error with respect to aversive stimuli, its parameters, and the parameters of contingencies for producing particular baselines can be minimized. Researchers can rely on that literature to determine experimental parameters and other procedures that are most suitable for creating the desired baseline performance, taking into account the advantages and disadvantages of each procedure for particular purposes (see also chaps. in Sahgal, 1993a; van Haaren, 1993). Investigators should be well informed about the reasons that a specific procedure is most appropriate for a given study, the advantages and disadvantages of the procedure, and the likely effect of the procedure on the animal. Although the use of pain alleviating drugs (at least during baseline or control conditions) is typically antithetical to the purposes of many behavioral experiments that involve aversive stimuli, there should be thoughtful consideration of ways to minimize pain without jeopardizing the experiment.

Escape, avoidance, and punishment. The basic behavioral paradigms of aversively motivated behavior are escape and avoidance (Baron, 1991; Clincke & Werbrouck, 1993; Sahgal, 1993b; Schulteis & Koob, 1993). An escape procedure is one in which an animal learns to make a particular response to terminate an aversive stimulus that is already present (e.g., electric shock through a grid floor that can be escaped by running to another compartment of the apparatus or by pressing a lever that turns the shock off). An avoidance procedure is one in which an animal learns that making a certain response will prevent the onset of an aversive stimulus. In many studies of avoidance or punished behavior, depending on the contingencies, once the animal acquires the response, it is common for few if any shocks to be delivered (i.e., the delivery is under the animal's control). This is particularly true of procedures that use conditioned aversive stimuli (e.g., tone or light paired with shock) to maintain behavior, such as the stimulus-shock termination procedure (Morse et al., 1977).

In a punishment procedure (sometimes termed *conflict procedure*), making a response occasionally produces a positive reinforcer (e.g., food), but some or all of the responses also produce an aversive stimulus, which has the effect of reducing the overall rate of responding maintained by the positive reinforcer. Different degrees of suppression can be produced by varying parameters such as intensity of the aversive stimulus, the number of responses followed by the aversive stimulus, and so forth (Azrin & Holz, 1966; Baron, 1991; Commisaris, 1993). Even in many punishment paradigms, judicious choice of the schedule of reinforcement and the schedule of punishment to be superimposed can permit a well-trained animal to learn to suppress behavior sufficiently to obtain most or all of the available reinforcers without regularly contacting the aversive stimulus (Morse et al., 1977).

Electric shock. Whether a particular stimulus (e.g., an electric shock, a loud noise, a cold environment) will serve as a negative reinforcer is evaluated empirically by presenting it and determining whether a laboratory animal will learn a response that terminates it, diminishes its intensity, or decreases its frequency of occurrence. In parallel with research on positive reinforcers, stimuli that function as negative reinforcers for some organisms may not do so for others. As with positive reinforcers, some stimuli function reliably as negative reinforcers across a wide range of conditions for most or all individual organisms and across species. Electric shock is such a stimulus, which largely accounts for the prevalence of its use as an aversive stimulus in behavioral research. Other characteristics of electric shock have made it particularly useful (Azrin & Holz, 1966; Baron, 1991). The following are summarized from Azrin and Holz (1966):

1. In the range used for behavioral research, electric shock does not produce tissue damage. Shock produces its noxious quality by directly stimulating nociceptive fibers, not by producing injury.

2. The sensation produced does not persist beyond the period of stimulation. Delivery of the shock thus does not interfere with the ability to make responses, such as those that prevent the next shock delivery.

3. Physical aspects of the shock stimulus are specifiable and con-
    trollable by the experimenter, which permits precise control
    of all the parameters within and across studies and replication
    by other investigators.

Experimental control over the onset and termination, as well as the intensity, of an aversive stimulus is an absolute requirement of much research on aversively motivated behavior.

The concept of using minimal levels of intensity of shock, as with any stressor, is an important one, but there are important caveats. Punishment research has shown that using gradually increasing shock intensities results in habituation such that the level of shock ultimately required to produce the desired suppression of responding likely will be higher than it would have been if a higher shock level had been used initially (Azrin & Holz, 1966).

Stress. Not all research that uses aversive stimuli seeks to produce stress. Animal models have been developed specifically to study the effects of stress on immune function and other physiological and behavioral systems. In stress research, subjects (or a group of subjects) often do not have control of the aversive stimulus as they do in studies of avoidance, escape, and some studies of punishment. This is because many of the phenomena of interest occur only, or most readily, if the subject does not have control over the stressful event.

The development of reliable, objective indices of stress is important to stress research, and information from such studies can also inform research-ers' understanding of the effects of behavioral procedures that use aversive stimuli or those that might be considered stressful. A number of behavioral and physiological responses have served as dependent measures in studies of stress (Paré & Glavin, 1993). No single physiological or behavioral measure can be taken as uniquely indicating the occurrence of stress in the intact animal. Even situations in which a constellation of signs permits the occur-rence of stress to be concluded, the variable responsible for the stress may require empirical verification. In stress research, it has been particularly clear that inclusion of carefully designed control conditions is essential for appro-priate interpretation of the results (Paré & Glavin, 1993). Because stress research, by its very nature, must be presumed to cause pain and distress, attention to careful design so that the results will be clearly interpretable is critical.

DRUGS OR TOXICANTS

Psychoactive drugs are those that act via the central nervous system to affect mood and behavior. Many research areas in psychology involve the study of the effects of classes of psychoactive drugs and in turn use the effects of the drugs as a tool to understand behavioral processes (Branch, 1991; Goldberg & Stolerman, 1986; Goudie & Emmett-Oglesby, 1989; van Haaren, 1993). Some research in psychopharmacology compares and contrasts the effects of drugs on behavior to better understand the behavioral effects of clinically useful sedatives, stimulants, antipsychotics (also called *neuroleptics*), and antidepressants, and how ongoing behavioral baselines or environmental contexts can produce effects different from what might otherwise be expected (Barrett, Glowa, & Nader, 1989; Thompson, Dews, & McKim, 1981). The effectiveness of many new drugs as analgesics, antidepressants, and anxiolytics in people has been determined by behavioral studies using aversive stimuli in animals.

Behavioral toxicology experiments characterize the effects of relatively low levels of toxicants, such as lead and carbon monoxide, to which people may be exposed (e.g., Krasnegor, Gray, & Thompson, 1986). Behavioral toxicology and behavioral pharmacology are distinguished primarily by the particular chemical they investigate. The arbitrary nature of the dividing line is made clear by studies in which abused inhalants, such as toluene, are investigated.

Some research focuses on better understanding of pharmacological and behavioral variables related to drug abuse. Drug taking, or the ability of drugs to serve as reinforcers, is studied experimentally in self-administration procedures (Ator & Griffiths, 2003; Meisch & Lemaire, 1993). If animals are outfitted with chronically indwelling venous catheters, then a drug is delivered intravenously as a consequence of behavior. This and the oral self-administration procedure are most common for studies related to abuse liability or drug abuse and dependence. Some studies may use chronically indwelling intragastric or intracranial catheters. In most such procedures, the tubing exits from a site on the back or the top of the head (depending on the species) and is threaded through a protective device, referred to as a tether, to a swivel or other connection permitting attachment to the pump that will deliver the drug. A similar arrangement is used for experiments that involve implantation of intracranial stimulating or measuring devices. In any procedure in which an animal is outfitted with a chronically indwelling device, a program of frequent, regular, inspection and maintenance is critical to the health of the animal and the success of the experiment. Good understanding of aseptic procedures (e.g., when connecting the end of the catheter to the swivel) is important to preventing infection. Good understanding of the dangers of indiscriminate use of antibiotics is important to avoiding the development of resistant strains of bacteria.

To obtain and use drugs that have been scheduled under the Controlled Substances Act, researchers must have a license from the Drug Enforcement Administration (DEA). Psychoactive drugs such as alcohol, caffeine, and nicotine, many of those used as antidepressants, and some other psychoactive chemicals can be used in research without such a license, but most sedatives, stimulants, analgesics, and drugs with psychotomimetic effects, whether clinically useful or not, require a drug license. Separate licenses are required for drugs approved for medical use (Schedules II–V) and those that have no approved medical use in the United States (Schedule I).

In designing studies of drug effects, a number of considerations related to animal welfare apply. Most behavioral studies with psychoactive drugs are not studies of toxicity. Researchers should assemble enough information about the effects of the drug from other studies to understand the range of doses likely to be behaviorally active but safe. Also, it is important to understand considerations in translating doses across species that vary greatly in body weight to avoid toxicity when going from a very small to a very large animal (Dews, 1976). If the study is one of chronic administration, the researcher should understand the conditions under which physical dependence (i.e., manifested by a withdrawal syndrome when the drug is stopped) might develop and determine what might be done, consistent with the goals of the experiment, to alleviate the withdrawal syndrome. One should choose a solvent for the drug that is the least likely to damage tissue if the drug is to be given intramuscularly, subcutaneously, or intraperitoneally. Finally, the researcher should consider developing methods for oral drug delivery, when appropriate, that might be used reliably for long-term studies (cf., Turkkan, Ator, Brady, & Craven, 1989).

SURGICAL PROCEDURES

The USDA regulations require "appropriate provision for pre- and postoperative care of the animals in accordance with established veterinary medical and nursing practices." It further states that "All survival surgery will be performed using aseptic procedures, including surgical gloves, masks, sterile instruments, and aseptic techniques." Although it is common for behavioral scientists to learn to do surgical procedures themselves, receiving some portion of the training from someone who has been formally trained (e.g., in medical school or veterinary school) in operating room procedures and in good aseptic and surgical technique is of great benefit.

Scientists should use up-to-date methods for anesthesia and analgesia (including postoperative analgesia) that are appropriate for the species (Flecknell, 1996; see ILAR, 1992). They can prevent infection by performing the surgery under aseptic conditions and by use of antibiotics appropriate to the species. Also, they need to keep records of the treatments used in conjunction with the surgery and have a plan for frequent postoperative monitoring of the animal and a contingency plan for action if the animal's condition deteriorates.

The USDA regulations state that "Major operative procedures on nonrodents will be conducted only in facilities intended for that purpose which shall be operated and maintained under aseptic conditions. Nonmajor operative procedures and all surgery on rodents do not require a dedicated facility, but must be performed using aseptic procedures." A "major operative procedure" is defined as "any surgical intervention that penetrates and exposes a body cavity or any procedure, which produces permanent impairment of physical or physiological functions." The regulations prohibit an animal from having "more than one major operative procedure from which it is allowed to recover. . . ." Exceptions can be made, including "for scientific reasons," if justified in writing "by the principal investigator."

THE END OF THE EXPERIMENT

Much research in psychology involves training animals under a particular procedure and continuing to use the well-trained animal in research across the lifespan. For some experiments, naive animals are critical. In all circumstances, though, laboratories need to have policies established about what happens to animals that no longer can serve in research or are sick. The methods of euthanasia appropriate for a species must always be understood even when a researcher considers it unlikely that it will be needed. The USDA regulations require that the IACUC determine that euthanasia be by "a method that produces rapid unconsciousness and subsequent death without evidence of pain or distress, or a method that uses anesthesia produced by an agent that causes painless loss of consciousness and subsequent death." (See chap. 4 for more details on euthanasia.)

An alternative to euthanasia for animals that have not undergone surgical procedures and are otherwise in good health is to release them as pets. This is common in laboratories in which long-term behavioral experiments have resulted in students or research assistants becoming attached to a particular animal. Although this is recognized as a reasonable alternative by attending veterinarians and the professional ethics of the APA, the head of the laboratory needs to consider carefully the ability of the individual to provide appropriate care. Because IACUCs may require information about the disposition of animals at the end of the study, it is important to include this option in the protocol at the outset.

CONCLUSION

Healthy animals are critical to replicable research. Thorough training of students and other personnel, clearly defined laboratory practices with respect to treatment of animals, and consistent overall supervision are critical not only to the humane treatment of laboratory animals but also to excellence in a research program.

Neither the requirements of the USDA regulations nor those of the PHS Animal Welfare Assurance (see chap. 9) may govern work in a laboratory at the present time. Those sets of requirements do reflect, however, current consensus of the scientific community about good laboratory practices in the use of animals. As such, they provide a reasonable framework within which psychologists who work with laboratory animals can formulate their own laboratory practices and to which they can refer in training students, who one day may work in such a laboratory.

REFERENCES

Animal Welfare Act, 7 U.S.C. § 2132 (2002).

Ator, N. A. (1991). Subjects and instrumentation. In I. H. Iversen & K. A. Lattal (Eds.), *Techniques in the behavioral and neural sciences: Vol. 6. Experimental analysis of behavior, Part 1* (pp. 1–62) Amsterdam: Elsevier Science.

Ator, N. A. (1999). Statistical inference in behavior analysis: Environmental determinants? *The Behavior Analyst, 22,* 93–97.

Ator, N. A., & Griffiths, R. R. (2003). Principles of drug abuse liability assessment in laboratory animals. *Drug and Alcohol Dependence, 70,* S55–S72.

Azrin, N., & Holz, W. C. (1966). Punishment. In W. K. Honig (Ed.), *Operant behavior: Areas of research and application* (pp. 380–447). New York: Appleton-Century-Crofts.

Bacotti, A. V. (1976). Home cage feeding time controls responding under multiple schedules. *Animal Learning and Behavior, 4,* 41–44.

Baron, A. (1991). Avoidance and punishment. In I. Iversen & K. A. Lattal (Eds.), *Techniques in the behavioral and neural sciences: Vol. 6. Experimental analysis of behavior, Part 1* (pp. 173–217). Amsterdam: Elsevier Science.

Barrett, J. E., Glowa, J. R., & Nader, M. A. (1989). Behavioral and pharmacological history as determinants of tolerance- and sensitization-like phenomena in drug action. In A. J. Goudie & M. W. Emmett-Oglesby (Eds.), *Psychoactive drugs: Tolerance and sensitization* (pp. 181–219). Clifton, NJ: Humana Press.

Bordens, K. S., & Abbott, B. B. (1996). *Research design and methods: A process approach* (3rd ed.). Mountain View, CA: Mayfield.

Branch, M. N. (1991). Behavioral pharmacology. In I. H. Iversen & K. A. Lattal (Eds.), *Techniques in the behavioral and neural sciences: Vol. 6. Experimental Analysis of Behavior, Part 2* (pp. 21–78). Amsterdam: Elsevier Science.

Branch, M. N. (1999). Statistical inference in behavior analysis: Some things significance testing does and does not do. *The Behavior Analyst, 22,* 87–92.

Clincke, G. H. C., & Werbrouck, L. (1993). Two-way active avoidance. In A. Sahgal (Ed.), *Behavioural neuroscience: A practical approach* (Vol. 1, pp. 71–79). Oxford, England: IRL Press

Commisaris, R. L. (1993). Conflict behaviors as animal models for the study of anxiety. In F. van Haaren (Ed.), *Techniques in the behavioral and neural sciences: Vol.*

10. *Methods in behavioral pharmacology* (pp. 443–474). Amsterdam: Elsevier Science.

Craft, R. M., Heideman, L. M., & Bartok, R. E. (1999). Effect of gonadectomy on discriminative stimulus effects of morphine in female versus male rats. *Drug and Alcohol Dependence, 53,* 95–109.

Davidson, M. (1999). Statistical inference in behavior analysis: Having my cake and eating it? *The Behavior Analyst, 22,* 99–103.

Dews, P. B. (1976). Interspecies differences in drug effects: Behavioral. In E. Usdin & I. S. Forrest (Eds.), *Psychotherapeutic drugs. Part 1* (pp. 175–224). New York: Marcel Dekker.

Ellenberger, M. A. (1993). The use of animal models in behavioral pharmacology. In F. van Haaren (Ed.), *Techniques in the behavioral and neural sciences: Vol. 10. Methods in behavioral pharmacology* (pp. 1–21). Amsterdam: Elsevier Science.

Falk, J. L. (1977). The origins and functions of adjunctive behavior. *Animal Learning and Behavior, 5,* 325–335.

Fisch, G. S. (1998). Visual inspection of data revisited: Do the eyes still have it? *The Behavior Analyst, 21,* 111–123.

Flecknell, P. (1996). *Laboratory animal anaesthesia: An introduction for research workers and technicians* (2nd ed.). San Diego, CA: Academic Press.

Gleeson, S. (1991). Response acquisition. In I. H. Iversen & K. A. Lattal (Eds.), *Techniques in the behavioral and neural sciences: Vol. 6. Experimental Analysis of Behavior, Part 1* (pp. 63–86). Amsterdam: Elsevier Science.

Goldberg, S. R., & Stolerman, I. P. (Eds.). (1986). *Behavioral analysis of drug dependence.* Orlando, FL: Academic Press.

Goudie, A. J., & Emmett-Oglesby, M. W. (Eds.). (1989). *Psychoactive drugs: Tolerance and sensitization.* Clifton, NJ: Humana Press.

Graves, J. A. M., & VandeBerg, J. L. (Eds.). (1998). Comparative gene mapping. *ILAR Journal, 39*(2, 3).

Hineline, P. (1977). Negative reinforcement and avoidance. In W. K. Honig & J. E. R. Staddon (Eds.), *Handbook of operant behavior* (pp. 364–414). Englewood Cliffs, NJ: Prentice-Hall.

Hughes, J. E., Amyx, H., Howard, J. L., Nanry, K. P., & Pollard, G. T. (1994). Health effects of water restriction to motivate lever-pressing in rats. *Laboratory Animal Science, 44,* 135–140.

Institute of Laboratory Animal Resources, Committee on Pain and Distress in Laboratory Animals, National Research Council. (1992). *Recognition and alleviation of pain and distress in laboratory animals.* Washington, DC: National Academy Press.

Kazdin, A. E. (1984). Statistical analyses for single-case experimental designs. In D. H. Barlow & M. Hersen (Eds.), *Single case experimental designs: Strategies for studying behavior change* (2nd ed., pp. 265–316). New York: Pergamon Press.

Krasnegor, N. A., Gray, D. B., & Thompson, T. (Eds.). (1986). *Advances in behavioral pharmacology: Vol. 5. Developmental behavioral pharmacology.* Hillsdale, NJ: Erlbaum.

Krishef, C. H. (1991). *Fundamental approaches to single subject design and analysis.* Malabar, FL: Krieger.

Lane, M. A., Ingram, D. K., Ball, S. S., & Roth, G. S. (1997). Dehydroepiandrosterone sulfate: A biomarker of primate aging slowed by calorie restriction. *Journal of Clinical Endocrinology and Metabolism, 82,* 2093–2096.

Loftus, G. R. (1996). Psychology will be a much better science when we change the way we analyze data. *Current Directions in Psychological Science, 5,* 161–171.

Masoro, E. J. (1985). Nutrition and aging. A current assessment. *Journal of Nutrition, 115,* 842–848.

McNaughton, N. (1993). Automatic shaping of responses. In A. Sahgal (Ed.), *Behavioural neuroscience: A practical approach* (Vol. 1, pp. 9–12). Oxford, England: IRL Press.

Meisch, R. A., & Lemaire, G. A. (1993). Drug self-administration. In F. van Haaren (Ed.), *Techniques in the behavioral and neural sciences: Vol. 10. Methods in behavioral pharmacology* (pp. 257–300). Amsterdam: Elsevier Science.

Morrison, A. R., Evans, H. L., Ator, N. A., & Nakamura, R. K. (2002). *Methods and welfare considerations in behavioral research with animals: Report of a National Institutes of Health Workshop* (NIH Publication No. 02-5083). Washington, DC: U.S. Government Printing Office.

Morse, W. H., McKearney, J. W., & Kelleher, R. T. (1977). Control of behavior by noxious stimuli. In L. L. Iversen, S. D. Iversen, & S. H. Snyder (Eds.), *Handbook of psychopharmacology: Vol. 7. Principles of behavioral pharmacology* (pp. 151–180). New York: Plenum Press.

National Research Council. (1995). *Nutrient requirements of domestic animal series: Nutrient requirements of laboratory animals* (4th rev. ed.). A *report of the Board on Agriculture, Subcommittee on Laboratory Animal Nutrition, Committee on Animal Nutrition.* Washington, DC: National Academy Press.

National Research Council. (1996). *Guide for the care and use of laboratory animals.* Washington, DC: National Academy Press.

Paré, W. P., & Glavin, G. B. (1993). Animal models of stress in pharmacology. In F. van Haaren (Ed.), *Techniques in the behavioral and neural sciences: Vol. 10. Methods in behavioral pharmacology* (pp. 413–441). Amsterdam: Elsevier Science.

Perone, M. (1999). Statistical inference in behavior analysis: Experimental control is better. *The Behavior Analyst, 22,* 109–116.

Poling, A., Nickel, M., & Alling, K. (1990). Free birds aren't fat: Weight gain in captured wild pigeons maintained under laboratory conditions. *Journal of Experimental Analysis of Behavior, 53,* 423–424.

Rosnow, R. L., & Rosenthal, R. (1996). *Beginning behavioral research: A conceptual primer* (2nd ed.). Englewood Cliffs, NJ: Prentice Hall.

Sahgal, A. (Ed.). (1993a). *Behavioural neuroscience: A practical approach* (Vols. 1–2). Oxford, England: IRL Press.

Sahgal, A. (1993b). Passive avoidance procedures. In A. Sahgal (Ed.), *Behavioural neuroscience: A practical approach* (Vol. 1, pp. 49–56). Oxford, England: IRL Press.

Schulteis, G., & Koob, G. F. (1993). Active avoidance conditioning paradigms for rodents. In A. Sahgal (Ed.), *Behavioural neuroscience: A practical approach* (Vol. 1, pp. 57–69). Oxford, England: IRL Press.

Sidman, M. (1960). *Tactics of scientific research: Evaluating experimental data in psychology.* New York: Basic Books.

Thompson, T., Dews, P. B., & McKim, W. A. (Eds.). (1981). *Advances in behavioral pharmacology* (Vol. 3). New York: Academic Press.

Toth, L. A., & Gardiner, T. W. (2000). Food and water restriction protocols: Physiological and behavioral considerations. *Contemporary Topics in Laboratory Animal Medicine, 39,* 9–17.

Turkkan, J. S., Ator, N. A., Brady, J. V., & Craven, K. A. (1989). Beyond chronic catheterization in laboratory primates. In E. F. Segal (Ed.), *Housing, care, and psychological wellbeing of captive and laboratory primates* (pp. 305–322). Park Ridge, NJ: Noyes Publications.

van Haaren, F. (Ed.). (1993). *Methods in behavioral pharmacology.* Amsterdam: Elsevier Science.

Van Sluyters, R. C. (Ed.). (1997). Understanding and using the Internet and the World Wide Web [Special issue]. *ILAR Journal, 38*(4).

Wilcox, R. R. (1996). *Statistics for the social sciences.* San Diego, CA: Academic Press.

4

CONDUCTING BEHAVIORAL RESEARCH WITH ANIMALS AT SMALLER INSTITUTIONS: VETERINARY CARE AND FACILITIES

CHRISTINE M. PARKS

The establishment and maintenance of a laboratory animal program at small institutions such as 4-year colleges or high schools may entail challenges not encountered at larger academic research centers. These challenges may be the result of limited availability of resources at smaller institutions. In developing an adequate program of animal care and use, smaller institutions should consult the *Guide for the Care and Use of Laboratory Animals*[1] (Institute of Laboratory Animal Resources, National Research Council, 1996) along with the considerations reviewed in this chapter. The *Guide* defines the components of a program of animal care and use, as well as provides a description of the physical plant recommended for the housing of research or teaching animals. For small institutions with limited resources, careful consideration of the individual situation and thoughtful deployment of available resources along with professional consultation should allow these institutions to comply with the *Guide*.

---

[1]Hereafter referred to as the *Guide*.

The *Guide* is the source document to use in self-assessment of an animal care and use program. The Association for Assessment and Accreditation of Laboratory Animal Care, International (AAALAC; described in detail in Appendix D, AAALAC Accreditation Program) also uses the *Guide* as the primary reference when it evaluates a program for consideration for accreditation. AAALAC provides an expert review and evaluation of animal care and use programs, and achievement of accreditation by an institution is a prominent sign to granting agencies and the general public about the quality of an animal care and use program. The components of a satisfactory animal care and use program are as follows, as outlined in the *Guide*.

INSTITUTIONAL POLICIES AND RESPONSIBILITIES

Institutional Animal Care and Use Committee (IACUC)

The IACUC is responsible for the oversight of the entire animal care and use program. The institution must consider the IACUC's composition, protocol review procedures, and program and facilities review processes. The proper composition may be more difficult for small institutions. Appropriate scientific members are needed, as well as a veterinarian, and a community member. The IACUC needs to review and approve nonstandard husbandry procedures that are experimentally necessary, in addition to the research or teaching use of the animal (see chaps. 8 and 9 and Appendix I, this volume, for more information about IACUCs).

Veterinary Care

Key elements in the development of a program of veterinary care include the intensity of the research or teaching at the institution, clear delineation of the responsibilities and authority of the veterinarian, and the veterinarian's direct involvement in the care and use of animals. Other issues specific to veterinary care at smaller institutions are addressed in detail here.

Personnel Qualifications and Training

Personnel qualifications include veterinary and management staff members as well as the animal caretaking staff and the research investigative staff. At smaller institutions, students may participate in the basic care-taking chores, or the investigator or instructor may be responsible for the direct day-to-day care of the research and teaching animals. Issues in personnel qualifications include continuing professional education, education of new personnel, and education in the use of hazardous agents. Educational opportunities for students, employees, and faculty members may be obtained through local branches of the American Association of Laboratory Animal Science (AALAS), journals, commercially available books, tapes, or slide sets, or by including staff members of the small institutions in training programs of larger area institutions that may be willing to include persons other than their own staff in their training programs. Training can be provided in house on a case-by-case basis by knowledgeable individuals. Training in a task should be provided before an individual is asked to do that task using an animal without supervision.

Staffing

At small institutions, the animal caretaking staff may be quite small. It may consist of one supervisor and a caretaker, only a caretaker who is supervised by an investigator, or only student help, with the investigator or instructor taking responsibility for animal care. No matter who does the caretaking, adequate training is necessary. The hiring of professional laboratory animal science personnel is encouraged. AALAS certifies personnel nationally at three skill levels of knowledge and experience in laboratory animal care. In many locales, local branches of AALAS have continuing education meetings for all levels of personnel involved in laboratory animal medicine. Training may be provided on site on an as-needed basis, as long as knowledgeable instructors are available. As mentioned in the Personnel qualifications and training section, contacts may be made with nearby larger institutions that may be able to accept other personnel into their program. When training new personnel to take care of animals, close supervision is critical. The investigator or the instructor and the institution are the responsible parties, and they are accountable for the proper care and use of the animals.

Personnel Hygiene

Work clothing, laundry, and change facilities should be provided. Work clothing can be as simple as laboratory coats, gloves, and dedicated shoes. It is not recommended to take clothing home to launder. Clothing taken home to launder may expose other members of the household to potentially zoonotic diseases, that is, diseases that are communicable to humans from nonhuman animals. A commercial laundry or an on-site laundry can be used to clean work clothes.

Occupational Health and Safety Program

The content, program oversight, and risk assessment of all personnel having animal contact, including the veterinarian, animal care staff members, investigative staff members, students, and faculty are key components of an occupational health program. The program should be risk based, managed with the input of a human health professional, and include information and training on zoonotic diseases (diseases transmissible from animals to humans). The occupational health program should be prepared to deal with possible exposure to animal research based hazards. For a small program using domestically reared rodents, the occupational health plan may include provision of information on zoonoses, a tetanus vaccination, information on allergy, and education on what to do in case of a bite or scratch. For institutions using primates or hazardous agents, a more extensive program is required. First aid kits, including a bite kit and eye wash, should be made easily accessible in case of a bite or scratch. If primates are housed, then tuberculin testing of the handlers (and the animals) should be performed to detect tuberculosis. In addition, the institutional health clinic should be made aware that research personnel might require emergency antiviral medication in the event of bite by a macaque. Macaques can carry the Herpes B virus that can be fatal to humans. The Institute of Laboratory Animal Resources (ILAR; 1997) has published a book entitled *Occupational Health and Safety in the Care and Use of Research Animals*, which addresses the issue of occupational health in animal facilities. This document is a resource for planning an occupational health program. Because the occupational health program should be risk based and tailored to the needs of the institution, someone with a background in human health should be identified to assist in the development of the particular plan needed for the institution.

Hazardous Agents

If the institution uses infectious agents, radiation, recombinant DNA, or chemical hazards, then policies and procedures to ensure review and monitoring of the use of such agents in animal research are a necessary part of the program. If an institution's research involving such hazards is minimal, then consultants can be engaged to review the use of the agent in animals as necessary. Personnel who work with the animals must be aware of the hazard, wear appropriate protective clothing, and have access to information on what to do in case of exposure. Animal room doors must be labeled with the appropriate hazard symbol.

Miscellaneous Policies

Other policies include issues such as prolonged restraint and multiple major survival surgeries. The IACUC should review and the researcher justify all such types of procedures.

ANIMAL ENVIRONMENT, HOUSING, AND MANAGEMENT

Whenever a teaching project or a research study requires housing animals in nonstandard housing, or involves food or water deprivation, the IACUC must approve these deviations from standard practices for scientific cause. If the animal's cage cannot be cleaned at least every 2 weeks, then this should be justified and approved by the IACUC. Unless otherwise stated, the assumption is that animal husbandry practices will follow the *Guide*.

Housing

The types of caging in which animals are housed should allow for sanitization and should be appropriate for the species. Solid bottom caging with bedding is recommended for rodent housing. Wire flooring may be used if scientifically justified. Larger animals may be housed in cages made of stainless steel (or other rustproof material), runs, or pens. The dimensions of the caging should be adequate to meet the standard of the *Guide* and the Animal Welfare Act (AWA) regulations (U.S. Department of Agriculture [USDA], 2001, 9 CFR, Part 3). The social and environmental enrichment for the animals should be carefully considered. The U.S. Department of Agriculture (USDA) animal welfare regulations (USDA, 2001) require a written exercise program for dogs and an environmental enrichment program for nonhuman primates. If animals must be housed in unusual caging, this should be scientifically justified and approved by the IACUC. Housing in laboratories or areas other than animal rooms meeting *Guide* standards must also be justified, reviewed, and approved by the IACUC.

Feed

The type of feed provided, the storage of the feed, and quality control of the diet are important issues. Animals generally have feed ad lib, or may be fed once a day. Most animal feeds start to lose nutritional quality with time. The milling dates of feed should be known, and most feed should be discarded 6 months post milling; feed containing vitamin C, such as guinea pig and primate chow, should be discarded 3 months post milling.

Bedding

The type of bedding should be appropriate for the species housed and should be compatible with the research. The storage of the bedding should keep it free from contamination to keep the bedding from being a source of disease for the animals. Some bedding may contain volatile oils (such as pine shavings) that can induce hepatic enzymes and lead to invalid results for some types of research.

Water

Water should be from a reliable clean quality source, treated with chlorine, or hyperacidifed if necessary. Animals are provided free access to water unless water restriction is scientifically necessary. Water may be provided from water bottles, pans, or automatic watering devices.

Sanitation

The animal cages, food and water containers, and the room or secondary containment barrier must be sanitized on a regular basis. The animals' home cages should be sanitized at least every 2 weeks. If a cage washer is not available that can sanitize using hot water at 180° F, then a program of microbiological monitoring should be in place to ensure sanitation. Cages that are washed by hand should be sanitized using chemical methods and rinsed thoroughly before use. Any testing apparatus that comes into direct animal contact must also be sanitized. Ideally, this should be between each animal if used for different animals on the same day, or at least at the end of each testing day. Waste disposal should be appropriate and a vermin control program in place. Rodent cages and caging pans should not be emptied of bedding in the animal room because this creates aerosols. Cages can be dumped in the same area where they are washed or adjoining areas. Care should be taken to minimize personnel exposure to aerosolized dirty bedding, which can induce allergies in workers.

Animal Records and Identification

Animal records can be kept by the veterinarian, research or teaching staff members, caretaking staff members, or some combination of these. For certain species, such as cats, dogs, and primates, individual records must be kept. Procedural, anesthetic, surgical, and recovery records must be kept, as well as records for treatment of any disease or experimentally induced condition. These records should be available on request to the veterinarian, the USDA inspectors, or AAALAC site visitors. Animal identification should include cage cards for rodents and tattoos or tags for other species. The *Guide* contains recommendations for information to be kept on research or teaching animals. USDA regulations require specific types of identification for dogs and cats (see also Appendix C for specific record-keeping requirements).

Care for Weekends and Holidays

All vertebrate animals must be observed daily. The person observing the animals must be adequately trained to care for the species housed and to recognize changes in animal well-being. This person can be an investigator or instructor, a technician, or an animal caretaker. Emergency veterinary care should also be available, and emergency contact information such as telephone numbers should be posted near the laboratory telephone or in a prominent location.

VETERINARY MEDICAL CARE

General Issues

The first issue for a smaller institution to determine is the intensity of veterinary care necessary for their program of animal care and use. Researchers in a very small program who use only rodents in noninvasive studies might need a consulting veterinarian who visits periodically and is available by telephone. Researchers in a larger program who use rabbits, cats, dogs, or primates or perform invasive procedures would need more intense veterinary involvement, and they may need a part-time or a full-time veterinarian. A program with an active surgical component, especially involving animals such as cats, primates, and rabbits, would also require increased veterinary participation. Institutions with large programs often employ more than one veterinarian.

Type and Qualifications of Veterinarian Needed

The minimum qualification for the job is a doctorate in veterinary medicine (DVM, VMD) degree. A license to practice in the state, along with a Drug Enforcement Administration (DEA) license, would be necessary if the veterinarian will order controlled substances. Appropriate USDA certification is necessary for the veterinarian to sign interstate health certificates. The laws and regulations regarding use of animals in research state that the attending veterinarian at a research facility must have experience in the species held at the facility (USDA, 2001, 9 CFR, Part 1). The veterinarian also needs to be familiar with the regulations and laws governing animal research. Local practitioners can be used, as long as they have knowledge of the species and the applicable laws and regulations (or are willing to learn).

A veterinarian with interest and knowledge in laboratory animal medicine is the best choice, if available, for most institutions. Most private veterinary practitioners do not have in-depth knowledge of common laboratory animal species, the laws and regulations governing research, or research techniques and methods. Private practitioners can function in regular care or the emergency care of animals when a consulting or part-time laboratory animal veterinarian is unavailable.

There are two organizations that list veterinarians with interest or knowledge of laboratory animal medicine. The first is the American Society of

Laboratory Animal Practitioners (ASLAP). Membership is open to any veterinarian who is engaged or interested in laboratory animal practice and who maintains membership in the American Veterinary Medical Association (AVMA), or any other national veterinary medical association recognized by AVMA. The second organization is the American College of Laboratory Animal Medicine (ACLAM). ACLAM is recognized by the AVMA as a specialty organization. ACLAM tests and certifies qualified veterinarians in laboratory animal medicine. A listing of ACLAM certified diplomates is contained in the AVMA Directory.

Locating Veterinary Services

One of the best places to look for a veterinarian is to first contact the nearest large research institution that uses animals and ask to speak to their laboratory animal veterinarian. This veterinarian may do consulting or have knowledge of other laboratory animal veterinarians in the area. An institution may also advertise to obtain veterinary services. Places to advertise include the ACLAM or ASLAP newsletter and the AVMA journals.

Relationships Between the Veterinarian and the Investigative Staff

As in most other human relationships, it pays to have good communications between the veterinary and investigative staff members. Both investigators and veterinarians have the same goals—humane, appropriate animal care and use, and good research. Both the investigator or the instructor and the veterinarian need to keep the laboratory animal care and use program at the institution in compliance with laws and regulations so that the institution can legally conduct animal research. The veterinarian should have the knowledge and experience to assist the researcher and the institution to achieve this goal. It is a joint effort requiring communication, knowledge, and good will. The investigator may have to educate the veterinarian as to the particular research needs. The veterinarian may have to educate the investigator about the needs of the animals, the institutional animal care and use program, or about the measures needed to prevent disease. The laws, regulations, and standards for accreditation are also a fact of life in modern animal research. Again, one should assume good intent on both sides and keep the channels of communication open.

Authority and Responsibilities of the Veterinarian

The authority and responsibilities of the veterinarian should be clearly delineated in advance of hire or contract and understood by everyone involved in the program. The authority should match the responsibilities. The AWA regulations state, "Each research facility shall assure that the attending veterinarian has appropriate authority to ensure the provision of adequate veterinary care and to oversee the adequacy of the other aspects of animal care and use" (USDA, 2001, 9 CFR, Part 2, Subpart D).

COMPONENTS OF A VETERINARY CARE PROGRAM

Preventive Medicine

Preventive medicine programs should include the following components:

- *Animal procurement.* The veterinarian and the investigators should work together to determine the source of animals (vendor selection) and the evaluation of these sources. As few a number of sources as possible should be used for animal health reasons. The source or sources should be reliable, dependable providers of healthy animals of the proper genetic background, and meet all legal requirements of licensing and shipment of animals. If a larger research institution is in the area, then they may be able to advise and help smaller institutions in the purchase of animals from commercial vendors for teaching and research. Rats or mice can be used from sources that are not commercial vendors of laboratory rodents, but these animals are generally conventional animals that may harbor pathogens that can affect the research or infect other animals in the colony. The genetics of noncommercial rodent stock is usually not known. Commercial laboratory animal vendors should be used whenever possible. In most circumstances, the use of pet store rats or mice is not advisable or recommended.
- *Quarantine and isolation.* These considerations depend on the source of the animals and the nature of the research or teaching project. If nonconditioned dogs and cats are used, then incoming animals should be separated from conditioned animals. If a new vendor of rodents or other animals is used, or rodents or other animals are received with an unknown health status, then it is advisable to quarantine them. If animals ill with suspected contagious disease must be kept in the facility and treated, they should be isolated from healthy animals to prevent disease transmission, if possible.
- *Separation by species and source.* For animal health reasons, animals of different species should not be housed together. One species of animal may carry organisms that cause it no harm, but these organisms might cause disease or death in another species. If different species must be housed in the same animal

room together, some means to separate them is strongly advised, such as microisolator cages and change hoods. The same concerns (i.e., disease transmission) may also exist for animals of the same species but from different sources housed in the same room.

Surveillance, Diagnosis, Treatment, and Control of Diseases

Programs and resources for the surveillance, diagnosis, treatment, and control of diseases include the following:

- Daily observation of the animals by responsible trained personnel must be performed and adequate procedures must be in place to report health problems and provide veterinary care if necessary.
- Medical records should be maintained that document procedures, observations, and treatments.
- Preventive medicine programs appropriate for the species, such as vaccinations, teeth cleaning, periodic examinations, and so forth should be provided.

Animal health monitoring for rodent species often includes serology of representative samples of animals from the colony for pathogenic organisms, especially viral diseases that may not cause clinical illness but may destroy or delay research. This is especially important with breeding or long-term rodent colonies. Monitoring for nonviral organisms such as pinworms, mites, and bacterial infections should also be a part of the health monitoring program.

Anesthesia and Analgesia

The use of these agents in research animals is also part of a program of veterinary care. Concerns include the following:

- Agents and dosages of anesthetics and analgesics used in each species is an area in which veterinary input can be critical, especially in research that requires prolonged anesthesia or painful procedures. It should be noted that anesthetic and analgesic agents may be controlled substances and as such require one or more government licenses, secured storage, and logs of their use. It is the veterinarian's responsibility to provide guidelines for use and assist in the monitoring of the use of these agents.
- The training and experience of the personnel who perform anesthesia is also very important. The investigators or instructors, the veterinarian, and the IACUC should all be involved

in monitoring the training and experience of personnel using anesthetics and analgesics.

- Safety concerns are also important in the use of anesthetics and analgesics, from a personnel point of view as well as for the animal subject. Some agents are flammable or explosive, can be toxic if inhaled or taken internally, or may be drugs of potential abuse that should be kept in locked storage facilities.

Survival surgery and postsurgical care is yet another aspect of proper veterinary care. The following are some issues involving surgery:

- The qualifications of the personnel performing the surgery should be assured by the IACUC, with veterinary input.
- The techniques used during survival (or long nonsurvival) procedures are critical. Sterile technique should always be used in survival surgery. For rodents, this usually includes sterile preparation of the animal (with shaving of hair and scrubbing of site), sterile instruments, sterile gloves and supplies, and a surgical mask. For rabbits, cats, dogs, and other nonrodent species, full aseptic techniques are required, such as surgical suites of rooms, sterile gowns, and draping.
- Postoperative care of all species is critical. The animals should be observed until they can maintain sternal recumbancy, or longer if necessary. Careful, complete records of the anesthesia, the surgery, the postoperative recovery period, the use of analgesic agents and the longer term recovery period should be kept, especially for those species regulated by the AWA regulations.

Euthanasia

Proper methods of euthanasia are also considered a veterinary care issue. The agents or methods used, and the training and experience of the personnel performing the euthanasia must be carefully reviewed by the veterinarian and the IACUC. The AVMA has produced a *Panel Report on Euthanasia* that is generally considered to be the standard for research animals (American Veterinary Medical Association, 2000). Physical methods of euthanasia without prior sedation or anesthesia generally must be justified for scientific reasons and reviewed and approved by the IACUC. The proper training and experience of the personnel performing physical methods of euthanasia is particularly critical to the humane death of the animal.

Euthanasia of animals may not be required at the end of an experiment or research project. In some cases, animals may be reused in another project, so long as the previous project was noninvasive and not painful, and the IACUC approves the reuse. Adoption of animals may be possible with institutional agreement, but care must be taken to match adoptable animals with suitable owners.

Animal carcasses are usually incinerated, but in some areas of the country disposal in landfill may be allowed to some extent. Animals that are euthanized by the use of carbon dioxide may be used as food for raptors or snakes. Institutional policy and applicable laws should guide the disposal of research and teaching animals.

FACILITIES

The *Guide* provides information on the structure and operation of the physical facilities for animal housing. These standards should be met whenever possible. In small institutions with limited space and budgets, some degree of deviation from the *Guide* may be necessary. Professional consultation should be sought when making such deviations from the *Guide*, and the IACUC should be involved in the decision-making process.

General Issues

For smaller institutions using research animals, lack of appropriate animal housing and support space necessary for an animal care program can be a primary problem. Mixing of functions that, ideally, should be physically separated sometimes occurs, as well as mixing of species or sources of animals. Another common problem is less than ideal heating, ventilation, and air conditioning (HVAC) systems in animal housing areas. Smaller animal quarters may not have cage washing facilities, adequate storage areas, or proper surgical suite areas. Some mixing of functions may be acceptable, and special caging can sometimes help with the problem of mixing of species, but extreme care and professional judgment needs to be carefully applied.

Key Components of Animal Facilities

- *Animal rooms.* The surfaces of animal rooms should be sealed and impervious. The walls, floors, and ceilings should be smooth and allow for sanitization. The paint should not be peeling, and any wooden surfaces in the room should be sealed.

  The light cycle should be regulated by a timer, and there should be no windows in the room. The light intensity should be high enough for the care-taking staff to do their work, but low enough that the eyes of sensitive species (such as albino rodents) are not damaged by too intense light.

  The HVAC system should ideally provide 100% fresh air without recycling of air. The room air exchange rates should be at least 10 changes per hour. The temperature and humidity should be controlled to stay within the ranges suggested in the *Guide* and monitored by the facility. If air exchanges are low, animal populations in the room can be reduced to levels more compatible with the HVAC system if no other solution is possible. Ventilated caging systems can also be used. These systems can provide adequate levels of ventilation at the individual cage level.

- *Support areas.* Separate areas should be provided for cage storage, food and bedding storage, general storage, waste disposal area, lounge area for personnel, administrative space, cage sanitation facilities, and surgery facilities (if surgery is performed). All these areas do not necessarily have to be located within the animal facility, although such a location is ideal.

- *Other features.* Emergency power is needed if the geographic area has a history of frequent or prolonged power outages. Environmental monitoring of animal room airflow, relative air pressures, temperature, and humidity is also desirable. "High–Low" thermometers should be placed in animal housing rooms so that daily temperature fluctuations can be monitored.

- *Security.* Security systems can range from simple measures such as locked doors with limited key distribution, to sophisticated alarm systems with such features as motion detectors, computer access by card reader, hidden cameras, and local alarms. The extent of the system depends on many factors such as the nature of the research, the types of animals held, the activity in the area, and the budget allowed for it. One of the most cost-effective measures is education of the personnel inside the animal facility, the institution, and even the local public about the benefits of humane animal research, teaching and testing.

- *Animal laboratories.* If animals must be kept in laboratory environments for longer than 12 hours, then the housing arrangement must be reviewed and approved by the IACUC and included in the semiannual facility review. The laboratory environment must come as close as possible to the standards for animal rooms if housing is approved. If survival surgery on rodents or other procedures using other animal species occur in laboratory animal environment, then an animal area for such use should be delineated and kept neat and clean and free of clutter for at least the period of time it is used as an animal area. USDA inspectors will examine selected laboratories, and AAALAC site visitors will also tour laboratory areas used for live animals.

Federal Regulatory/Compliance Agencies Site Visits

- *U.S. Department of Agriculture (USDA)*. The Veterinary Medical Officers (VMO) perform unannounced inspections under the AWA. The USDA inspects research facilities that house species covered under the Act. These animal species include wild mice and rats, guinea pigs, hamsters, gerbils, ferrets, dogs, cats, nonhuman primates, rabbits, and farm animals used in biomedical research, and excludes birds, rats of the genus *Rattus*, and mice of the genus *Mus* that have been bred for research purposes. The USDA inspectors must be allowed access to animal facilities and laboratories, as well as access to all records related to the AWA regulations (animal protocol, IACUC minutes, IACUC semiannual program and facility evaluations, health, and purchase records). These unannounced visits occur at least yearly, or more often if the VMO has time to do so. The USDA also requires an annual report to be filed by research institutions (see chap. 8, this volume, for more information on USDA regulations).
- *Public Health Service (PHS)*. The PHS has a policy document in which there are numerous requirements for research institutions receiving PHS funds (Public Health Service, 1996). These include an approved assurance statement, IACUC approval letters for grants, and annual reports. The Office of Laboratory Animal Welfare (OLAW) is the agency within the PHS that regulates animal care and use. OLAW retains the right to visit institutions that have valid assurance statements, for cause or randomly, with a week or so of notice to the institution. The institution's own assurance statement, the PHS policy, and the AWA regulations are the main documents used in these evaluations. These visits are usually focused more on the IACUC functions and the program of animal care and use, and less on the facilities than have the USDA inspections (see chap. 8, this volume, for more information PHS policy and OLAW).
- *Association for Assessment and Accreditation of Laboratory Animal Care, International (AAALAC)*. AAALAC is a private, voluntary, confidential organization that provides peer evaluation to animal care and use programs and facilities. AAALAC will accredit any size institution if it meets the standards (see Appendix D, this volume, for specifics about this voluntary accreditation program).

In summary, small institutions using animals in teaching and research can establish excellent programs for animal care and use. The key documents used for evaluation of programs and facilities are the *Guide*, the AWA, the PHS Policy, and the PHS *Institutional Administrator's Manual for Laboratory Animal Care and Use* (U.S. Department of Health and Human Services, 1988). The Applied Research Ethics National Association (ARENA)/OLAW IACUC guidebook (Applied Research Ethics National Association, 2002) is another resource document that may be used. The key components of an animal care and use program are administrative commitment to animal care and use, appropriate veterinary input, investigator support, technical support, and adequate funding.

REFERENCES

American Veterinary Medical Association. (2000, March 1). 2000 report of the American Veterinary Medical Association panel on euthanasia. *Journal of the American Veterinary Medical Association, 218,* 669–696.

Animal Welfare Act, 7 U.S.C. § 2132 (2002).

Applied Research Ethics National Association. (2002). *Institutional animal care and use committee guidebook* (2nd ed.). Bethesda, MD: Office of Laboratory Animal Welfare, National Institutes of Health.

Institute of Laboratory Animal Resources, National Research Council. (1996). *Guide for the care and use of laboratory animals* (7th ed.). Washington, DC: National Academy Press.

Institute of Laboratory Animal Resources, National Research Council. (1997). *Occupational health and safety in the care and use of research animals.* Washington, DC: National Academy Press.

U.S. Department of Agriculture. (2001). *Code of Regulations, title 9, chapter 1: Animal and plant health inspection service, subchapter A—animal welfare.* Washington, DC: U.S. Government Printing Office.

U.S. Department of Health and Human Services. (1988). *Public health service institutional administrator's manual for laboratory animal care and use* (NIH Publication No. 88-2959). Rockville, MD: Author.

U.S. Department of Health and Human Services. (1996). *Public health service policy on humane use and care of laboratory animals.* Rockville, MD: Author.

III

LESSONS FROM THE FIELD

5

CONDUCTING BEHAVIORAL RESEARCH WITH ANIMALS AT SMALLER INSTITUTIONS: A CASE HISTORY

JESSE E. PURDY

As discussed in chapter 4 of this volume, smaller institutions may have fewer resources and therefore have more difficulty justifying the establishment and maintenance of a laboratory animal research program. With the increased costs of conducting such research attributed to increased regulations (Domjan & Krause, 2002) and the increased challenge to maintain animal laboratories brought about by animal activists (Turville-Heitz, 2000), it seems likely that the number of small institutions that offer animal research programs will decrease. Thus, it appears imperative that small colleges train undergraduates in the methodology and the value of behavioral research with animals.

Laboratory animal research is a fundamental component of psychology. Much has been written regarding the importance of animal research and its contributions to psychological science (e.g., Domjan & Purdy, 1995, 1996; Miller, 1985). Indeed, the experimental analysis of behavior in animals has been carried out for more than 100 years. Examples include Spallanzani (1729–

1799) in 1793 who blinded or deafened bats and showed that they were capable of orientation through echolocation (Grier, 1984), and Thorndike (1898) who is often credited with initiating the controlled experimental analysis of behavior. The contributions of animal research to psychological science are pervasive across all subdisciplines, including the biological bases of behavior, sensation and perception, motivation and emotion, learning and memory, developmental psychology, psychopharmacology, psychopathology, treatment, and health and stress.

The American Psychological Association (APA) remains a strong advocate for research with animals. Numerous articles addressing the use of animals in research have appeared in the *American Psychologist* (e.g., Gallup & Suarez, 1985a, 1985b; Miller, 1985; Rollin, 1985). Recent editions of the *APA Monitor on Psychology* (October 2001; December, 2003; March, 2004) have acknowledged these contributions and pointed out that animal research has strong educational value. Not only do students learn a great deal about anatomy, physiology, and behavior from conducting research with animals but also students learn to care for and maintain healthy animals, to recognize the subtle cues that indicate an animal is sick or stressed, and to treat animals ethically and responsibly. In addition, students learn to design experiments that meet federal and local guidelines for the ethical treatment of animals, to be conversant with the published guidelines for such research, and to prepare proposals for submission to an institution's committee on animal welfare. Graduate students in biopsychology programs and other subdisciplines in which research with animals is probable benefit from training as undergraduates in the procedures for the ethical treatment of animals and in the conduct of research with animals. Such training strengthens the students' competitiveness in a tight graduate school market and their effectiveness in the graduate program.

The approach of this chapter is that of a case history of the program offered at Southwestern University located in Georgetown, Texas, a baccalaureate one national liberal arts college with an enrollment of 1,200 students. This chapter consists of four sections relating to the development, maintenance, and operation of an animal laboratory. In the first section, I consider the means by which the aquatic animal research program at Southwestern University was established. I also suggest potential sources of funding for the development and maintenance of an animal research laboratory. Discussion in the second section centers on keeping current within the field and offers suggestions for those who desire to broaden their experiences. In the third section, I offer tips and encouragement on the process of presenting and publishing data, followed by suggestions for communicating one's results to the outside community. In the fourth section, I focus on maintaining an active animal research program in light of high teaching, advising, and committee loads. The chapter concludes with a justification for establishing an animal research program at the home institution and stresses the importance of undergraduate training.

ESTABLISHING AN ANIMAL RESEARCH LABORATORY

There is value in establishing animal research laboratories at small institutions. Undergraduate students benefit a great deal when they take advantage of opportunities to engage in research with animals. In addition, the knowledge acquired from such research experiences contributes to the advancement of the science of psychology. In this section, I describe the trials and tribulations encountered in establishing the aquatic animal research laboratory at Southwestern University. I describe the process, discuss the various sources of funding, and offer suggestions for establishing an animal laboratory.

Getting Started in Animal Research

The job market in the academic sector in psychology for those interested in conducting research with animals was tight in 1978 and remains so today. The promises that were given in 1978 by those professors who predicted that retirement and attrition would ease the situation have not come true. In those days, as is now, one applied for all positions for which one seemed even remotely qualified. For example, at Southwestern University, a position was posted for a "human experimental psychologist." Being human, I applied.

During the 2-day interview, the vice president for fiscal affairs informed me that the newly renovated psychology laboratory could not be used for the conduct of research with rats. The ventilation within the 72-year-old building would not support such a facility. Given the laboratory constraints and the fact that all of my graduate work had been with rats, the dean asked me if I could develop a program of research that used human participants. I indicated that I was extremely allergic to rats and I informed him of my interests in cognitive psychology. I then assured him that I could develop a human experimental program.

When I arrived on campus at the start of the academic year, I toured the psychology lab, which had three rooms totaling 560 square feet. One of the rooms contained cabinets and a sink. I was informed that there was $1,000 for the purchase of new equipment. The $1,000 was spent quickly to obtain traditional psychophysical equipment, and I sent memos to the department chair and to the dean indicating the need for more equipment. I also gave thought to preparing an equipment grant for the National Science Foundation (NSF). The NSF Instructional Scientific Equipment Program (ISEP) had a March 2, 1979 deadline.

I obtained permission from the administration to apply for the matching funds grant and prepared an application in the spring of 1979. The first proposal was not particularly strong. Reviewers commented that the proposal read as if the principal investigator had simply taken the catalog from the Lafayette Instruments Company and had chosen equipment that looked good. There were several major problems. First, reviewers commented that the equipment requested was neither flexible nor sophisticated and recommended the acquisition of microprocessors. Second, the reviewers were not convinced that I had determined what I wanted students to learn and had then developed a list of equipment that would meet those objectives. One of the reviewers commented, "Rethink your objectives! Shoot for teaching more advanced concepts in the advanced courses with more sophisticated equipment." All reviewers commented that a strong need had been demonstrated and that the evaluation section was particularly strong.

Although I was developing a program using human participants, I missed working in an animal laboratory. I was determined to prepare a stronger NSF proposal and to develop an animal research program. With the university administration's approval, I spent the fall semester in 1979 determining the options for an animal research program at a place where rats or pigeons were not an appropriate choice. The solution appeared to lie in the selection of an alternative research organism, the goldfish. Goldfish had served as subjects in a wide range of research activity and could learn to strike a target, to traverse a swim way, and to shuttle in a shuttle box. Goldfish had been subjects in experiments on auto shaping, learned helplessness, probability matching, and simultaneous contrast. Goldfish also responded well on complex schedules of reinforcement including multiple and mixed schedules and differential reinforcement of low rates of response. In addition, goldfish had been shown to discriminate on the basis of color, light intensity, auditory stimuli, and position.

The use of fish provided a clear solution. The lab's size and the ventilation system were adequate for the large aquarium and for the swim ways, shuttle boxes, and operant apparatuses. The water in the home tank and in the other apparatuses could be kept at a constant temperature with small thermostatically controlled heaters. In addition, maintaining a fish laboratory was significantly less costly than a rat laboratory. Fish were inexpensive, they ate less food and it was cheaper, and their environment was more easily controlled.

The second attempt at an ISEP grant from the NSF focused on the development of an aquatic animal research facility, which could support an animal laboratory component for the course in animal learning and independent research projects by students. The grant requested the equipment necessary to develop four stations for avoidance learning (shuttle box apparatus), four operant conditioning stations (controlled by microcomputers), and four T-maze/swim way apparatuses. In addition, I requested a large aquarium to house the animals.

In October 1980, the reviewers commented that the proposal had not explained how the animal learning laboratory component fit within the rest of the program. Overall, the proposal was too narrow in its scope and it did not allow reviewers to determine whether the proposed animal learning laboratory was "the most appropriate way to remedy the described deficit in research experience in experimental psychology." I spent the remainder of the semester thinking about the third revision of the grant proposal.

In the middle of the year, the dean sent me to a grants writing seminar held in Washington, DC. One of the speakers, who was from the NSF, offered several useful tips for developing grant proposals. In preparing the third grant proposal, care was taken to consider the entire experimental program and to determine more specifically what information and experience students needed from the beginning of the program to the end. The purposes of the project were fourfold: (a) to increase the amount of laboratory experience for each student in psychology; (b) to obtain modern and sophisticated research equipment, which attracts and retains students in psychology; (c) to improve the students' science education and appreciation through hands-on experience; and (d) to increase the students' competitiveness with respect to admission to quality graduate programs in psychology. I carefully described the need, the current program, and the various laboratory exercises students would conduct in detail. The proposal showed how students would be introduced to the equipment in lower level courses and as seniors how students would learn to be proficient in the design and conduct of an experiment using modern and sophisticated equipment.

After submitting the proposal, I received from the dean a brochure describing the Sam Taylor Fellowship Program. The program was administered by the Division of Higher Education within the United Methodist Church and provided funds for the continuing education of faculty members of colleges and universities in Texas. Any full-time faculty member of a United Methodist institution of higher education within Texas or any full-time faculty member of any accredited institution of higher education within Texas who is a member of the United Methodist Church could apply. The program provided funds for expenses incurred in academic work pursuant to a graduate degree or for expenses incurred in academic work beyond the doctoral level. In addition, funds could be used for research expenses incurred in the writing of a doctoral thesis, or for expenses incurred in a research project that specifically addressed the improvement of the quality of individual community or religious life.

Earlier in the fall, I had written to M. E. Bitterman, a well-known comparative psychologist at the University of Hawaii, and asked him about developing an aquatic animal research laboratory. He replied that it would be difficult in a letter to discuss such matters and he asked if I were going to the next meeting of the Psychonomic Society. I talked to the dean, and he agreed to fund my attending the meeting. At the meeting, I discussed with Bitterman the possibility of establishing an aquatic lab. He offered a great deal of advice, and at the end of the conversation he suggested that there would be no better way to learn about the conduct of research with goldfish than to be a visiting scientist in his lab. The Sam Taylor Fellowship Program appeared to be an ideal way to fund my working in Bitterman's laboratory. I prepared the one-page application and submitted it in July 1981. Funds were requested to defray expenses to spend 2 months at the Bekesy Laboratory of Neurobiology at the University of Hawaii. The purpose of the proposal was to provide a full understanding of how a research laboratory using aquatic organisms is designed, operated, and maintained, and to obtain the skills necessary to develop a program of research that would involve undergraduate students.

In September 1981, the reviewers' comments for the NSF ISEP proposal made for more interesting reading than did the previous grant reviews. The proposal received strong support with comments suggesting that there should have been greater emphasis on the conduct of independent and individual research projects and that the exercises for the research methods course should include research in social psychology, personality, and other areas of human research. One reviewer commented that the use of goldfish resulted in a limitation of the animal program, but one panel of reviewers commented, "In particular, the panel wishes to recognize the creativity of using goldfish where a standard rat lab is physically impossible." The grant proposal for $21,870 was funded.

A letter was mailed to the Sam Taylor Fellowship Program committee informing them that the NSF grant had been awarded. About a month later, the results of the Fellowship Program were announced. The proposal was funded. After 3 years, the animal program at Southwestern University was beginning to take shape. I had the money necessary to develop an animal laboratory using fish as the subjects of choice and I was going to spend 2 months at the Bekesy Laboratory of Neurobiology in Honolulu, Hawaii learning the intricacies of fish research.

From these beginnings, the aquatic animal research program has grown in size and stature. An impressive number of students have worked in the laboratory and have gone to graduate school, professional schools, and jobs in which they are using the skills they acquired in the laboratory. Currently, between 8 and 10 students participate in animal research annually. These students are learning about all phases of research including developing the research question, securing approval from the animal welfare committee to conduct the study, constructing the apparatus, developing the procedure, collecting and analyzing data, and writing and presenting a manuscript. Over the years, work in my lab has resulted in more than 70 professional presentations at regional and national meetings of the American Psychological Association and other organizations, and in more than 30 professional publications. In addition, more than 60 students have served as coauthors on these presentations or publications. Although the records are not overly systematic, a perusal of grade books revealed that of the students who worked in the aquatic animal research lab, 68 went on to graduate school and of these 43 have either completed or are completing their doctoral degrees. Of the 43 doctoral degree-seeking students, 8 were training to be lawyers, medical doctors, dentists, or veterinarians. Eighteen students were studying in the area of biopsychology or physiology; 5 students were in the areas of developmental, cognition, education, or human computer interactions; 7 students were in social psychology, industrial/organizational psychology, or sociology; and 5 students continued study in clinical or counseling psychology. Of the students who authored or coauthored presentations for publications from the aquatic animal research lab, 66% went on to graduate school.

Suggestions for Establishing an Animal Research Laboratory

I turn now to suggestions for developing an animal research facility. There are three major problems to solve: knowledge, space, and money. Most colleges and universities are willing to work with researchers on these matters, but one should not get too demanding or too impatient. Knowledge is best obtained through experience. For those researchers who wish to develop an animal program similar to that found in their graduate program, the knowledge is already available. However, for researchers who seek to develop a program outside their area, it is best to spend as much time as possible at a laboratory where such experiences can be obtained. Opportunities can be established usually by making contacts with the individuals at the laboratories in question. Funding can be obtained through the home institution or from private sources that fund continuing education projects such as the Sam Taylor Fellowship Program. Although certain funding opportunities are discussed in this chapter, the reader is reminded that it is likely that there is an office or officer on campus where information concerning funding sources is available.

Adequate space can be a limiting factor in the development of an animal laboratory. Many science buildings are configured to house animals, but often the space crunch prohibits one from taking over such space. The best approach may be to work with faculty members in other departments who have access to these facilities. Often, with a little diplomacy, one can share space. Even if the psychology department has laboratory space, it may not have been designed to house animals and consequently it may require some creativity to develop.

In general, one would start with a small program and then increase the capacity as the program builds. At Southwestern University, the animal program began in three small rooms that were inadequate for housing rats. After 8 or 9 years, space became available in the men's locker room of a gym that was not being used. The locker room provided concrete walls and floors with drains and the shower room provided numerous sources for water. Although slightly smaller in square footage, the space was much better designed for aquatic research. Three years later, the program was moved to a small house that the university had acquired. The carpet was removed and a linoleum floor was installed. The ventilation and heating and cooling systems were redesigned to better handle a humid environment. Presently the animal program has moved for what I hope is the last time. In the summer of 1996, the entire Department of Psychology moved into a new academic classroom building funded by the F. W. Olin Foundation. The academic classroom building houses an aquatic laboratory that for the first time in 18 years provides adequate and appropriate space. The 1,800 square foot laboratory houses rooms for saltwater and freshwater animals, an operant conditioning laboratory, and an observational lab. The laboratory has additional space for students and a workshop for constructing apparatus. The point is that one can conduct research in less than adequate space, and with time, effort, and just a little complaining on a daily basis, one may finally end up with ideal space.

Equipment is more difficult to acquire, but it too comes in degrees of sophistication. Much of the equipment needed can be built for far less money than what is required to purchase from commercial distributors. Many of the aquatic tanks and much of the electronic equipment found in the Southwestern University's aquatic laboratory have been constructed locally. On virtually every campus, there are individuals, faculty and staff members, and students who truly enjoy building electronic equipment. Befriend these people and let them help construct the needed equipment.

It is also possible to borrow and recycle equipment. Several years ago, the physics department upgraded their equipment and the psychology department inherited four Apple IIe computers. Although more sophisticated computers were available, the Apple IIe computers were adequate for the control of operant and maze apparatus. In addition, several pieces of laboratory equipment have been loaned to the department for use in the aquatic laboratory. Through contacts made while I worked in several major research laboratories (including the Marine Biomedical Institute in Galveston, Texas and the National Marine Fisheries Service in Seattle, Washington), it was possible to secure pieces of equipment that were not in use.

However, not all of the materials and equipment necessary to set up a program can be borrowed or recycled; researchers will also need money. The NSF is one major source of funding for animal research programs. Some of the programs within the NSF that have supported or still support animal research are described later. For up-to-date information in NSF programs, see http://www.nsf.gov.

The Multi-User Biological Equipment and Instrumentation Resources (MUE) enables one to acquire equipment for an animal research laboratory. This program provides support for the purchase of major pieces of equipment that will be shared by several investigators with actively funded research projects as well as single items or several items of equipment with a related purpose. Grants typically are made in the range of $40,000 to $400,000 and at least a 30% match by the host institution is expected. This program may have limited appeal to psychologists in the beginning stages of developing an animal laboratory. However, there may be researchers who find themselves in situations in which people in other departments have established laboratories in the previously described areas, and need and are willing to share equipment.

For small institutions that have biological field stations or marine laboratories, researchers may be able to obtain equipment through another program entitled Improvements in Facilities, Communications, and Equipment for Research at Biological Field Stations and Marine Laboratories (FSML). This program provides funds to enable a field station or marine laboratory to fulfill its role in biological research and education. To this end, funds are available to provide modern laboratories and educational spaces, up-to-date equipment, appropriate personal accommodations for visiting scientists and students, and user-friendly communication and data management systems for a broad array of users. Proposals focus on specific and definable projects of physical plant improvement, major scientific equipment acquisition, and data management and communication system implementation. Requests for funds may not exceed $250,000. The grant is a cost-sharing grant depending on the size of the request. For institutions that have not received support from this program, up to $50,000 may be requested with no required match.

The Collaborative Research at Undergraduate Institutions Program was designed to encourage multidisciplinary research efforts at predominantly undergraduate institutions. Research projects may either be carried out entirely within the principle investigator's (PI) home institution or may support collaborative projects with institutions other than predominantly undergraduate institutions. Collaborative research groups must consist of three or more faculty members from more than one disciplinary area and up to 10 undergraduates from the predominantly undergraduate institution. Annual budgets for collaborative research projects are expected to average $200,000, although they may be higher. In addition to the operating budget, up to $50,000 may be requested for the acquisition of well-justified research equipment.

The NSF Course, Curriculum, and Laboratory Improvement (CCLI) Program was developed to improve the quality of science, technology, engineering, and mathematics (STEM) education for all students. The four-track program targets activities affecting learning environments, course content, curricula, and educational practices. The four tracks include Assessment of Student Achievement in Undergraduate Education (CCLI–ASA), Educational Materials Development (EMD), National Dissemination (ND), and Adaptation and Implementation (A&I). Although acquisition of equipment may be possible under any of the four tracks, the A&I track is probably best suited for this purpose. According to NSF published guidelines, "projects are expected to result in improved education in science, technology, engineering, and mathematics at academic institutions through adaptation and implementation of exemplary materials, laboratory experiences, and/or educational practices that have been developed and tested at other institutions. Proposals may request funds in any budget category supported by NSF, or may request funds to purchase only instrumentation" (National Science Foundation [NSF], Overview, Paragraph 4, 2004a). Proposals within the CCLI–A&I track are of two types, but researchers interested in obtaining equipment for their laboratory will likely submit Type I proposals. According to the guidelines, Type I projects adapt and implement high-quality STEM curricula, materials, and techniques to effect specific curricular change. Acquisition of equipment for this purpose is appropriate and expected. The minimum budget request is $5,000 and projects are typically completed within 2 to 3 years. Depending on scope, up to $100,000 for a single course and up to $200,000 for comprehensive projects is available.

The National Science Foundation's Major Research Instrumentation (MRI) Program was designed to improve the condition of research and research training facilities. The MRI Program replaces the instrumentation component of the Academic Research Infrastructure (ARI) Program. The MRI program supports the acquisition or development of major research instrumentation or the improvement of research facilities. As stated in the announcement, the goals of the program are to (a) promote the modernization of science and engineering research laboratories and related facilities at institutions of higher education (including graduate and undergraduate institutions), independent nonprofit research institutions, research museums, and consortia thereof; and (b) assist graduate and undergraduate academic institutions, including those that historically have received limited Federal research and development funds, to improve their academic science and engineering infrastructure. The program encompasses repair, renovation, or replacement of scientific or engineering research equipment and research training facilities. Awards range from $100,000 to $2 million, and matching funds are not required.

STAYING CURRENT AT SMALL INSTITUTIONS

Occasionally, one hears professors at major research institutions tell their graduate students that to go to a small teaching-oriented institution is a fate worse than death. The argument is that it is not possible to develop a strong program of research at such a place, nor is it possible to keep current. Nothing could be farther from the truth. There are significant advantages to those individuals who are faculty members at small institutions. First, there is often a great deal of support from the institution's administration particularly if one involves students. This means that professors are not constrained by what is hot and what is not in the funding world. Thus, if external funding is not available, then they are not out of business, which can be the case at major research institutions. Second, and perhaps more important, because professors at small institutions are not tied to the funding world, they are free to undertake any kind of problem they find interesting. This means that they are free to conduct research that may be more risky and perhaps can lead to interesting discoveries that would be more difficult to undertake as a beginning professor at a major research institution.

There is a bit of truth to the notion that one can become stagnant at a small university. A professor can find himself or herself isolated and without some effort can get behind in one's research interests. The trick is how to avoid this problem. In the following paragraphs, I discuss the means by which I attempted to remain current in light of a heavy teaching and committee load and I offer suggestions for how one might avoid the pitfalls of stagnating waters.

Avoiding Stagnancy in a Small Pond

In 1978, the Department of Psychology at Southwestern University had two faculty members: the chair, a humanistic psychologist who offered a strong internship program, and me. Southwestern University was a comfortable institution that placed a great deal of emphasis on quality teaching and less on the conduct of research. I worried about the possibility of becoming stagnant at such a place and once expressed this concern to the chair of the mathematics department, Ralph Whitmore, who had been at the university since 1944. Whitmore offered sound advice, "Get out of town as often as possible and spend your summers at other institutions." The solution to getting out of town is funding and to this end, one needs to watch for opportunities from federal and private funding sources.

During the fall semester of 1982, I received a brochure describing the Resident Research Associate Program that was offered by the National Research Council (NRC). The Resident Research Associate Program provided funds for recent postdoctoral and senior level scientists to serve as guest investigators at federally sponsored research laboratories. Among the participating laboratories was the Northwest and Alaska Fisheries Center within the National Marine Fisheries Service in Seattle, Washington. I mailed a letter to H. O. Hodgins proposing a series of investigations. Hodgins indicated interest in the project, made suggestions regarding the proposal, and encouraged me to apply for a NRC Associateship.

In January 1983, I submitted an application proposing to assess the effects of aromatic hydrocarbons on foraging and avoidance behavior in salmonids. In March, I learned that I had been selected as an alternate for the program and in June 1983 received notification that my proposal had been rejected. In August, I surprisingly learned that one of the associates had accepted a tenure track position, and thus I was offered an NRC Associateship. After deliberation with the dean and the department chair regarding teaching assignments and finances, a sabbatical leave was approved. I spent one year at the Mukilteo Biological Field Station, Mukilteo, Washington, which was operated by the National Marine Fisheries Service. I constructed apparatus, trained salmon to strike a target for food, and collected data on the effects of aromatic hydrocarbons on foraging and avoidance learning.

In June 1989, I met with Lee Fuiman at the University of Texas Marine Science Institute (MSI) in Port Arkansas, Texas. We developed a proposal and submitted it to the Sam Taylor Fellowship Award Committee. The proposal was funded, and in the summer of 1990 I spent 8 weeks at MSI conducting experiments with larval red drum.

In June 1991, John Forsythe, senior research associate and laboratory manager at the National Resource Center for Cephalopods (NRCC), contacted me. The NRCC was established to develop the methodology and technology necessary to culture octopus, squid, and cuttlefish for biomedical research. Forsythe indicated an interest in a project to develop a system whereby cephalopods could be fed automatically and on demand. I reasoned that one approach to developing an automatic feeding system might be to first demonstrate that cephalopods would exhibit sign tracking or auto shaping. I submitted a third proposal for the Sam Taylor Fellowship Program. The proposal was funded, and in the summer of 1992 I spent 7 weeks at the NRCC conducting experiments on sign tracking with squid and cuttlefish.

In recent years, I have spent summers working at the Bamfield Center for Marine Science, in Bamfield, British Columbia and in McMurdo Sound, Antarctica working with Weddell seals. These opportunities to conduct research at different places have been intellectually challenging and have kept my interest for the past 25 years. Certainly, my teaching and my enthusiasm have been positively affected by such experiences.

Suggestions for Staying Alive at Small Institutions

Whitmore was correct. It is important to "get out of town" but there are other means of staying alive. One good way is to establish contacts with major research universities. Southwestern University is located 28 miles from Austin, Texas and it was possible to develop relationships with the people at the University of Texas (UT). I have invited several prominent people from UT to give talks at Southwestern University, and they have made it possible for several of Southwestern University students to conduct research at UT. In addition, I have collaborated on several projects with the faculty members there. I also attend a weekly seminar in biopsychology offered for graduate students and faculty members. These contacts and others that I have made through attendance at meetings have provided a rich source of ideas and information.

In addition to local options for keeping active and private sources of funding such as the Sam Taylor Fellowship Program, the NSF and other federal programs offer numerous programs designed to keep one abreast of the latest developments in psychology. Several of these programs are described as follows. (For current information in NSF programs, see http://www.nsf.gov or for a list of relevant publications related to faculty development see www.ehr.nsf.gov/ehr/due/publications/pub_by_year.asp.)

- The NSF Chautauqua Short Courses are an annual series of forums throughout the United States in which scholars at the frontiers of various sciences meet with undergraduate college teachers of science intensively for several days. The forums provide an opportunity for invited scholars to communicate new knowledge, concepts, and techniques directly to college teachers, and in ways that are immediately beneficial to their teaching. The primary aim is to enable undergraduate teachers in the sciences to keep their teaching current and relevant. In addition to this program, faculty development funds may be available through the CCLI Program previously described. Readers may wish to peruse the CCLI–ND Program at www.nsf.gov/cgi-bin/getpub?nsf03558. As the programs under the CCLI–ND Program are developed, one may wish to take advantage of these faculty development opportunities.
- The NSF Research in Undergraduate Institutions (RUI) Program encourages research by faculty members at predominantly undergraduate institutions, where such research contributes to basic knowledge in science and engineering and strengthens the quality of undergraduate training for graduate study and careers in science and engineering. According to the announcement by the NSF, the specific objectives of the RUI Program are to "(1) support high-quality research by faculty members at predominantly undergraduate institutions, (2) strengthen the research environment in academic departments that are oriented primarily toward undergraduate instruction, and (3) promote the integration of research and education" (NSF, Paragraph 3, 2004b). Normal duration of these awards is from 1 to 3 years and award size ranges from $5,000 to $250,000. Proposers are advised to consult with the NSF discipline program officer prior to final preparation of a RUI proposal. There are two general thrusts of the program: (a) faculty research projects, and (b) multi-investigator/user research instrumentation grants.
- The NSF Research Opportunity Awards (ROA) Program, which is a component of the RUI Program, enables faculty members at predominantly undergraduate institutions with limited research opportunities to participate in research under the aegis of NSF-supported investigators at other institutions. The intent of the program is to increase the visitor's research capa-

bility and effectiveness, improve research and teaching at the home institution, and enhance the NSF-funded research of the host PI. Proposers for this program must initiate contact with NSF-supported investigators who have been awarded or who are applying for funding from NSF. The PI of the host institution submits the application and the research proposal must enhance or extend the NSF-funded research project. Any item acceptable for inclusion under a regular grant application may be included in the request, but most NSF programs limit support to moderate amounts ($10,000 to $15,000).

- The Small Grants for Exploratory Research (SGER) Program was established by the NSF for funding small-scale, exploratory, high-risk research. Proposals are internally reviewed and typically are funded for one year. The grant request cannot exceed $50,000. The program is not always available and one should determine the status of the program by contacting the appropriate director of the relevant disciplinary program officer. This program may be useful to those who wish to conduct a series of pilot studies, which can then be used to develop a full research proposal.

- The American Society for Engineering Education (ASEE) co-sponsors a summer faculty research program and sabbatical leave program. According to the 2003 announcement, the U.S. Navy–ASEE summer faculty research program provides science and engineering faculty members from colleges and universities the opportunity to participate in research at U.S. Navy laboratories during the summer. Participants work with professional peers in the U.S. Navy laboratories on research tasks of mutual interest. Participants have an opportunity to establish continuing research relations with the research and development personnel, which may result in sponsorship of the participants' research at their home institutions. The period of appointment is 10 weeks and stipends range from $1,400 to $1,900 per week depending on the level of the appointment. Of particular interest to psychologists, the program supports research concerned with human factors engineering, training systems research, computer technology for training equipment, intelligent training systems development, and human–computer interfaces. Additional research opportunities exist for signal and image processing, information processing, group dynamics, cross-cultural communications, workforce management, personnel assignment, assessing behavioral and physiological responses during sustained performance, and neuroelectric and neuromagnetic assessment and cognitive performance. (For more information, contact ASEE Projects Office, 1818 N Street, NW, Suite 600, Washington, DC 20036-2479; telephone: (202) 331-3500; Web site: http://www.asee.org/fellowship.)

- A similar program from the ASEE is cosponsored with the National Aeronautics and Space Administration (NASA). This program is designed to further the professional knowledge of qualified engineering and science faculty members, to stimulate an exchange of ideas between teaching participants and employees of NASA, to enrich and refresh the research and teaching activities of participant's institutions, and to contribute to the research objectives of the NASA center. The programs are for 10 weeks and stipends are $1,000 per week. (More information on each of these programs and the sabbatical programs can be obtained from the ASEE office. Inquiries can be directed to personnel at (202) 331-3500, or check the Web site at http://www.asee.org/fellowship.)

- For individuals who teach at domestic private or public minority/minority serving institutions, the National Institute of Health (NIH) offers opportunities for individuals to spend an academic year updating their research skills at a research-intensive institution. The purpose of the Minority Access to Research Careers (MARC) Faculty Senior Fellowship Program is to enhance the research and research training capabilities of the home institution by offering faculty members the opportunity to update or retool their research skills through high-quality research experiences. It is hoped that such experiences will enhance the research and teaching environment of the home institution and lead to long-term collaborations between the faculty member and the host researchers. Funds are available to cover salary for the period of time spent at the host institution and up to $4,000 for supplies and direct expenses related to the applicant's research training. Applications are accepted April 5 and December 5. (Information is also available on the Web at http://grants2.nih.gov/grants/guide/pa-files/PAR-02-145.html.)

THE COMMUNICATION GAME: PUBLISHING AND PRESENTING WITH AND WITHOUT STUDENTS

To have the data from experiments locked in a file cabinet where they cannot be seen is a serious misuse of resources. Data are meant to be shared, and this involves presentations at conventions, seminars, restaurants, and so forth as well as publishing in journals. In this section I discuss the trials and tribulations encountered as I attempted to communicate the results of experiments conducted in my lab. In addition, I discuss various opportunities for faculty members and their students to present or publish the results of their work.

Communication of Results

The four keys to the presentation and publication of data include remembering that the process is not easy for anyone, that one cannot take personally reviewer's comments, that one cannot allow himself or herself to get discouraged, and that one must be persistent. I learned these four keys over the course of many years, and I still find it useful on occasion to remind myself of them. My first attempt at publishing an article was not successful. I had completed a study for my master's degree and sent a manuscript to the *Journal of Experimental Psychology* (JEP). The editor informed me that single-shot experiments were not typically published in *JEP* and he advised me to read the journal before submitting a second manuscript. I then submitted the manuscript to another journal and although the reviews were more positive, the manuscript was rejected. Two years later, after having completed the fourth related experiment, the manuscript was submitted to *Learning and Motivation*, where it was accepted with minor revision (Purdy & Cross, 1979). In all, it had taken only 3 1/2 years to conduct the experiments and get a manuscript published. I admit to a strong sense of satisfaction when I received a reprint request for the paper from the editor of *JEP* who had rejected the manuscript a few years previously.

In the fall 1979, I submitted an abstract for presentation at the 1980 annual meeting of the Southwestern Psychological Association (SWPA). I received two postcards. The first indicated that the abstract had been received and the second simply said, "SWPA proposal rejected." I was devastated. I did not think that the study was going to change the way the world works, but I did think that it was worthy of presentation. For the next several years I presented material at the annual meetings of the Texas Academy of Science and did not submit an abstract for presentation at SWPA until fall 1982. I had committed two errors. I had taken the rejection personally and feeling that perhaps I did not have much to offer the science of psychology, I had gotten discouraged. Eventually I decided to try again. I submitted an abstract for the 1983 meeting of SWPA. The abstract described the studies I had conducted in Bitterman's laboratory at the University of Hawaii and it was accepted for presentation. The acceptance did much to improve my confidence.

In the fall 1984, I completed the observing response manuscript and sent it to the *Journal of Comparative Psychology* (JCP). Both reviewers recommended against publication though I was encouraged to continue the work. I revised the manuscript on the basis of those comments and resubmitted it to a second journal. One of the reviewers recommended publication, but the other two reviewers recommended against. I conducted two more studies before attempting publication. The manuscript was submitted to the *Journal of Experimental Psychology: Animal Behavior Processes*. Reviewers indicated that the paper was not sufficiently theoretical to warrant publication in *JEP* and one of the reviewers commented that the manuscript belonged more appropriately in *JCP*. I revised again and sent the paper to *JCP*.

The editor of *JCP* accepted the paper with revision, but there was one major problem. I had to address the concerns of Reviewer 3 who had written a three-page, single-spaced review. I thought about the comments for days and discussed the issues with several individuals. My only conclusion was that another study was required to satisfy the third reviewer. The study was conducted and 9 months later submitted for review. It was accepted for publication 3 days later (Purdy & Peel, 1988). The entire process took only 5 years.

In the meantime, I had submitted to the *Journal of Fish Biology* the manuscript describing the two experiments examining the effects of aromatic hydrocarbons on foraging and avoidance learning in salmon. On the day that marked one year since I had heard from the editor that he was sending the paper out for review, I wrote to inquire as to the status of the paper. The manuscript had been misplaced and there had been a postal strike in Europe. The good news was that the manuscript had been accepted for publication without revision (Purdy, 1989). In the following years, I submitted several more papers for publication with similar results. One reviewer would recommend publication and a second would recommend against. I once submitted a manuscript to the *International Journal of Comparative Psychology*. The journal was going through a change of editors and my paper was caught between outgoing and incoming editors. The review process took 2 years to conclude with a publication (Purdy, Bales, Burns, & Wiegand, 1994).

The publishing game is not easy. The final product does little to indicate the amount of effort and problems that were encountered. I am not alone in this conclusion. Michael Domjan, who is at the University of Texas at Austin, has informed me more than once that my experiences are not atypical. He even went to the trouble to read me a few of his reviews. It was completely gratifying, in a sick kind of way, to discover that even highly regarded animal learning psychologists, at least on occasion, receive the same kind of reviews that I have. The key, as I mentioned before, is not to get discouraged, not to take reviewer's comments personally, and to be persistent.

In addition to publishing, attending and presenting at conventions is an important activity. Conventions are great for sharing data, meeting people, and making contacts. Equally important is having students attend and present at conferences. Students learn about the various subdisciplines within psychology and the cutting edge developments in these areas. Students also learn that the experiences they are receiving at their home institutions are not unlike the ones others are receiving. Finally, at conventions students are able to meet other faculty members and students, which provides opportunities to assess graduate programs and career options, and to develop further possibilities for conducting research.

Suggestions for Publishing and Presenting Animal Research Results

It is not my intent in this section to provide the names of all the possible journals that publish animal research. This list would be quite long. I instead offer options for publishing that may not otherwise have been considered. There are a growing number of journals whose purpose is to publish psychological research that was conducted and written by students. The *Psi Chi Journal of Undergraduate Research* is published quarterly by Psi Chi, The National Honor Society in Psychology. The journal's first issue was published in 1996 and included manuscripts representing many of the various subfields within psychology. The purpose of the journal is to "foster and reward the scholarly efforts of undergraduate psychology students as well as to provide them with a valuable learning experience" (*Psi Chi*, 2004, Paragraph 1). (For more information, contact Psi Chi directly at Psi Chi, The National Honor Society in Psychology, P.O. Box 709, Chattanooga, Tennessee 37401-0709; telephone (423) 756-2044; e-mail: psichi@psichi.org; Web site: www.psichi.org.)

The journal *Modern Psychological Studies* (MPS) was founded in 1993 and publishes biannually research conducted by undergraduate students. (Submission information can be obtained by contacting the editor at MPS, Department of Psychology, University of Tennessee at Chattanooga, 615 McCallie Avenue, Chattanooga, Tennessee 37403-2598; telephone (423) 785-2238; e-mail: mpsedit@cecasun.utc.edu;Web site: http://www.utc.edu/mps.).

The *Journal of Psychology and Behavioral Sciences* was founded in 1966. One issue is published annually and authors may be undergraduate students with a faculty mentor. (For information, consult the Web site at http://www.alpha.fdu.edu/psychweb/JPBS.htm.)

Finally, the *Journal of Psychological Inquiry* was founded in 1996 by the Great Plains Behavioral Research Association. Authors must be undergraduate students and submissions must come from students enrolled at institutions that sponsor the Great Plains Students' Psychology Convention or from students who have had papers accepted for presentation at either the Great Plains Student's Psychology Convention, the Association for Psychological and Educational Research in Kansas, the Nebraska Psychological Society, or the Arkansas Symposium. (For more information, see http://puffin.creighton.edu/psy/journal.JP/inscon.html.)

The reader may feel that publishing in a traditional journal is a better experience for the faculty member and the student. One would not want all of one's publications in student research journals, but do not make the mistake of thinking that the papers published in these journals are of low quality that could not have been published elsewhere. The quality of research conducted by many of these students may not achieve the level of sophistication found in some professional journals, but the work often adds to the knowledge base in psychological science and represents the efforts of some of the best undergraduate students in the country. Graduate advisors in doctoral programs would do well to peruse these journals and recruit the authors for their graduate programs.

A major advantage of having students submit their manuscripts to such journals is that the experiences by students who have submitted the results of their research are typically positive. Students learn a great deal about the review process and about what constitutes publishable work without the experience of having an extremely negative review.

In a similar vein, there are numerous opportunities for students to present their work in the form of either posters or oral presentations. Psi Chi offers such opportunities at national meetings including the annual meetings of the American Psychological Association and the American Psychological Society. In addition, Psi Chi annually supports programs at the meetings of the various regional psychological associations of the APA. Currently, Psi Chi sponsors cash awards for the best paper or poster presented at a regional or national meeting. Such awards can be used to defray the cost of attending the convention. Contact the local Psi Chi Regional Vice President or call the National Office at (423) 756-2044 for details.

In addition to Psi Chi programs, most states offer student conventions. As mentioned previously, students can present the results of their efforts at the Great Plains Student's Psychology Convention, the Association for Psychological and Educational Research in Kansas, the Nebraska Psychological Society, or the Arkansas Symposium. Another outlet for student work is the annual Texas Christian University (TCU) Psi Chi Student Convention.

Students get excited about presenting their work at these conventions and they learn a great deal about the process. If possible, it makes sense to have students present their papers or posters at a student convention and then present again at a regional or national meeting. Student conventions can serve as training grounds for the student and are quite student friendly. Such an experience lessens considerably the anxiety attached to presenting at a regional or national meeting for the first time.

BALANCING TEACHING WITH RESEARCH

Perhaps one of the biggest problems facing faculty members at small institutions is finding the time to develop an animal research program. With heavy teaching loads, advising loads, committee loads, and family commitments, one finds the prospect of developing a research program a bit daunting. For beginning faculty members at such institutions, the task may seem impossible. For me, the initial process was a bit like graduate school. The first year was the most difficult. Teaching and advising took a great deal of time and I had no idea where the energy would come from to start a research program. In the second and third years, it became a little clearer. As I taught courses for the second and third time I became more comfortable and I found that I had more time to devote to research. In this section, I again take a case history approach on the means by which I balanced teaching with research, and I offer suggestions for others.

THE CONDUCT OF BASIC RESEARCH IN LIGHT OF HEAVY TEACHING LOADS

When I arrived at Southwestern University faculty members were expected to teach four courses each semester, advise students, and, as I was to discover, serve on committees. I had little notion of what teaching four courses entailed, little sense of what advising students meant, and absolutely no idea of what constituted a committee assignment. I discovered that teaching load, advising load, and committee load seriously cut into one's time to conduct research. The trick was to find ways of reducing these loads and to find ways to conduct research less time intensively.

At Southwestern University in the early 1990s faculty members welcomed the dean's decision to adopt a three-course teaching load. At about the same time, the Department of Psychology was scheduled for a 10-year review. The outside reviewer, James Motiff, chair of the department of psychology at Hope College, Holland, Michigan, recommended that each faculty member teach a course that involved students in research projects of publishable merit. Prior to this time faculty members had been involving students in their research, but they were not getting course credit for it. In essence, faculty members were working with students on an independent study basis in addition to their usual load. With Motiff's suggestion and his credibility as an outside reviewer, psychology faculty members at Southwestern University established independent research courses, which became a regular part of each faculty member's teaching load. The course enrolled no more than eight students who actively participated in all aspects of a research project including research design, construction of apparatus, collection and analysis of data, and manuscript preparation.

Through these courses, students gain an appreciation for the need for research and they come to understand more fully the scientific method. This is critical to the student's education. To be competitive for graduate programs, students must be able to participate in all aspects of a research project. They should be able to read critically the literature, determine problem areas that lend themselves to empirical test, formulate hypotheses, test hypotheses using the various methods of science available to psychologists, statistically analyze data and prepare it for presentation, and prepare manuscripts for presentation and publication. In addition, it is imperative that students be able to use computers to control sophisticated apparatus, analyze visual and auditory data, conduct complex statistical analyses, and present data. These skills are best taught through hands-on research experience.

By having the conduct of research with students as part of the teaching load, the faculty member also benefits. In addition to having more time for research, having student assistants allows the faculty member to carry out more experiments than would otherwise be possible. Faculty members will find that student interest in research grows exponentially. This has the effect of challenging one to devise more ways to get more students involved. In addition, students will begin to read the literature and will want to discuss their findings. This in turn challenges the faculty member to keep current. With students conducting more and more research, which results in more and more presentations and publications, the faculty member's reputation grows and the program becomes one that is known to produce strong undergraduate candidates for graduate programs. These outcomes cannot help but make one more competitive for tenure and promotion.

It is also possible to design research questions that can be answered through less time intensive means. In graduate school it was common to carry out rat studies for 4 to 6 hours per day, 7 days a week, for 7 to 10 weeks at a time. With heavy teaching, advising, and committee loads, this kind of time commitment is difficult, if not impossible, to make. Students too have strong time pressures and typically cannot afford that level of commitment. Much of the animal research conducted at Southwestern University uses operant methodology. The methodology can be used to answer a number of interesting questions concerning foraging decisions that animals make and basic questions within the area of animal learning, including questions concerning secondary reinforcement, observing, and paradoxical effects of reward. These types of studies typically do not require the constant presence of the researcher and conform nicely to class schedules, which revolve around 50-minute periods. A number of studies conducted in the aquatic lab require the use of videocassette recorders. Such studies, which have included examination of the role of endogenous alarm substances on predator defense strategies in fishes, daily foraging patterns in fishes, predator–prey interactions in fishes, and social and vocal interactions in Weddell seals typically do not require extensive and consecutive periods of time to conduct. In addition, the videotape analysis can be accomplished within the time constraints faced by students.

JUSTIFICATION FOR THE ESTABLISHMENT OF AN ANIMAL RESEARCH PROGRAM

There is a growing political movement to bring all nonhuman animal research to cessation. In many ways, the outcome of this political movement has been positive. Researchers are required to justify the use of animals in their experimental protocols and they have to assess critically the number of animals needed. This requirement reduces the number of animals used in experimentation and it helps to ensure that the animal model chosen is appropriate for the questions asked. Researchers are also required to maintain their animals in larger, cleaner, and healthier environments and conduct their research in a manner that is minimally invasive. These outcomes are laudable and they have likely resulted in decreases in animal abuses. Conversely, the bad publicity and the difficulty that is encountered in conducting animal research could eventually eliminate animal research or at a minimum alter the direction of such research. In the end, this stifling of research questions could have an enormous negative impact on the acquisition of knowledge.

Justification for the use of animals in research has come from a variety of individuals in a number of different disciplines. Rollin (1985) contended that humans have largely worked out a set of ideals for how humans ought to be treated and that a similar set of ideals could be developed for animals. Rollin argued that psychologists should devote more effort to theory construction and less to invasive animal experimentation, and psychologists must give more consideration to the study of consciousness and awareness. For Rollin, research in these areas of animal cognition is morally defensible and hence justifiable. At the conclusion of his article, Rollin repeats two principles from his 1981 paper to guide animal research. These principles are as follows:

1. *The utilitarian principle*. Before embarking on a piece of research, one ought to determine, to the best of one's ability, that the potential benefit to humans (or to humans and animals) clearly outweighs the pain and suffering to be experienced by the experimental animals.
2. *The rights principle*. In cases in which research is deemed justifiable by the utilitarian principle, it should be conducted in such a way as to maximize the animal's potential for living its life according to its nature, or telos, and certain fundamental rights should be preserved as far as possible given the logic of the research, regardless of cost considerations. (p. 926)

In essence, Rollin suggested that research that has potential to benefit the animal itself is defensible as well as research that benefits humans. If deemed defensible by either criterion, then such research should be conducted so as to preserve the animal's lifestyle. However, to conduct research in a manner that preserves the animal's lifestyle, it must be assumed that one knows what the animal's nature or telos is. It would appear that research that examines the ecology and ethology of the animal is also justified.

Gallup and Suarez (1985a) outlined several reasons that justify the conduct of animal research. Gallup and Suarez maintained that often it was only possible to use the appropriate control groups to establish cause and effect relationships using nonhuman subjects. Animal subjects can be used to control for genetic background, biological mechanisms, prior experience, and others. The use of animals in research also allows for the investigation of the role of maturation and development in behavioral changes. The use of animals in research also allows for the conduct of research, which can assess the effect of genetic manipulation on behavior. This line of research is invaluable in an attempt to determine the interaction between nature and nurture and the extent to which behavior is genetically determined.

As nonhuman animals typically are less complex than humans both structurally and functionally, animal researchers may be better able to identify basic principles of learning and behavior, which can then be tested against a human model. Currently, considerable work is being conducted on the biological basis of learning and memory in aplysia, a marine invertebrate. This simple model of learning is having a tremendous impact on the nature of research related to learning and memory. Gallup and Suarez (1995a) pointed out that animal research provides the foundation for many issues, including child abuse, mental illness, suicide, drug addiction, brain damage, and sexual assault. Finally, behavioral research on animals has led to the development of techniques that benefit animals, specifically models for improved housing and care, the protection and breeding of endangered species, the care of domestic farm animals, and the control of harmful insects.

CONCLUSION

The conduct of research with animals is justifiable. In addition, it is appropriate at the undergraduate level and at small colleges and universities. As mentioned previously, training undergraduates to conduct research with animals offers several major advantages. Students learn firsthand about the anatomy, physiology, and behavior of animals. They learn to care for and maintain an animal colony, and they learn to treat animals responsibly and ethically. Students also learn the various guidelines for the conduct of research with nonhuman animals.

It is important to note that by being involved in animal research, students acquire a better understanding of the scientific method particularly as it relates to the methods of science commonly used in psychology. Students learn to design better experiments and to determine the control groups necessary to establish cause and effect relationships. By being involved in research and in the presentation and publication of their results, students will be exposed to conferences and conventions within psychology. Attendance at meetings keeps students informed regarding the latest developments in the field and provides students with information regarding graduate programs including admissions requirements and the various programs of research. Clearly, the advantages of establishing an active program of research that uses nonhuman animals as the subjects of choice outweigh the efforts required to develop such a program. It behooves investigators to ensure that future generations of students derive the same benefits of exposure to such programs that they enjoyed as undergraduates.

REFERENCES

Adelson, R. (2003). Kick-starting extinction through massed exposure helps mice overcome conditioned fear faster. *Monitor on Psychology, 34*(11), 20.

Adelson, R. (2004). One fundamental learning process. *Monitor on Psychology, 35*(3), 20.

Ballie, R. (2001). Animal sleep studies offer hope for humans. *Monitor on Psychology, 32*(9), 20.

Domjan, M., & Krause, M. A. (2002). Research productivity in animal learning from 1953 to 2000. *Animal Learning & Behavior, 30*, 282–285.

Domjan, M., & Purdy, J. E. (1995). Animal research in psychology: More than meets the eye of the general psychology student. *American Psychologist, 50*, 496–503.

Domjan, M., & Purdy, J. E. (1996). Teaching about animal research in psychology. *American Psychologist, 51*, 979–980.

Gallup, G. G., Jr., & Suarez, S. D. (1985a). Alternatives to the use of animals in psychological research. *American Psychologist, 40*, 1104–1111.

Gallup, G. G., Jr., & Suarez, S. D. (1985b). Animal research versus the care and maintenance of pets: The names have been changed but the results remain the same. *American Psychologist, 40*, 968.

Grier, J. W. (1984). *Biology of animal behavior.* St. Louis, MO: Times Mirror/Mosby.

Miller, N. E. (1985). The value of behavioral research on animals. *American Psychologist, 40*, 423–440.

National Science Foundation. (2004a). *Course, curriculum, and laboratory improvement (CCLI).* Overview, paragraph 4. Retrieved March 8, 2004, from http://www.ehr.nsf.gov/due/programs/ccli/

National Science Foundation. (2004b). *RUI/ROA: Research in undergraduate institution and research opportunity awards.* Paragraph 3. Retrieved March 8, 2004, from http://www.ehr.nsf.gov/crssprgm/rui/start.shtm

Psi Chi. (2004). *Psi Chi journal of undergraduate research.* Paragraph 1. Retrieved March 8, 2004, from http://www.psichi.org/pubs/journal/home.asp

Purdy, J. E. (1989). The effects of brief exposure to aromatic hydrocarbons on feeding and avoidance behavior in coho salmon (*Oncorhynchus kisutch*). *Journal of Fish Biology, 34*, 621–629.

Purdy, J. E., Bales, S. L., Burns, M. L., & Weigand, N. (1994). Assessing the rewarding aspects of a stimulus associated with extinction through the observing response paradigm. *International Journal of Comparative Psychology, 7*(3), 100–115.

Purdy, J. E., & Cross, H. A. (1979). The role of R-S* expectancy in discrimination and discrimination reversal learning. *Learning and Motivation, 10*, 211–217.

Purdy, J. E., Eimann, D. G., & Cross, H. A. (1980). Persistence of a briefly presented visual stimulus in sensory memory. *Bulletin of the Psychonomic Society, 16*, 374–376.

Purdy, J. E., & Peel, J. L. (1988). Observing response in goldfish (*Carassius auratus*). *Journal of Comparative Psychology, 102*, 160–168.

Rollin, B. E. (1985). The moral status of research animals in psychology. *American Psychologist, 40*, 920–926.

Thorndike, E. L. (1898). Animal intelligence: An experimental study of the association processes in animals. *Psychological Review Monograph, 2*(8).

Turville-Heitz, M. (2000). Violent opposition. *Scientific American, 282*, 32.

6

USING LABORATORY ANIMALS IN TEACHING AND RESEARCH WITH LIMITED RESOURCES

DONALD F. KENDRICK

The use of laboratory animals in teaching and research when resources are limited has historically defined experimental psychology. Thorndike (1874–1949) began his animal research in the basement of William James's house and the James's children were his lab assistants (Leahey, 1991). In the summer of 1919, Tolman (1886–1959) obtained six rats from the Anatomy Department (where they were housed). He was not positive. "I have begun with my rats. At present, I am merely playing with them every day. I have six to begin with. I don't like them. They make me feel creepy" (Tolman, 1919; as cited in Innis, 1992, p. 191). Nonetheless, by October, Tolman had 50 rats, cages he built himself, 2 students working with him, and his own re-search in progress (Innis, 1992). In November, he received grant funds of $150. From such modest beginnings began one of the most prolific careers in psychology.

It may be too much to hope that by reading this chapter, one could emulate Thorndike's or Tolman's careers, but the common theme of animal research, from the least to the greatest, is modest beginnings. This chapter comprises four sections that describe how to get started, how to improve and expand, how to integrate resources and facilities of both research and teaching, and how to cope with issues and controversies of the ethical treatment of animals. My objective is to provide a set of instructions for the psychology instructor's beginning years of academic appointment, in an environment in which teaching objectives come first, and research, if encouraged, is traditionally not funded.

GETTING STARTED

The first thing to do is to set up the Institutional Animal Care and Use Committee (IACUC). It may seem odd to create a committee as a first step. However, the IACUC accomplishes two purposes. First, it is important that more than one faculty member is aware of the care and use of animals and approves the protocols. Second, the committee is the liaison between the faculty member using animals and the general community. (Refer to Appendix C for the structure of IACUCs and their specific responsibilities.)

With the IACUC in place, the next step is to decide whether to maintain and house animals or to use animals on a temporary basis. Pets (e.g., caged birds, dogs, hamsters, and gerbils) can often be used in demonstrations of basic learning principles in the classroom and then returned home. It is important to be aware that, legally, an animal used in the classroom is not considered a pet. This means the animal is considered a laboratory animal and the regulations controlling the use of laboratory animals are in effect. When the pet is returned home, it becomes a pet again. A researcher must get approval from the IACUC to bring animals into the classroom for any purpose.

Housing and Maintenance

For researchers who are considering housing animals, it is necessary to review local laws and institutional policies (see chap. 9, this volume). Approval from the IACUC to house the specified number of animals is also required. Most small schools may not have a policy. It is then a good idea to seek advice and opinions from colleagues, administrators, and students on how to set up the colony. It is also a good idea to post a copy of the approval for housing in the housing facility. Funding for consumable supplies must be established. Regular veterinary care, with at least semiannual visits, is essential. Funding may come through the researcher's department or school, or one may decide to independently fund a small colony. It is no more expensive than keeping pets, based primarily on the number of animals housed and maintained. Institutions with agricultural departments may have a veterinarian on staff. Local groups (e.g., Pigeon and Dove Club and the Caged-

Bird Club of America), are good resources to consult. Wildlife management divisions usually have state-employed veterinarians or lists of local veterinarians (see chap. 2, this volume, for more details about veterinary care). I once convinced a local veterinarian to donate his time. With no prior experience with lab animals or with pigeons, he quickly read and studied them and became quite adept. Employees at local pet stores may provide information about area veterinarians who have experience with rats, mice, and exotic animals (e.g., reptiles and caged birds).

Once funds for consumable supplies and veterinarian care are determined, there remain three major considerations to housing animals: cages, feeding, and cleaning. All three are discussed throughout the chapters in this volume; for the beginning instructor there are some basic considerations.

- *Cages.* Small colonies can be housed very inexpensively. Four goldfish can be kept in a bowl or a 5- or 10-gallon aquarium; kits and supplies purchased from pet stores may be adequate. Rodents (rats, mice, gerbils, or hamsters) and pigeons are the next most likely lab animals. Pet store kits for rodents may suffice when only two or three animals are involved. For example, aquariums with cedar chip bedding and wire screen covers (that can be secured) could be used. Pigeons require larger cages and are more expensive in other ways. I have caged them in large Plexiglas boxes with screen tops and cedar chip bedding. Cleaning these cages on a daily basis can be a major chore. Better cages allow waste to fall through the cage floor to a catch pan. Hardware cloth, galvanized steel, or stainless steel with 1-inch **x** 1/2-inch openings can be cut and shaped to make cages and set on cedar chips in a metal pan (made from galvanized sheet metal). Commercially available standard wire cages and racks, too expensive for the unfunded researcher, may be available from other universities on an interinstitutional loan. This is all the more likely because, sadly, some large universities are closing their animal labs and others are decreasing in size. For example, in the early 1990s Michigan State University discontinued maintaining the pigeon laboratory for undergraduate instruction (Rilling, personal communication, November 23, 1994) and the equipment was boxed, stored, and may still be available. Regardless of the species and caging decisions, do not use wood or any porous material. The cage must be dry and well ventilated, and it must provide a safe, comfortable environment as similar as possible to the one the animal would seek of its own accord.
- *Feeding.* Pet store foods are readily available. Larger quantities may be obtained from a feed store or farmer's co-op. They have

catalogs of feeds and can special order what is needed. Food and water must be provided daily and the water replaced daily, unless food or water restriction have been approved by the IACUC. The researcher should occasionally provide small quantities of fresh foods. Most species will eat leaf vegetables, carrots, peas, and corn. Pigeons may be fed a pellet food supplemented with mixed grains, or they may be fed just the mixed grain. Pigeons also eat greens, especially the young shoots germinated from the mixed grains. With a veterinarian, one can determine the foods that will provide complete nutrition; do not rely on commercial foods because they are often inadequate alone. Certain foods have expiration dates that should be adhered to for both nutritional and regulatory reasons.

- *Cleaning.* The cleaning agent used for the cages must kill bacteria and fungus. Clorox, or any household bleach, may be added to water for cleaning. Sanitizing soaps are also readily available. Please be aware of chemicals that may be toxic to some species. Read the warning labels for chemicals and ask a veterinarian about them. Daily attention to the animals is required to maintain a clean and healthy environment. Cleaning the cages is also a good time to inspect the appearance of each animal. By systematic examination of each animal, one will become familiar with the healthy appearance of the animals. Should health problems develop, the researcher will be able to notice them earlier. Exhibit 6.1 is a list of cleaning requirements, which I keep posted on the wall beside the door to my pigeon laboratory. The laboratory houses 20 pigeons. Every animal lab should have a similar list of duties, with the frequency of how often they should be performed, posted near the lab. This is true even if there is only one person working with the animals. Eventually, a researcher should have students working as well. If the students do not clean, it might benefit them to know the procedures that are involved. Exhibit 6.1 may also be used as a checklist for students responsible for cleaning pigeon colonies.

Classroom Demonstrations

Once the IACUC is established and the animals selected, the next step is to decide what to do with them. One interesting classroom demonstration is a replication of the Clever Hans effect. A description of the method is generally available (Marshall & Linden, 1994). This section discusses three example demonstrations for classroom use. I have used them in my classes, so they are specific to the animals available to me. However, they can be easily

EXHIBIT 6.1
Checklist for Cleaning Pigeon Colonies

Daily
1. Rinse and refill water cups.
2. Inspect animal. Look at eyes, nostrils, beak, neck, chest, back, tail feathers, legs, feet, and belly.
3. Sweep or vacuum floors (do not mop).
4. Clean sink.
5. Clean lids of food and grit containers.
6. Wipe off weight scales with damp cloth.
7. Wipe off table with damp cloth.

Tuesday and Thursday Additional Cleaning
1. Clean shelves under pigeon cages.
2. Check each cage and clean if needed.
3. Mop floor if needed.
4. Clean walls (especially around pigeon cages) as needed.

Weekly Cleaning Checklist
1. Remove table and weight scales.
2. Sweep or vacuum floor.
3. Wash individual cages and rack.
4. Wash food and water cups.
5. Clean vacuum cleaner (if used during the week).
6. Clean drain hole in floor.
7. Take all garbage (sealed in plastic bags) outside and put in cans. Put lids on cans.
8. Wash doors, door frames, and windows (both sides).
9. Perform daily cleaning duties.

modified for other animals. Students are given copies of protocols written according to American Psychological Association (APA) style and format, with spaces to record their observations, report methods, graph data, and answer discussion questions.

The first demonstration, "Behavioral Observation," is a simple behavioral observation and recording. This is a typical exercise for students in a research methods course, an introduction to animal learning, and first-year biology or ethology. I have used my spouse's two pet cockatiels, although any caged birds will do; cockatiels are particularly active and social. There are many toys (bells, ladders, and playgrounds) for cockatiels sold commercially that can be added to the situation to encourage activity. The birds are brought to class and students keep running records of their behavior for approximately 15 minutes. From these records, specific behavior is selected and for the next 15 minutes, students count the number of times and the duration of the behavior. These data are then tabled or graphed. Discussion and interpretation follow.

Objective observation rather than interpretation has always been the focus of this demonstration. In a more advanced field observation, in which the students performed a naturalistic observation on a species and location of their choice, one student returned to class completely disgusted with the behavior of ducks on a local pond. She had no idea, she said, that those cute ducks were in reality so vicious. They fought, they bit, and she sat horrified as one tried to drown another by climbing on its back and grabbing it by the neck. I suggested that perhaps she was not being objective, but was guilty of interpretation. Maybe so, she said, but it was pretty obvious what was going on, anyone could see it. It was a delight to see her enlightened face when I suggested that perhaps she had witnessed sexual behavior instead of aggression. The importance of objective observation was discovered by at least one student that semester.

The second demonstration, "A Goldfish Learning Experiment," takes an untrained goldfish and conditions a blue versus red discrimination in a water-filled Plexiglas shuttle box. One or two goldfish are needed and should not be fed for 24 hours prior to the demonstration. Goldfish and most tropical fish can go without food safely for up to 2 weeks (Mills, 1982). For about $25 one can buy a 2-foot x 3-foot sheet of Plexiglas from a home-building supply store. From this piece, cut a bottom, sides, and end pieces, which can be easily cut with an electric circular saw (use a blade designed for cutting plywood). Next cut two extra end pieces and drill large holes in them close to one edge. A hole saw and an electric drill make this step easy. Glue the box together using a silicon caulk; make sure it is suitable for aquariums because some silicon is toxic to fish. Insert the two pieces with the holes in the box about 4 inches from the ends. These pieces form the walls that separate the box into three chambers: two chambers that are 4 inches long and one main center chamber about 16 inches long. The holes are for the fish to swim through. I like putting one hole down and one hole up so that as the fish swim from end to end, a sine wave swim pattern results.

With a goldfish placed in one end, the instructor or student places a blue card or colored construction paper against the backside of the box. This card should be the full height and length of the goldfish shuttle box. When the fish swims to the opposite end, a small piece of flake food is dropped on the surface of the water. The fish eats it. Now a red card replaces the blue card and the fish must swim to the opposite end to get a second piece of flake food. The first few trials will take a few minutes, but rather quickly, the fish will learn to swim rapidly to the left end in the presence of the blue card and to the right end in the presence of the red card. Wait until the goldfish is in the main chamber before providing a color cue, and use a quasi-random left-right pattern.

Students record shuttle times and the classical Thorndike learning curve is exhibited. Generalization gradients may also be obtained. Goldfish learn quickly. This demonstration is easily done within a 50-minute class period.

The third demonstration, "Operant Conditioning," requires an operant chamber. A researcher can build an operant chamber (a box with a funnel and tube to deliver food). Simple schedules of reinforcement, extinction, and discrimination can be demonstrated. Rats or pigeons may be used here and a well-trained animal can be used for several semesters. Mary L, a demonstration pigeon, served for 5 years. Her name was actually the name of the student who first trained her. Students are required to write their first names and last initial on the ID card attached to the pigeons' cages. After Mary L, the student, completed the course, her pigeon became her namesake. Mary L, the pigeon, pecked on a variety of schedules of reinforcement and quickly learned reversal discriminations. At the end of the demonstration, I opened the door and Mary L would come flying out of the operant chamber and fly around the room. I would pretend she had escaped. Students were sure that animals do not want to be in the chamber. As the students jumped and yelled, Mary L would fly about the room, then fly directly to me when I called her name. She would land on my shoulder, give me a bird kiss, and then hop back into the chamber. It was an exciting and dramatic demonstration of the power of positive reinforcement in behavior control. It also led to many discussions of whether Mary L was being controlled or had entered the chamber of her own free will.

I have also demonstrated basic principles of reinforcement using a pet dog that had been trained to sit, stand, or roll over on command. I have found that small dogs are best for this exercise (I use my mother's miniature red dachshund). Training a new behavior cannot usually be done in the allotted class time. However, it is possible to transfer the training to a student and to demonstrate generalization. With small bits of cheese or other treats, the dog quickly learns to sit for any student. Then it is shaped to sit for *set* and *sat*. When the student uses a low voice tone, the dog will also lower its ears and head as it sits. From *sat* it is easy to train a dog to sit for *stat* and finally for *statistics*. Students are amused to see a dog sit and hang its head when they say *statistics*.

GETTING MORE INVOLVED

It has been my experience that once one gets involved in providing students with live animal experiences, the positive reinforcement produces even more involvement. The faculty member begins to generate new ways to use animals, university administrators begin to provide more aid (because of positive feedback from students), and students want to leave their chairs, stop observing, and get direct control over the procedures and manipulations. At this point it becomes necessary to obtain funding, to find space to house animals, and to encourage students' original research projects.

Funding

The lack of funding is an overused excuse for not pursuing the use of animals in teaching and research. However, funds are available. Several chapters in this volume discuss how to get funds. In this section, I briefly mention the sources I have used. There are some basic guidelines for the person in a small institution: One, never say no. Any amount is useful. A little here, a little there, and it all adds up. Two, purchase in part, not whole. I had to purchase individual cages (about $60 each) in small lots (one to five at a time) over a 3-year period. This was not so bad. However, the rack to hold them was prohibitively expensive and I was continually told that no money was available, nor would be forthcoming. Nevertheless, I purchased as many cages as possible with whatever funds were available. When a faculty member took an unpaid leave of absence, other faculty members were able to convince the dean to use some of the unused salary to purchase the expensive rack. Three, talk with administrators in person when requesting funds, then follow it up in a memo. Four, provide justification and the benefits of spending their money on your projects. Follow this with post hoc evaluations. Administrators are more likely to provide future funds to someone who has written to them about how past funds were spent and the relative success of the venture.

There are at least five funding sources. First, and perhaps the most overlooked, is slush funds. The chairperson, dean, or other school official will have money that is not designated for any particular purpose or is unspent. It is the researcher's job to find that person and convince them that a few hundred dollars would go a long way to enhancing students' education.

Second, most institutions or departments and schools within institutions have some sort of funding available for developing new teaching techniques or for new research efforts. These in-house grants are typically small: hundreds of dollars, rather than thousands. This is quite sufficient to get started.

Third, many agencies at the state and federal level have grant funds available for the researcher or educator at smaller institutions to build and equip a laboratory for undergraduate instruction. Several chapters in this volume provide the necessary references.

Fourth, do not overlook the students. Researchers may charge them a lab fee or have students purchase their own animals and supplies. I once had students purchase hardware cloth. A part of their lab experience was to build pigeon cages. They, of course, donated the cages to the school on completion of the course. One year, students purchased a printer for the lab computer, which they then used to type and print their reports. It cost less then $5 per student and it is still in use 6 years later.

Fifth, consider splitting costs with another department. Anatomy, biology, and other departments typically purchase and house animals. Psychology departments requiring the temporary use of live healthy animals may be allowed to use the animals in demonstrations or research, then return them for their original intended purposes.

Housing and Maintenance

It is most likely that researchers will need to house and maintain an animal colony. General guidelines for housing, cleaning, and feeding are discussed in chapter 2 of this volume. There are two basic approaches to housing animals: short term and long term. One may wish to acquire and use animals only for the duration of the demonstration or research project. This reduces maintenance costs, especially during term breaks and summer, when there would be no animals to care for. However, one must then dispose of the animals in an ethical fashion. Although euthanasia is one obvious and ethical choice, please consider finding homes for the animals. It is perfectly acceptable for students to adopt lab animals that are healthy. This of course depends on the species; lab rats do not usually make good pets. However, I have successfully placed lab rats and mated pairs of pigeons with students. The pigeons require a farm environment or a family with experience with keeping a pigeon loft. One pair of pigeons became an accepted part of the farm animal life and joined the chickens for the morning feed. It is the researcher's responsibility to ensure that the animal will be treated ethically in its adopted home. This requires that the researcher train students in animal ethics. Incorporating animal ethics training within the animal-use demonstrations and research projects is discussed in the section, Integrating Research and Teaching, in this chapter.

If one decides to maintain an animal colony throughout term breaks and summers, then assistance in cleaning and feeding the animals is needed. The researcher will need funding to hire an assistant. Many schools have a form of financial aid that requires students to work on campus for administrators and faculty. One of these work–study students may be available and willing to clean the animal facilities. A psychology major would be particularly apropos. Researchers may be able to convince administrators to hire a part-time worker. Another option is to require students who are working on research projects to care for their animals themselves. Indeed, this may be an important part of the research experience.

Research Space

A fundamental commonality among schools, colleges, and universities is the lack of space. Whether or not there is an established animal colony or demonstration animals are kept at home or in the office, space for students to pursue their projects will be needed.

Discovering unused space is an art. It requires a nosy person. Peek into every nook and cranny of every building on campus. Record room numbers, location, and the current use of each room. Do not trust the lists produced by the administrators. Actual use of space is rarely on their lists. One will discover a room, perhaps more than one room. It may be filled with stored items that can be distributed and put in use; it may be a forgotten closet under a stairwell; it may be an old garage on the edge of campus, forgotten and abandoned. I have found and used all three. At one university, by comparing the outside appearance of a building with the rooms inside, I discovered a small room that had been walled in. My colleagues and I put a doorway in a hall wall, punched a hole through to the outside for a small ventilation fan, and created research space. It should be noted however, that research space should be adequate and able to be sanitized for conducting experiments with nonhuman animals. In addition, housing nonhuman animals in areas other than those designated for animals requires justification, review, and approval by the IACUC.

Administrators also often think that animal space could be better used for other purposes. My pigeon lab was reviewed annually the first few years just to see if there was not something better to be done with the space. Administration and building-service personnel, for example, would arrange a visit and I would be available to conduct show and tell. On the walls of the student area of the laboratory are the research posters that students presented at local, regional, and national meetings, such as the National Undergraduate Research Conference, Regional Psychology Association meetings, and so forth. Everyone can easily see the products of the previous students. Often administrators and other visitors spend as much time reading and asking questions as they do looking around the facility.

In one particularly harrowing instance, the university president was looking for space for one of his pet projects. He was noticeably unimpressed by the posters, by the students working diligently at operant chambers, and by the amount of time and effort I had obviously spent setting it all up. Then he walked away and asked, "What is this room used for?"

"It's a small project I'm working on, nothing much really, a modified student operant chamber interfaced to an old Model III, Tandy, microcomputer. Pigeons are being trained in a discrimination task," I told him. Suddenly, he was all ears. He wanted to see it, so I led him into the darkened room and pointed out the peephole to view the pigeon as it worked. He got down on his knees and peered in. I left the room and shut the door. He came out in about 10 minutes grinning from ear to ear. "That's the damnedest thing I ever saw," he said, "that pigeon knows that red will get it food!"

I do not believe there are any specific guidelines for keeping space or justifying the use of it. My emphasis on the students and teaching was not impressive, but one look at a small personal research project saved the day. In general, one should be flexible and perhaps not emphasize one aspect of one's use of space to the exclusion of other uses. Creativity and enthusiasm for a research also may help to maintain research space.

Once a researcher has set up an animal colony, either a short-term colony or a long-term colony, he or she will most likely be doing in-class demonstrations and promoting student projects. If so inclined, this is a good time to add a personal research project. The desire to conduct original research coupled with the educational benefits of demonstrations and student projects is a compelling argument to justify the space and funds needed to house and maintain animals.

A plan is needed. It should include class demonstrations, student projects, and original research. The plan should be a systematic, detailed approach to the ethical use of animals, showing clearly how students will be trained and how the animals will be used.

It is important to develop students' awareness of ethics. Merely assigning ethical documents to be read (e.g., APA, 2002; *Ethical Principles of Psychology and Code of Conduct*) is not sufficient. Faculty members should encourage students to discuss ethics and to develop their own rules for ethical treatment. Naturally, faculty members must ensure that local laws and general guidelines are followed. These should be the foundation on which students develop their own guidelines for their own behavior with respect to animals. Exhibit 6.2 provides an outline of this process, as it would apply to class demonstrations and to research projects. It is a basic three-step process of awareness, establishing rules of conduct, and reviewing and revising the rules.

Using Animals in Teaching

There has been much said about the use of alternatives to live animals in teaching (and research), but the basic message seems to be a rather vague "there are other ways." Just what the other ways are is not often stated. There are three approaches to using animals in teaching: living animals, computer-simulated animals, and videos and films. It might be both prudent and instructive to use all three options.

- *Videos*. First, show videos or films demonstrating the topic of study. There are excellent, although rather old, films demonstrating a variety of behavior principles using animals (e.g., Skinner, 1975). Try videotaping an in-class demonstration one term, then using it in class thereafter. At Middle Tennessee State University (MTSU), educators show two basic films. One reviews principles of classical and operant conditioning (Zimbardo, 1990, 2001) and the other discusses the relationship between animal research and human behavior. After viewing the short films, students listen to an audiotaped interview

EXHIBIT 6.2
Outline of the Process for Ethical Training With Animals in Classroom
Demonstrations and Research Training

Classroom Demonstration
1. Ethics review and discussion including
   a. Obtaining and housing animals
   b. Experimental procedures
   c. Euthanasia
2. Classroom demonstration
3. Evaluation of demonstration including
   a. Principles demonstrated
   b. Ethical treatment (was this demo ethical?)
4. Revision of ethics as determined in 1 above

Research Training
1. General ethics lecture and seminar
2. Ethics of specific projects/research procedures as related to 1 above
3. Institutional review and approval (or colleagues review and recommendations)
4. Conduct research projects (monitor and discuss ethical concerns during project)
5. Conclude research; reconsider ethics with suggestions of changes in protocols and procedures for future lab projects

with the president of Funds for Animals, which is a radical animal rights group (Gianelli & Crawford, 1981). It is much more effective to have students view such films before raising ethical issues. Seeing the research that is portrayed in the films establishes the conditions for ethics in the context of animal behavior and psychology. More recent videos include the APA series on "The Contributions and Importance of Nonhuman Animal Research in Psychology"(American Psychological Association, 1998). The first two segments, "Perception and Action" and "Psychopharmacology," are currently available and the production of additional videos is in progress.[1]

- *Live animal demonstration.* Second, perform an in-class demonstration using a live animal. After seeing a film, students are much more impressed by the live demonstration and they are more prepared to understand what is happening as the demonstration progresses. In my classes, students observe a pigeon on a fixed ratio (FR) schedule of reinforcement. I provide them with a *Learning Theories Manual* written for the specifics of my demonstration, which is loosely modeled after Michael (1963). In the past, I have taken a rat or pigeon to class in an operant chamber for a demonstration. THX-1138 was a pet rat (named for the title of a movie about a future in which people live boring lives in boxes and perform meaningless dehumanizing tasks

---

[1]Videos can be purchased via APA's Web site at http://www.apa.org/books or by calling the order department at (800) 374-2721.

for the state) who would bar press in a small homemade chamber for bran pellet reinforcers. THX-1138 (pronounced *Thex* for short) was so well trained at home that food deprivation and weight reduction were not necessary (or maybe he just liked bran). Lacking money to purchase an electronic chamber, I built one from Plexiglas. The bar was a piece of metal on a fulcrum, and I dropped pellets by hand through a rubber tube in the wall. During the demonstration, students were invited to drop pellets in the box on various simple schedules of reinforcement and record responses per minute. Extinction and discrimination were demonstrated as well. Simply turning off the classroom lights was the stimulus associated with extinction; lights on indicated reinforcement availability. After the session, I would open the door and THX would come out to visit, walking up students' arms, digging into their pockets, and so forth. Students loved it. THX was eventually retired. At home, he lived in a large wire box. He was mated and his offspring became the new demonstration rats.

- *Computer simulations.* Third, have students train a computer rat in a maze or operant chamber, or classically condition a computer dog (see Cunningham, 1993). Even the best computer simulations are poor representations of live animals, but seeing the real thing first makes it easier to grasp the essential characteristics of the computer animal. A computer-resources book is now being published annually; it is an excellent source of information on computer-based simulations, software packages, Internet sites, and so forth (Wallace, 1997).

At MTSU, students use Sniffy[2] MacLab's simulated rat (Alloway, Krames, & Graham, 1995). Sniffy is available in MAC or IBM versions for about $40 per copy. A site license is available for computer labs. Sniffy is a very convincing rat; it behaves like a rat. Students in the lab are required to hand shape Sniffy to bar press, maintain continuous reinforcement, and then to move on to simple schedules of reinforcement and extinction. They save Sniffy on a diskette as he learns. All the student behavior one sees in a live rat lab can be seen in the Sniffy lab. For example, they name their rats and claim that some rats are dumb, some are smart, and they protest about putting the rat on extinction because it is cruel. One student came to my office in tears. She forgot to save her rat at the end of the session and in her rush to

---

[2]The most recent versions of Sniffy can be purchased through Wadsworth–Thomson Learning. The Sniffy Lite version can be trained to perform basic operant and classical conditioning phenomena and costs $15.95. The Sniffy Pro version allows for training of more advanced phenomena and can be purchased for $25.95. A demonstration can be downloaded from http://www.wadsworth.com/psychology_d/special_features/sniffy.html or 1-800-354-9706.

correct the error had reformatted the diskette, thereby erasing all previously trained and saved versions. "I am so sorry, I killed my rat!" she cried. Although back-up copies of rats trained to various stages are kept so students do not have to retrain a new computer rat from scratch, but she said, "It's just not the same; my rat was smart and he was nice too." Sniffy is the closest thing to a live rat I have seen.

This three-step process (films, demonstration, and computer simulations) enhances learning considerably. Watching demonstrations on film allows one to stop and ask questions, to rewind and review, and to proceed at whatever rate is necessary to satisfy students. The live animal demonstration moves quickly without time for questions and answers, but it is likely to be the single most convincing and memorable event of the course. Finally, the computer simulation allows students to individually explore animal behavior and learning. They can try out different parameters, set individualized conditions, or even design and conduct their own experiments in animal learning.

Animals for Research Training and Faculty Research

In the live pigeon laboratory, beginning students observe demonstrations of pigeon operant conditioning (learning theories), and more advanced students conduct canned experiments with pigeons (operant conditioning). Some students continue with independent research in which they assist on research projects of graduate students' theses or faculty members' original research. The animals thus serve in all capacities: demonstration, training, theses, and original research for publication. Purchasing animals and equipment, training students, and conducting research are discussed in this section.

The pigeons are purchased with departmental funds at the discretion of the departmental chair. Funding is also available from MTSU's in-house granting committee. Funding from federal agencies are generally unavailable to small institutions, but there are several special programs for small schools. On occasion, I have driven to other universities to pick up animals that other researchers no longer wanted. I have also purchased locally bred pigeons for much less than commercially available birds.

The pigeons first serve in a beginning animal learning class, then in graduate or faculty research, then in the advanced animal learning class, and then go back in the beginning class. First, the pigeons are used in the beginning animal learning class, in which a graduate teaching assistant (GTA) hand shapes a pigeon while students observe and record the pigeons' behavior. The GTA thus gains experience in hand shaping and maintaining behavior (and teaching others), while the beginning students benefit from the real-life, real-time, live animal demonstration. Because space is limited, only a small group of two to four students observe at a time. The same pigeon may be hand shaped while one group observes and then the pigeon may be placed on an increasing FR schedule while another group observes. Finally, the pigeon may be maintained at some maximum FR schedule (e.g., FR 30) while the remaining students observe. This same bird may be used for several semesters with retraining on the FR schedule or placed on some other simple schedule. The birds thus trained are experienced peckers, and when research calls, the demonstration bird is promoted to research bird. Having the pigeon trained to peck the white response disk facilitates early training on the research project. Because the bird has not been trained in discriminations or other complex procedures, there is no contamination of prior learning on current learning; the bird is naive with respect to the experimental procedures.

When the research project is concluded, the pigeon may return to the beginning class or it may be assigned to a student in the advanced class. In the advanced class, the pigeons are trained on simple discriminations, concurrent schedules, and other advanced topics, ending with the students' single-subject original research project (e.g., training the pigeon to play Ping-Pong). The bird may then be returned to the beginning class for demonstrations of basic schedules of reinforcement.

Because pigeons live quite a long time, about 15 years on average, a long-term care plan is required, such as the multiple-use plan previously discussed. Ultimately, the animals must be given to other departments (e.g., biology) for other purposes or euthanized.

The pigeon lab resorts to euthanasia in three situations: severe health problems, old age, and inability to provide adequate care. The first two, health problems and old age, are obvious and just causes for terminating the life of a faithful research companion. The third, inability to provide adequate care, is not so noble. Unfortunately, there are times without funds, without student workers, and without adequate resources to maintain the animals properly. For example, several years ago, most of the animals were very old, the student worker had graduated and no one else had even applied for the caretaker job, and there was no room for new younger animals. No new research was possible, and the birds were so old that my colleagues and I questioned the ethics of using them as demonstration birds. I decided to euthanize them.

Some lab animals, especially those of behavioral studies that are drug free and surgery free, could be placed in homes if they are not too old. Students have asked to place my pigeons on the their parents' farms. I have received telephone calls from parents supporting the requests. This is perfectly acceptable, only if all involved are well aware of the ethics and the legal responsibilities. With proper ethics training, researchers can release lab animals into students' care; the very people whom they have had the best opportunity to properly educate in animal ethics. This does not violate any state or federal regulations; however, it does entail special concerns that must be considered (see chap. 8, this volume). Also, the IACUC must approve the release of animals to students and other caretakers.

ISSUES AND CONTROVERSIES

There are two primary sources of issues and controversies: Specific student problems and the animal rights activists. Specific student problems include students with phobias and those with specific problems regarding participation in particular experiments. For these students, it is best to provide alternatives. The student who has a phobia of birds may be permitted to observe in a nonparticipating way. Students who conscientiously object to particular experiments should be encouraged to suggest and implement procedural changes that reduce or eliminate their concerns. The amount of work involved in producing a well-researched written protocol could well be the substitute activity. The student who opposes all use of animals in education should be encouraged to investigate the extent of usage using library resources or to provide written protocols of alternatives to the use of animals.

The concerns of the animal rights activists are a different matter. I have had animal rights activists call on the telephone demanding access to my lab and colony for inspection by concerned citizens. I have had telephone interviews from student reporters and town reporters. I have had students and other people come into my lab wanting to see what goes on and why. In all cases, it is most important to open the lab; nothing is gained by denying students and others access to the lab. Plan on having to open the lab. Develop a plan for dealing with students' concerns in the classroom and lab, for dealing with the media, and for dealing with animal rights activists. The campus media should be informed regularly of your activities. An annual or term memo from the animal lab is a good way to indicate one's willingness to use animals ethically and openly. Provide open lab days each term—days when students and the general public are invited to the lab to see what goes on and why. Provide tours of the lab and animal colony to youth groups, campus organizations, elementary schools, and other classes.

When confronted with objections to animal research, do not become defensive. Emphasize that researchers are learning what is and is not good for animals, and what the more ethical alternatives may be. Researchers are attempting to experiment with the animals, not on them, to form a more perfect understanding of them and of ourselves. None of these things will dissuade the hard-core activist. Usually, the activists' issues are larger than the lab or the animals. Activists assert that the use of the animals by humans for human interests must be stopped, and that researchers have no right to cage animals and use them for any human-designed purpose. There is little one can do in this situation. Merely having animals is a violation of their rights in the eyes of the activist. It is best to refer the activist to the IACUC. It is their responsibility to deal with the public on researchers' behalf, to describe the legal uses of animals, delineate university policies, and ensure the well-being of the animals and the legality of the lab.

However, when confronted, I like to tell the activists what happened at Michigan State University in the late 1970s. Activists released nearly 60 White Carneaux pigeons from the student labs. I was the teaching assistant for the lab and when I arrived the next day, the campus was in an uproar. White bird bodies littered the streets. The poor lab pigeons had never learned about cars, dogs, or cats. They flew low across streets and were hit by cars. They landed in the middle of intersections and were run over. Dogs and cats merely walked up to them and bit them, then chased them down as they helplessly flopped with broken wings. It was a sad thing. The animals were not saved by being released, but instead suffered the cruelest of deaths. A similar incident occurred at the University of Minnesota in April 1989, when activists broke into two research facilities. Not only did they destroy millions of dollars worth of research equipment and research data, but they also released 116 animals, including some transgenic mice, most of which were killed.

CONCLUSION

Setting up animal laboratories and providing live animal demonstrations in the classroom need not require large outlays of money. Many people spend more on their pets than is needed to set up a small animal colony for classroom demonstrations of basic behavioral principles. I have attempted in this chapter to report what I have done in small, 2-, 4-, and 6-year colleges, with limited resources. It is my hope that, no matter the paltry size of funds, researchers are encouraged to set up their own labs and get their students involved in animal demonstrations and research. Despite the misgivings of the animal rights activists, there is much to be learned by the respectful, ethical, research with animals. Humans of all ages seem to be naturally curious about animals, and only by encouraging ethical animal investigations can researchers ensure the continued growth of their understanding of life and behavior.

REFERENCES

Alloway, T., Krames, L., & Graham, J. (1995). Sniffy, the Virtual Rat [Computer software]. Pacific Groves, CA: Brooks/Cole.

American Psychological Association (Producer). (1998). *Perception and action: The contributions and importance of nonhuman animal research in psychology* [Motion picture]. (Available from the American Psychological Association, 750 First Street, NE, Washington, DC 20002-4242)

American Psychological Association. (2002). Ethical principles of psychologists and code of conduct. *American Psychologist, 57,* 1060–1073.

Cunningham, M. (1993). CC.Dog, ALLEY.RAT, MAZE.RAT, OP.RAT [Computer Software]. Sarasota, FL: Crofter Publishing. (Also available at http://www.thecroft.com/psych.html)

Gianelli, M. (Interviewee), & Crawford, C. (Interviewer). (1981, October 15). Do animals have rights? [Television interview]. In C. Kuralt (Producer), *CBS Nightly News.* New York: CBS News.

Innis, N. K. (1992). Tolman and Tyron: Early research on the inheritance of the ability to learn. *American Psychologist, 47,* 190–197.

Leahey, T. H. (1991). *A history of modern psychology.* Englewood Cliffs, NJ: Prentice-Hall.

Marshall, M. J., & Linden, D. R. (1994). Simulating Clever Hans in the classroom. *Teaching of Psychology, 21,* 230–232.

Michael, J. (1963). *Laboratory studies in operant behavior.* New York: McGraw-Hill.

Mills, D. (1982). *You and your aquarium.* New York: Knopf.

Skinner, B. F. (1975). *A demonstration of behavioral processes by B. F. Skinner* [Film]. (Available from Insight Media, 2162 Broadway, New York, NY, 10024)

Wallace, P. M. (1997). *Psych online 97.* Chicago: Brooks & Benchmark.

Zimbardo, P. (1990, 2001). Learning [Television series episode]. In WGHB in association with the American Psychological Association (Producer), *Discovering psychology.* Boston: WGBH for Public Broadcasting Service.

7

USE OF LABORATORY ANIMALS FOR TEACHING UNDERGRADUATE BEHAVIORAL SCIENCE

DAVID A. ECKERMAN

Although a variety of techniques can be used in the classroom to teach students about behavior, only by working with live subjects can a student truly test what is known about behavior. Computer simulations, just as written descriptions, provide only a sketch of the subject matter. Students appropriately treat simulations as practice rather than as a true encounter with what is known. Educational projects are sometimes intended to offer training in carrying out a particular procedure or to merely review what is known about a subject. Simulation may in some cases be the best approach for such training. Conversely, work with live subjects is superior if the project seeks to pique students' interest, to encourage students to critically evaluate established ideas, or to help students rise to the challenge of creating new ideas about biological and experiential influences on behavior. Susan Offner (1993) captured this effect in the following quotations from an article advocating the importance of continuing to allow students to carry out dissections in biology laboratories:

I can still remember my first dissection of a mammal. It was a mouse, and I thought it was 'yucky' and I didn't want to touch it. But, being too proud to admit this to my teacher, I cut it anyway. What ensued was a tremendous explosion of consciousness and understanding. All the things I had been learning were suddenly real. It was a profound experience. But it was something more. By confirming all the things I had been taught, it helped me understand that the world was a rational place, and that knowledge and understanding can come from serious study of real specimens and real data. Every year, I see this same kind of learning occur in my own students. This is what teaching is all about. (p. 147)

I am distressed with the amount of time and energy spent looking for 'alternatives to dissection.' The alternative to dissection is ignorance, and let us never forget that ignorance comes at a terrible price. There was a time in history when dissection was forbidden, when even medical students and doctors could not see the insides of animals. We call those times the Dark Ages. They were not a time of respect for life. They were a time of ignorance, and along with the ignorance came tremendous insensitivity and cruelty. In the absence of real medical knowledge and understanding, superstition prevailed and all kinds of grotesque mutilations were performed in the name of science. One of the most important lessons to come out of the Dark Ages is that love of and respect for life come from knowledge and understanding and not from ignorance and its invariable handmaidens, fear and superstition. If this sounds farfetched, imagine what this country would be like if nobody had dissected in the last 40 years.

Students who have been through a good biology course, who have studied both animals and their relationship with the world in a broad sense, will leave the course with an enduring respect and reverence for life. Dissection is an essential part of such an education. (p. 148)

Researchers have made great strides in understanding behavior. Yet, further increasing one's understanding of behavior is critical if one is to address most of the major problems in the world. For example, solutions to drug addiction, prevention of AIDS, control of the population size, and appropriate use of resources all involve behavioral change. The advances researchers have made in these areas were started, in many cases, with a careful inspection of animal behavior. The present understanding, however, falls woefully short of what researchers must know to address the problems previously discussed. Merely exposing students to current understandings, then, will not advance their knowledge. These students must learn where the present understanding falls short and be inspired to improve this state. Researchers cannot rely on simulations to encourage such reevaluation or to challenge students. Simulations merely provide opinion. In a review of the use of animals in education, the U.S. Congress Office of Technology Assessment identified the following goals for the educational use of animals (U.S. Congress Office of Technology Assessment, 1986):

(1) Development of positive attitudes toward animals. In the best instances, such development incorporates ethical and moral considerations into student's course of study. (2) Introduction of the concept of biological models, by which students learn to single out particular animal species as representative of biological phenomena. Such models vary in the degree to which they provide general information about a broader spectrum of life. (3) Exercise of skills vital to intellectual, motor, or career development. Familiarity with living tissue, for example, enhances a student's surgical dexterity. (p. 199)

The material presented here seeks to aid those who wish to help train the next generation of behavioral scientists by introducing educational projects that use live animals. Although I am aggressive in my belief that such projects are essential to continue the advances we have made, I am also circumspect regarding the many issues that need to be addressed as educational projects are developed, approved for use, and carried out. Some of what follows, therefore, is cautionary, and I take as my starting point the many statements that have been issued by professional and governmental agencies to frame what is and what is not judged appropriate for such educational projects.

REGULATIONS, GUIDELINES, AND POLICIES REGARDING THE INSTRUCTIONAL USE OF ANIMALS

Use of Animals in Research, Testing, and Education

The American Psychological Association provided one of the clearest general guidelines for the appropriate instructional use of animals for psychology (American Psychological Association, 1990). The more detailed regulations and guidelines that follow in subsequent sections follow from this general assertion.

> Be it further resolved that the use of animals by students can be an important component of science education as long as it is supervised by teachers who are properly trained in the welfare and use of animals in laboratory or field settings and is conducted by institutions capable of providing proper oversight.

Educational Use of Animals

In an earlier publication (American Psychological Association, 1985), the American Psychological association had detailed specific guidelines that should be considered when using live animal projects in education.

A. For educational purposes, as for research purposes, consideration should always be given to the possibility of using non-animal alternatives. When animals are used solely for educational rather than research purposes, the consideration of possible benefits accruing from their use vs. the cost in terms of animal distress should take into account the fact that some procedures which can be justified for research purposes cannot be justified for educational purposes. Similarly, certain procedures, appropriate in advanced courses, may not be appropriate in introductory courses.

B. Classroom demonstrations involving animals should be used only when instructional objectives cannot effectively be achieved through the use of videotapes, films, or other alternatives. Careful consideration should be given to the question of whether the type of demonstration is warranted by the anticipated instructional gains.

C. Animals should be used for educational purposes only after review by a departmental committee or by the local institutional animal care and use committee.

D. Psychologists are encouraged to include instruction and discussion of the ethics and values of animal research in courses, both introductory and advanced, which involve or discuss the use of animals.

E. Student projects involving pain or distress to animals should be undertaken judiciously and only when the training objectives cannot be achieved in any other way.

F. Demonstrations of scientific knowledge in such contexts as exhibits, conferences, or seminars do not justify the use of painful procedures or surgical interventions. Audiovisual alternative should be considered.

Humane Care and Use of Animals in Research

The American Psychological Association also provides guidance regarding the use of live animals in research projects (American Psychological Association, 2002, see also Standard 8.09). Many of the guidelines, including those regarding the care of the animals and the training of caretakers, also apply for educational uses.

(a) Psychologists acquire, care for, use, and dispose of animals in compliance with current federal, state, and local laws and regulations, and with professional standards.

(b) Psychologists trained in research methods and experienced in the care of laboratory animals supervise all procedures involving animals and are responsible for ensuring appropriate consideration of their comfort, health, and humane treatment.

(c) Psychologists ensure that all individuals under their supervision who are using animals have received instruction in research methods and in the care, maintenance, and handling of the species being used, to the extent appropriate to their role. (See also Standard 2.05, Delegation of Work to Others.)

(d) Psychologists make reasonable efforts to minimize the discomfort, infection, illness, and pain of animal subjects.

(e) Psychologists use a procedure subjecting animals to pain, stress, or privation only when an alternative procedure is unavailable and the goal is justified by its prospective scientific, educational, or applied value.

(f) Psychologists perform surgical procedures under appropriate anesthesia and follow techniques to avoid infection and minimize pain during and after surgery.

(g) When it is appropriate that an animal's life be terminated, psychologists proceed rapidly, with an effort to minimize pain and in accordance with accepted procedures. (p. 1070)

Instructional Use of Animals

Though the American Psychological Association has been a leader in guiding the appropriate use of live animals in education and research, many other voices have also been raised. Generally, these other organizations offer similar guidance (e.g., Applied Research Ethics National Association and Office for Protection From Research Risks, 1992).

> Any instructional use of live vertebrate animals that is supported by the PHS is governed by the *PHS Policy*. The applicability of the AWRs[1] depends upon the species used. Most institutions have chosen to require that all instructional use if animals, regardless of funding source or species, be reviewed by the IACUC.
>
> It may be appropriate for students, at both undergraduate and graduate levels, to participate in the conduct of experiments involving animals for the purpose of education. All instructional proposals should clearly justify the particular value of animal use as part of the course, whether it is demonstration of a known phenomenon; acquisition of practical skills; or exposure to research. In all cases, consideration must be given to alternative approaches to attaining the desired educational objectives, in accordance with the U.S. Government Principles.
>
> Adequate supervision and training are especially important, as the techniques learned by students are those that will be carried into subsequent research careers. It is recommended that students receive instruction on the ethics of animal research and applicable rules and regulations prior to undertaking any experimentation. When students work in an investigator's laboratory, the IACUC must ensure that the students receive appropriate supervision and training in animal care and use. The *PHS Policy* and AWRs have specific training requirements that apply to all animal users, including students. Student projects involving protocols different from those approved for the instructor's laboratory must be reviewed and approved on their own merits by the IACUC. (pp. 77–78)

---

[1]Animal Welfare Regulations (U.S. Department of Agriculture).

Examples of the Instructional Use of Live Animals

Experiments sometimes entail behavioral observation with no intervention, or minor painless interventions, such as choices of food or living accommodations. Such projects teach the rigors of conducting a research project and the variability inherent to biological and biobehavioral systems. These exercises generally involve little or no distress to the animals, but still require IACUC approval.

Some procedures present additional concerns. Selected examples are listed below:

- Behavioral studies that involve conditioning procedures in which animals are trained to perform tasks using mildly aversive stimuli, such as the noise of a buzzer, may be potentially stressful to the animals. For other behavioral studies, using non-aversive stimuli, such as running mazes, it may be necessary to maintain animals at a reduced body weight to enable food treats to be used as an effective reward. Experiments involving food and water restriction for teaching purposes must be rigorously justified and carefully monitored.
- Some behavioral studies produce potentially high levels of distress, including those using aversive stimuli, such as unavoidable electric shock, and surgical ablations or drug-induced lesions designed to affect the animal's behavior or performance. The educational benefits of such procedures should be carefully reviewed and clearly justified, bearing in mind that studies involving unrelieved pain or distress are generally inappropriate when employed solely for instructional purposes (U.S. Government Principle IX).
- Laboratory studies in physiology, neurophysiology, biology, and pharmacology often involve observations and experiments using animals. For all procedures, including those in which animals are euthanized to obtain tissues (e.g., in the teaching of anatomy or tissue harvest for *in vitro* procedures), the procedures and method of euthanasia, if any, must be reviewed by the IACUC. The number of animals used should always be the minimum necessary to accomplish the objectives of the proposed educational activity. (pp. 78–79)

DEFINING EDUCATIONAL USES OF ANIMALS AND THE APPROPRIATE REVIEW CRITERIA

A distinction may be drawn between projects designed to develop new knowledge (research projects) and projects designed to educate. An educational project seeks to change the behavior of the student rather than to develop new knowledge of the subject matter being studied. To the extent that new knowledge of the subject matter is to be developed, the proposal should be evaluated as a research project (as noted in other sections in this document). Many projects, of course, have both educational and research goals (e.g., undergraduate independent research project). It seems appropriate that such proposals be evaluated on their merits as research projects.

A further distinction might be drawn between educational projects for courses that are (a) offered to students as part of a general curriculum in a school, and (b) training offered to restricted populations such as preprofessional students or to laboratory staff members (e.g., to workers in an animal laboratory). The review process for educational projects in open enrollment courses should set different standards than those for specific training activities.

In evaluating educational projects, the Canadian Council on Animal Care asks that answers be provided to the following eight questions. Their approach has considerable merit. Tait (1993) offered especially helpful comments regarding this approach and how answers are evaluated.

1. What is the pedagogical value of the proposed protocol? An unsatisfactory response to this question precludes protocol approval. The educator is asked to identify the academic objectives of the exercise and convincingly state their importance.

2. Are there alternatives that can provide an equivalent pedagogical value? Why would a videotape or computer simulation not be equally effective?

3. How are students being prepared for the experience? Proper preparation regarding the role of animal research for this topic, the ethical decisions involved, and proper animal handling and care as well as preparation regarding the academic issues being addressed.

4. At what academic level are the students? The educator should defend the usefulness of the exercise for students at this specific level of preparation.

5. What are the future prospects of the students? Is the project appropriate for students who have this degree of commitment to the discipline?

6. Who will prepare the animals for the experience? The higher the category of invasiveness, the more important this question becomes.

7. Who will supervise the students when they are interacting with the animals? Again, this question is directed at ensuring that adequate animal care is maintained and also at assuring

that the students attain an appropriate educational experience.

8. What alternative exercise will be available for students that philosophically oppose the use of animals in teaching?

Tait's (1993) wisdom on this topic is as follows:

Increasingly, one finds some students who oppose the use of animals in class exercises. While such students may not enroll in some optional courses because the content of the course is closely related to the exercises (e.g., a course designed to train students in the proper use of animals in research), the concerns will be expressed in mandatory courses that contain exercises that use animals. The educator must be prepared to deal with such concerns.

The authoritarian 'do the exercise or fail' approach will not generally suffice. If this approach is taken, two consequences may follow. First, there may be adverse publicity for the course and institution. And second, a grade appeal may be filed by the student, which will require a lot of the educator's time and which will probably be successful. Initially, both consequences would be the responsibility of the educator. However, either could become a crisis that would involve the animal care committee. To avoid such consequences, the educator should be prepared to deal with the student's concern without compromising the educational goals of the course and the exercises for which the animals are to be used.

The New York Academy of Sciences (1988), in their statement on educational uses of animals, join Tait in recommending that alternative exercises be envisioned for some students. I also offer some personal comments on that topic, specifically, that the Institutional Animal Care and Use Committee (IACUC), in conjunction with the department concerned, should advise their administration on the need to establish a policy to deal with concerns of students who wish to absent themselves from participating in classroom experiments involving live animals.

TAIT'S SCALING OF LABORATORY PROJECTS

Tait (1993) provided an interesting scaling of protocols that might be used in laboratory courses. His scale includes four levels of project for courses that are arranged from least to most invasive. Before proceeding to describe some specific examples, I will include an extended quote from Tait's presentation at the annual meeting of the American Psychological Association.

A. *Observation of Animals:* In observational studies, students view animals that are housed in aquarium, aviaries, field stations, zoos or on farms. The purpose of the exercise tends to be to develop comparative or ethological data gathering techniques. The degree of student interaction with the animals is normally minimal. Nonetheless, students find such exercises interesting, helpful, and informative. Generally, the exercises are innocuous, however, the animal care committee should be alerted if the observational studies focus on conflict either between species (e.g., hunting) or within species (territorial defense) that could result in injury and death.

B. *Observation of Animals in Laboratories:* The second category of teaching protocols references situations in which students are taken into an experimental laboratory to observe a particular scientific phenomenon. A variant of this category of protocol would be a classroom demonstration of the phenomenon of interest. Laboratory demonstrations include illustration of operant conditioning effects, animal memory tasks, maternal behavior, or feeding behavior. The exercises normally involve more invasive procedures than those used in the previous category of teaching protocol. On the other hand, since the students are observing a contemporary experimental phenomenon, the basic protocol will likely have been approved previously as a research protocol. When combined with classroom discussion of the theoretical basis of the research, the exercise can be very stimulating for students.

C. *Collecting Data in an Experiment:* The third category is the first in which students actually interact with animals. Within Psychology, this experience is likely to occur in courses that focus either on experimental design (how to conduct a valid experiment) or on a specialty area of the discipline (e.g., learning). One of the classical exercises in Psychology is the use of positive reinforcement to condition a rat to press a lever. The exercise requires that the students learn to handle the rat, use mild deprivation regimes, and coordinate the delivery of food to the behavior of the rat in an experimental chamber. Because so many behaviors are sensitive to their consequences, the exercise provides a useful experience for students with either clinical or experimental interests. A major gain from the experience for the student is the discovery that while the concept is simple, to achieve the required behavioral change requires a high degree of patience and subtlety.

D. *Performing Surgical Procedures:* The fourth category is a subset of the third. Because surgery is involved, I think the category needs to be separated from the previous one because the level of invasiveness of the procedures are an order of magnitude above many other experimental procedures used in teaching laboratories.

Instructors of specialty courses that examine brain-behavior interactions typically request teaching protocols in this category. The courses are generally designed for students who have an interest in clinical neuropsychology or the neurosciences. The students may be required to examine the behavioral effects of either brain lesions, brain stimulation or removal of endocrine glands or gonads to elicit hormonal changes that affect behavior, or to record neural activity that occurs during a behavioral act.

Frequently, students find these exercises intimidating. They approach the tasks with trepidation and perform them with the utmost caution. Completion of the exercises provides the students with a tremendous sense of accomplishment and the values of the exercises are retained far longer than are the contents of most courses.

EXAMPLES OF LABORATORY PROJECTS AND PROTOCOLS

Introductory Psychology

There may still be colleges or universities where instructors include in their introductory psychology course a laboratory exercise or a series of laboratory exercises involving live animal projects. The first place that was done, to my knowledge, was at Columbia College (of Columbia University) in New York. The instructors were Fred S. Keller and Nat Schoenfeld. In the late 1940s, they added a weekly laboratory to the introductory course. In most of the projects in this course, students worked in pairs with a rat subject. The sequence of activities went something like this:

- they established the operant level of bar pressing before reinforcers were introduced;
- they shaped bar pressing with water reinforcers and produced a stable pattern of lever pressing under continuous reinforcement;
- they observed extinction of lever pressing as well as its spontaneous recovery and rapid reconditioning;
- they produced characteristic patterns of lever pressing under fixed-interval and fixed-ratio schedules of reinforcement;
- they observed extinction following intermittent reinforcement; and
- they trained a chained schedule of reinforcement.

Depending on student and instructor interest, other projects or modifications could be introduced into this sequence. By the end of the course, students were respectful of what a rat could learn, were convinced that the environment was important for behavior, and were ready to go on to their own research endeavors. They had learned how to carry out an experiment and how to summarize experimental effects.

The course at Columbia College inspired many individuals who later became well-known teachers and researchers in psychology. The course was duplicated in many other schools across the United States and in other countries, as graduates of Columbia College moved into the teaching profession. It is not difficult to produce testimonials to this approach. I, for one, consider such an experience to be the primary reason I entered psychology. As a discussant for a symposium not long ago, I had a chance to see this enthusiasm in one audience. Lewis Gollub (personal communication, April, 1993) was one of the speakers. Gollub described a Columbia-style course he had taught for many years. The audience numbered around 80. When asked how many had taken a course like this when an undergraduate, more than 60 hands went up and then applause burst forth. When asked how many were now at teaching institutions that had at least one course that included a live animal laboratory project, almost all those hands stayed up—they were carrying on that tradition. As one who has seen the light turn on in many undergraduate eyes when they have successfully shaped a rat to press a bar, I am very comfortable in advocating the educational importance of including live animal educational projects.

I expect, however, that there are few places where a Columbia-style animal laboratory remains a central part of the introductory course. The amount of work required of the instructor is considerable, and the costs are somewhat high. The popularity of introductory psychology courses has driven the live animal projects into higher and more specialized courses. These other roles are reviewed here.

Courses in Experimental Psychology and Research Methods

Observation of Animals

In many cases a field project in which students travel to a site to make observations will meet educational objectives for a project without the necessity of obtaining or directly caring for the live animals involved. Such observations can be made on campus, in field stations, or on farms as well as in zoos, aviaries, and aquaria. The observation might also be made in a research laboratory by either having students take notes on a phenomenon already being studied in the laboratory or having students take notes on activities of the animals while in their home cages.

As noted by Davis (1993):

> The advent of lightweight, portable video cameras enables students to venture into the field to observe and chronicle animal behavior. I routinely send my sociobiology students to the local zoo to record examples of behavior discussed in class. The student researchers then present their tapes and describe their observations to the entire class. A nearby lake, or wildlife refuge, or game preserve, and a bit or patience will yield admirable, perhaps even publishable, results. To illustrate, I recently heard an excellent experimental paper describing the observation and manipulation of the food hoarding behavior of a colony of ground squirrels (*Spermophilus tridecemlineatus*) inhabiting a cemetery. Such projects are, once again, limited only by one's creativity and imagination. (p. 8)

Good candidate projects would include exercises comparing approaches to making observations as well as exercises that show social or foraging activities. Four interesting examples developed by Verna Case of Davidson College, Davidson, North Carolina, are included as Appendix E.

Brief Trapping of Animals

An intermediate case involves briefly trapping wild animals for observation. An example protocol for a behavioral project carried out in a zoology course is included as Appendix F. In this exercise, students record the open field behavior of deer mice and compare this behavior to that seen during presentation of recorded sounds (e.g., predator sounds or automobile sounds).

Collecting Data in an Experiment

For a number of years I have taught a laboratory course at the University of North Carolina (UNC) at Chapel Hill required for psychology majors. Now, I am aware that UNC–Chapel Hill is not a small college. Yet, because the laboratory sections have 10 to 16 students and the projects use within-subject designs, I am confident that the approach would apply to small colleges as well. The goals in this course are to expose the students to data from several kinds of subfields of psychology and to train them to characterize and interpret findings in a broad range of psychological phenomena. Teachers also ask the students to address issues of research ethics and research design (for a description, see Eckerman, 1991). The course has several experimental or demonstration projects that the students carry out and then write up. I have included as Appendix G the approved IACUC protocol that describes the live animal project that has been included for more than 10 years. It is a miniature Columbia course sequence. Instead of working in pairs, however, teams of five to eight students work with a rat. Among them, students arrange for pairs or triplets of team members to work with their rat once per weekday for a little more than one month. In this arrangement, not everyone has the direct experience of shaping the lever press responding. Yet, everyone has an opportunity to see that the rat's behavior is in tune with its environment and everyone plays a direct role in developing part of that story for his or her team. The ratio of five to eight students to one rat seems to be educationally sound.

Many of the research methods courses taught in the United States include a live animal project modeled after this classic operant training of lever pressing in rats or key pecking in pigeons. Typically these projects use either food or water reinforcement. There are, however, many other approaches that can be taken to provide useful educational experiences. Recently there has been an explosion of interesting procedures that highlight the abilities of animals to sense and learn from their surroundings. Many of these procedures translate naturally into student projects. Rats run radial arm mazes, swim to submerged platforms, and so forth. A search of relevant journals and textbooks would produce a list of potential projects. Although mammalian or avian subjects provide engaging demonstrations of operant learning, invertebrate subjects also demonstrate good sensory contact and some forms of learning (e.g., habituation).

Courses in Learning and in Animal Behavior

Projects in courses on learning and animal behavior might range from observations made in field settings to the direct collection of data in experiments. Many of these possible exercises would readily meet the educational criteria outlined in the first section of this chapter—they provide excellent and unsubstitutable training in specific content or in research methods and do not involve undue stress to the animal subjects. The appropriateness of a specific project should be related to (a) the specific educational goal and (b) the kind of student involved. Many educational projects involve a minimum of stress and therefore would be reasonable were they included in a laboratory course that was open to a variety of students. For example, it is desirable to limit food or water deprivation only to a level that might commonly be encountered by animals in their natural environments. The use of highly palatable reinforcers may be possible to be even less restrictive. Alternatively, some projects do involve more stress and would be reasonable only for students with specific career or training goals—for example, those undertaking tutorial or independent research projects in preparation for graduate study in the field.

Because it is common for projects in learning and animal behavior courses to continue for a period of weeks or months, the quality of care given to the animal during its participation is a topic of special relevance. Students often provide a major part of this care; therefore, it is important to provide specific training and good supervision to ensure that students are good caretakers. I have included as Appendix H an excellent set of guidelines on pigeon care provided by Lewis Gollub to his students. As in other uses of animals reviewed here, it is important to use this opportunity to teach humane and sensitive use of animals. E. P. Reese of Mount Holyoke College in South Hadley, Massachusetts, provided good guidance is provided in offering this kind of presentation (Reese, 1984).

One way to include live animal projects for students in learning courses is to directly involve them in the instructor's research activities. This approach is exemplified by three projects carried out at Davidson College in Davidson, North Carolina, by students in a learning laboratory course taught by D. Cerutti. The students first complete two or three projects using human participants. They then take over a research project from Cerutti's research laboratory for a period of time. Three example projects are described in Appendix I. The projects test a rat's ability to carry out conditional discriminations or a pigeon's foraging behavior.

Courses in Physiological Psychology and Behavioral Pharmacology

Researchers understand considerably more about the biological bases of animal learning and animal behavior than they did just a decade ago. To continue this exciting progress, researchers need to train the next generation of scientists. Laboratory courses and laboratory training are essential to this task. To the extent that stress to the subjects is involved, however, special considerations should be addressed. I have included as Appendix J two approved course protocols: (a) effect of entorhinal cortex lesions on differential reinforcement low rate response (DRL) performance; and (b) methods in behavioral neurobiology. These two protocols effectively address what I see as the critical issues—that the students be recruited as having specific convincing reasons to receive this training (most likely related to preparing for research careers), that supervision be especially strong and be provided by well-qualified personnel, and that stress to animal subjects be minimized.

Each of these protocols also use the approach mentioned in the previous section—in which students in the laboratory course participate in a research project undertaken by the instructor as part of their research activities. This approach maximizes the likelihood that the instructor has the appropriate expertise and that current research practices are used. In the first example, J. Rameriz asks his students at Davidson College to participate in his research on the role of the hippocampus on behavioral control. In the second example, S. Mulvey asked her students at Duke University to participate in her research on the neurobiology of learning in rat pups.

CLASSROOM DEMONSTRATIONS

Skinner–Catania's Lever Press Force Demonstration

To represent responsible use of animals to the students in that room, a live animal demonstration should be memorable, useful, and unsubstitutable. I believe I have an example of such a demonstration—one used successfully by B. F. Skinner in his lectures and then by his student A. C. Catania. In this demonstration, a rat is trained to forcefully press a lever. I include a paraphrase of A. C. Catania's (1984) description of this project because he emphasized some of the special lessons contained. I am confident this event engaged students in a way that no mere simulation would allow:

> The apparatus was a large Plexiglas cylinder where a rat pressed on a counterweighted lever to produce food. At first it pressed using one or both forepaws on the lever and pushing down. Lever presses began with the counterweight set at a modest level. As successive presses were reinforced, the counterweight was gradually increased until a point at which

depression of the lever required a force exceeding the rat's weight. At that point, continued success in shaping depended on the emergence of a new topography of lever pressing. Whereas pushing down on the lever with both hind legs on the floor had previously worked, an effective press now required that the rat's feet lift to the wall of the chamber, on which a wire mesh allowed it a firm grip. By pulling and/or pushing between forelegs and hind legs, the rat could depress the lever even with the counterweight exceeding its own weight. This performance, usually shaped within a single class session, illustrated two kinds of selection, one gradual and the other sudden: the relatively continuous change in the rat's pressing while the counterweight remained less than its own weight, and the relatively discontinuous change when that weight was exceeded. The sudden part of this shaping made an important point about the source of new topographies: The likelihood of producing the foreleg–hind leg topography depended jointly on the rat's anatomy and on its environment (e.g., whether the chamber wall allowed a firm grip for its hind feet and whether the height of the lever made it likely that the rat would lift its feet off the floor as the counterweight approached its own weight). (paraphrased from p. 714)

It should be clear that to have a live animal classroom demonstration be useful, the subject would have to be isolated from or habituated to crowd noise. Crowd excitement could cause distress without adequate preparation of the animal. A special worry for many behavioral demonstrations would be the subjects' willingness to consume the reinforcer in this situation. Without adequate habituation, in the presence of a crowded room, the subject might be reluctant to put its head into the feeder, the audience would reasonably conclude that the animal was distressed, and the demonstration would fail on all grounds.

Brief Visits to or From Experimental Subjects

Although I have never obtained an animal expressly for a classroom demonstration, I have brought classes to my laboratory and have occasionally brought an animal experimental subject to the classroom for a brief visit. Such a visit can be useful in making phenomena come to life for students. Discussion becomes more personal and concrete, and issues that would have gone unnoticed are acknowledged. I remember, for example, the following questions and comments: "What do you hope to accomplish with this kind of work, Dr. Eckerman?" "Is the bird starving?" "Is it really smarter than I am?" When one encourages the direct contact that a live animal demonstration allows, one had best be prepared to have a real conversation. But, of course, that is the point. That is the reason for doing it. It seems worthwhile to seek IACUC approval for such in-class events.

Trained Pets and Untrained Pets

I have twice had students bring their well-trained dogs to a learning class to show off their mutual talents. They showed the tricks and then had an opportunity to say how they trained the tricks that they were showing off. One of the students said the right things. The other said things that disagreed sharply with the learning principles being promoted in the course. The interesting discussion that followed helped sharpen the points raised in the course. Regardless of the ease of fit with the course, these were memorable and useful classes. If I had a trained dog, then I would surely bring him or her to class each year.

I suppose that even untrained pets could provide useful material for a class exercise. For example, the students could be asked to observe and write down what they see the animal doing. A discussion could then follow on whether the language was descriptive or interpretive and what was gained and lost each way. Would that be memorable and useful? What would be changed were they to describe the actions of a fellow student? I would propose that animal observation would provide lessons that the fellow student observation would not. The students might, for example, be tempted to believe the self-description of their fellow student. To naively believe in such introspection would surely set back psychology by many years.

ALTERNATIVES TO THE USE OF LIVE ANIMALS IN EDUCATION

Changing the Way Researchers Use Animals in Courses

Alternatives to present practices can include reducing the number of animals used and refining the project to reduce stress (Smith, 1994). Many researchers have increased the number of students per animal in educational projects. The appropriate number to set is one that meets the specific educational objectives with the fewest animals.

A second animal-to-student topic to be considered is whether it is appropriate to develop alternative activities to substitute for a live animal project for some students. One may, in fact, judge that a few students would be harmed by participation in the live animal activity. Such judgment might be based on their heartfelt beliefs. I know of no absolute standards for such a judgment, but I would encourage researchers to actively explore the issue with students who raise objections. I have had perhaps 20 such conversations over the years. In only one case was it my judgment that the student would be better served by generating an alternative activity. This was a student whose life decisions were consistent with her interest in not participating and who had based her request on accurate information regarding the project and the welfare issues involved. As an alternative exercise, the student and I developed a human learning project that captured many but not all of the features that students gain through the rat project. She devoted considerably more time to the alternative project. Of course, so did I. Yet, I do believe psychology has gained a healthier professional because her deeply felt concerns were understood and acknowledged. I should note that this one exception stands in contrast to the many conversations that I have concluded by saying the students' worries did not require an alternate exercise and that they should proceed to participate in the live animal project if they wished to complete that part of the course—most if not all those conversations resolved in good spirit as well.

Even in this one case, and for all the reasons noted previously, the student missed an educational opportunity. I am saddened when an instructor decides that in the long run the added effort and occasional confrontation that comes with having a live animal project is not worth the trouble. Each decision of that sort reduces the number of individuals who will be prepared to deepen the understanding of animals and how they relate to humans.

Videotapes and Other Audiovisual Mass Storage Resources

Sometimes a good video can approach the impact of a good classroom demonstration. And, it is a lot easier to arrange. I have been especially taken with videos on animal training by Karen Pryor (*Growing Lifestyle*, 2004). For example, her demonstrations of the use of conditioned reinforcement and shaping principles are both engaging and academically sound. Good titles include *Click! Using the Conditioned Reinforcer*; *Shaping! How to Develop Precise Responses and Complex Behavior Using Positive Reinforcement*; *Sit! Clap! Furbish! How to Understand, Teach, and Use Conditioned Stimuli*; *Supertraining! How Modern Animal Trainers Use Operant Conditioning*; and *If I Could Talk to the Animals: Reinforcement Interactions as Communication*. The last title is a tape of a convention address. (These videos can be obtained from Sunshine Books, 44811 S. E. 166th Street, North Bend, Washington 98045; telephone: (800) 472-5425. I will not try to list other video resources in this chapter because available material changes rapidly.)

Computer Simulations

A good computer simulation can communicate effectively what a theory implies. It can graphically draw out implications that are difficult to put into words. These simulations can be helpful when the educational focus is on understanding the theory. Theories, however, are useful in the long run only if they are both celebrated and scoffed at. When a computer simulation appears too good, it gives a false sense of spontaneity. Although that is good showmanship, it is bad science training unless carefully explained. Researchers will not deepen their understanding of animals by training their students to be well-versed in current theories. They need to have real data to challenge these theories. Each and every computer simulation should, therefore, come with a warning label that says, "May be hazardous to the health of science if believed."

That worry aside, there are some useful simulations currently available.

1. *Behavior on a Disk.* I have been especially taken with A. C. Catania's gamelike programs that challenge the player to shape a rat to press a lever with greater force (see classroom demonstration described previously). This is available through CMS Software, 100551 Rivulet Row, Columbia, Maryland 21044.

2. *Sniffy the Virtual Rat.* This program was developed by Tom Alloway, Lester Krames, and Jeff Graham of the University of Toronto. Direct experience with the program and a discussion with one of the developers convinced me that the graphics are adequate, the simulation is engaging, but Sniffy is not very ratlike. Satiation, pace of shaping, and variation are not well sketched. I wish it would approach the quality of Catania's simulation in terms of virtuality. In the meantime, there are the words of the descriptive brochure: "Sniffy is meant to save money and be ethical, yet provide a realistic and freeform experience with operant conditioning. You can condition any one of 15 different behaviors in Sniffy's repertoire. You can establish different reinforcement contingencies. Sniffy's bar pressing responses are kept in a cumulative record." It is suitable for classroom demonstrations. (For an opposing view on Sniffy as well as information on the latest version, see chap. 6, this volume. Sniffy can be obtained through Wadsworth-Thomson Learning at http://www.wadsworth.com or (800) 354-9706.)

3. *The Box.* Developed by R. Wayne Bartlett and Elson M. Bihm, this is a program written for Microsoft Windows that includes a series of demonstration modules demonstrating operant and classical conditioning phenomena as well as a professional development system for developing one's own modules. Data are shown as a cumulative record. Both student-centered demonstrations and full experiments are possible. (For information, contact Triad Soft, #180, 813 Oak Street, 10A, Conway, Arizona 72032.)

4. *CyberRat.* Roger Ray developed this Internet/CD hybrid simulation of operant conditioning and shaping utilizing 850 behavioral clips drawn from actual video of rat behavior. This program is sophisticated and very ratlike in my experience. It offers a full range of experimenter behaviors required to accomplish behavioral change. Researchers can request an evaluation copy at www.CyberRat.net.

Other computer simulations available for currently common personal computers include the following:

1. *Classical Conditioning Simulation*. This program allows manipulation of a number of conditioning trials, conditioned stimulus (CS) and unconditioned stimulus (US) intensity, and number of extinction trials. (Available from Life Science Associates, 1 Fenimore Road, Bayport, New York 11705.)

2. *OP.RAT*. This program simulates operant conditioning with an on-screen rat that may be shaped to bar press and learn discrimination reversal. (Available from Psi & Eye, 4310 South Semoran, #690, Orlando, Florida 32822.)

3. *The World of Sidney Slug and His Friends*. A computer simulation for teaching shaping without an animal laboratory. (Available from Bram Goldwater, PhD, Department of Psychology, University of Victoria, P.O. Box 3050, Victoria, British Columbia, V8W 3P5, Canada; or e-mail bgoldwat@uvic.ca.)

4. *Animal Behavior Data Simulation*. Simulates 25 animal behavior experiments; students supply values of independent variables. (Available from Oakleaf Systems, P.O. Box 472, Decorah, Iowa 52101.)

5. *Hyper-Neuroanatomy*. Basic neuroanatomy of primate brain. (Available from Kinko's Academic Courseware Exchange, 255 W. Stanley Avenue, Ventura, California 93001.)

6. *ABI-1*. Animated simulations of psychological experiments. (Available from ABI, 2124 Kittredge, #215, Berkeley, California 94704.)

In the 1950s many thousand individuals whom we now release to home care were warehoused in United States institutions "for the retarded." I am pleased that behavioral approaches allowed training for these individuals so they could rejoin their community. Further, I am pleased that behavioral training continues to open doors for individuals who would be restricted except for such training. The behavioral approach that has opened many doors is firmly based on principles that derive from research on animal learning. In addition, starting in the 1950s and increasing until today, many individuals maintain a healthy mood and an accurate perception of the world because they have psychopharmacological treatments available. These treatments are also based on research with live animals. If you share my belief that one needs to understand considerably more about behavior before addressing many societal problems, I encourage you to consider that continued live animal research will be needed as a basis on which researchers will build this understanding. Investigators who will offer this basic research will be introduced to live animal research through educational projects. I hope this chapter has provided information to facilitate the education of future researchers and protect the other appropriate use of live animals in education. To protect these appropriate uses, one must be circumspect and protect against inappropriate educational projects involving live animals. It is imperative to find this balance.

REFERENCES

American Psychological Association. (1990). *Resolution on the use of animals in research, testing, and education*. Washington, DC: Author.

American Psychological Association. (1985). *Guidelines for ethical conduct in the care and use of animals*. Washington, DC: Author.

American Psychological Association. (1996). *Guidelines for ethical conduct in the care and use of animals*. Washington, DC: Author.

American Psychological Association (2002). Ethical principles of psychologists and code of conduct. *American Psychologist, 57*, 1060–1073.

Applied Research Ethics National Association and Office for Protection From Research Risks. (1992). Instructional use of animals. In *Institutional Animal Care and Use Committee guidebook*. Bethesda, MD: National Institutes of Health.

Catania, A. C. (1984). Summing up: Problems of selection and phylogeny terms, and methods of behaviorism. *The Behavioral and Brain Sciences, 7*, 713–724.

Davis, S. F. (1993). Animals in the classroom. *Psychological Science Agenda, 6*(5), 8.

Eckerman, D. A. (1991). Microcomputers in undergraduate laboratory training in psychology. *Behavior Research Methods, Instruments, & Computers, 23*, 91–99.

Growing Lifestyle. (2004). Retrieved March 15, 2004, from http://www.growinglifestyle.com/psearch/Manufacturer/Book/Sunshine_Books/index.html

New York Academy of Sciences. (1988). *Interdisciplinary principles and guidelines for the use of animals in research, testing, and education*. New York: Author.

Offner, S. (1993). The importance of dissection in biology teaching. *The American Biology Teacher, 55*(3), 147–149.

Reese, E. P. (1984, August). Teaching sensitivity to animal welfare will make students better scientists. In D. Tice (Chair), *Ways to minimize pain and suffering for laboratory animals*. Symposium conducted at the 92nd convention of the American Psychological Association, Toronto, Ontario, Canada.

Smith, C. (1994, March). AWIC tips for searching for alternatives to animal research and testing. *Lab Animal*, 46–48.

Tait, R. W. (1993, August). The use of animals in teaching under contemporary regulations. In D. Tice (Chair), *Use of animals in teaching*. Symposium conducted at the 101st convention of theAmerican Psychological Association, Toronto, Ontario, Canada.

U.S. Congress Office of Technology Assessment. (1986). *Alternatives to Animal Use in Research, Testing, and Education* (DHHS Publication No. OTA-BA-273). Washington, DC: U.S. Government Printing Office.

8

USE OF ANIMALS AT HIGH SCHOOL FACILITIES

CRAIG W. GRUBER

When examining the use of animals in the high school psychology curriculum, one must first address the question: Why use animals in the high school classroom? There are several ways to answer this question. Just as in a college or university setting, using animals in the high school setting allows for demonstrative learning. The current use of films in classes should be continued, but viewing films of classic experimental psychology studies, although useful, is not on par with the benefits derived from hands-on learning. In addition, the use of animals in the classroom allows the instructor to demonstrate variations in training techniques. The presence of an animal laboratory can also allow students to gain a better understanding of the research enterprise and may even enable them to participate in local as well as national and international science fairs such as the International Science and Engineering Fair (ISEF).

PROGRAM AT WALT WHITMAN HIGH SCHOOL

The prototype laboratory established at Walt Whitman High School (WWHS), in Montgomery County, Maryland, can be used as an example of a high school animal laboratory. The facility at WWHS is by no means perfect, but it demonstrates that training in basic laboratory procedures and exposure to classic behavioral experiments can be achieved in a high school setting. Walt Whitman High School has a total enrollment of 1,950 students, of which approximately 200 enroll in the Advanced Placement (AP) Psychology program. These students are offered three laboratory options: (a) conduct animal research, which is primarily learning oriented; (b) conduct research with human participants (primarily, observational or survey); and (c) write a thesis paper. Although psychology is taught within the social studies department, the laboratory is an interdisciplinary program comprising the social studies and science departments. Laboratory courses for advanced students are taught in the science department through a research based science internship program. On average, 60% of students enrolled in AP Psychology choose the lab animal research option per semester. Although specifics of the particular protocol determine the length of time each student spends in the laboratory, because of space constraints typical AP Psychology student projects last no longer than 8 weeks. The next course in the progression, the Psychology Science Internship, lasts the entire academic year. Students, in consultation with teachers and faculty members at a local university, develop their own protocols and collect and analyze the data with the goal of publishing their findings.

Students in AP Psychology are given the choice of conducting one of two types of experiments in the laboratory. The first consists of replicating classic psychology experiments. Examples include training animals to perform simple bar press responses, sniff responses, or physical movement training. This type of laboratory exercise enables students to gain a fuller understanding of the principles of operant conditioning and the application of these principles to new situations. In the second option, students develop their own protocols to investigate new or less well-established phenomena. The latter option is the one that most students in the Whitman Behavioral Science Laboratory choose. Students are required to generate a problem of interest and complete a thorough review of literature before developing an experimental protocol. Students then develop their own experiments. This includes subject selection (number of subjects needed and a rationale for their response), apparatus design and construction, and statistical analyses. The instructor and members of the Institutional Animal Care and Use Committee (IACUC) then review the protocols.

Given recent fiscal demands and restrictions that have been placed on public schools, securing funding for such a program is especially challenging. At WWHS, apart from the facility itself, which was built to specification during a recent school renovation, funding for the program is almost entirely run through the psychology department. Through silent auctions, gift wrap sales, and special events, the program generates roughly $8,000 per year in revenue. That money, coupled with a small lab fee of $15, provides adequate funding for laboratory operations and defrays some of the costs associated with students attending and presenting their research at meetings or conferences. Designating specially trained students to assume day-to-day lab animal care and maintenance responsibilities has further reduced the costs associated with maintaining a laboratory animal facility. Although students volunteer for these animal care positions, all students entering the program are required to undergo extensive training in lab animal care. Furthermore, students who are not enrolled in the AP program are also allowed to volunteer for these positions. One unanticipated benefit of offering all students this option has been that even students who are skeptical about the ethics of using nonhuman animals in research have become involved in the lab animal facility and thereby experience the true nature of such research.

The remaining sections of this chapter deal with local institutional policies, veterinary care facilities and laws, and teaching with limited resources as they pertain to using animals in high schools. What follows is by no means an all-inclusive description, nor an exclusive list, but merely strategies that have been successful at a suburban Washington, DC, high school.

LOCAL INSTITUTIONAL POLICIES

When establishing an animal laboratory at a high school, one of the first things to establish is a school IACUC. The IACUC should be charged with accountability for the research and the use of animals and oversight of the protocols, as well as ensuring that the research conducted within its facility is appropriate, beneficial, and caring (the ABCs of laboratory animal research). At WWHS, the IACUC is a six-member panel that comprises the instructor, the chair of the science department, chair of the social studies department, a member of the community, the consulting veterinarian, and the principal of the school. Our institutional panel received an opinion from our veterinarian, as well as from the compliance administrator from a local university, to not include a student on our IACUC for review and inspection purposes. We cited numerous university models to support our decision. Whereas in the past we had a student lab administrator, the function of that position has now been relegated to interns with experience in designing and conducting experiments. Students do remain involved in reviewing protocols. This has the benefit of involving more students in the educational and learning process of animal welfare, as well as providing more advanced students the opportunity to mentor others. The IACUC meets twice a year, assuming that no issues or problems arise during the course of the experiments. WWHS has established a sign-off procedure whereby potential protocols are routed to each member of the committee so that they may review and comment on the proposal. The IACUC exists primarily as an electronic community. Protocols are e-mailed and the full committee meets only to address unresolved issues or to discuss protocols on which IACUC members dissent. Of course, any member of the IACUC may request a full meeting at anytime.

The school district also plays a critical role in the high school animal laboratory. First, the district must approve the use of animals for instructional purposes. Second, the school district should provide administrative support. Without the support of both the district and the school administration, it is difficult, if not impossible, both academically and administratively to maintain an animal laboratory at the high school level. In the case of WWHS, this support has come directly from the principal. Over the years, this institutional support has taken many forms, from course relief and schedule reduction to supplemental pay. Third, the school system should provide facility support. In the case of WWHS, a recent renovation included the construction of a research facility that included HVAC systems and animal colony rooms. The school system also supported renovations that were required to customize the space for laboratory use. Last, the school district should be willing to provide some avenue for funding (this issue will be discussed more fully later).

VETERINARY CARE AND FACILITIES

The requirements for animal laboratory facilities elaborated on in previous chapters in this volume adhere to federal as well as Association for Assessment and Accreditation of Laboratory Animal Care, International (AAALAC) standards. Every effort should be made to attain these prescribed standards. However, it should be noted that the financial practicalities of small animal laboratory operations in high schools might well influence how closely these guidelines are followed in a particular high school setting.

Perhaps the most obvious component of an animal-based laboratory is veterinary care. Most high school projects are not invasive, nor do they present a risk to the health and well-being of the animal. Therefore, if the instructor, who is often also the principal investigator (PI), is well versed in animal care, then veterinarians may be used primarily on a consulting basis. In my experience, most veterinarians will agree to this arrangement as long as they have the final say on the health and use of the animals. In addition, they serve on the IACUC and are cosigners of all animal research protocols. In some schools, parents who are veterinarians may be willing to serve as consulting veterinarians to the local school. This has been the case at WWHS and has been a way of increasing parent and community involvement in the school. Local research colleges or universities may also be able to provide a veterinarian, or at the very least, advice on how to proceed. In the worst case scenario, a high school may have to hire an outside veterinarian to serve on the IACUC and monitor the health and well-being of the laboratory animals. It is important to remember that veterinary care is essential to the operation of an animal facility.

The next relevant issue is the acquisition of the animals. Animals intended for research may not be procured from pet stores. Documentation of health records of animals provided by pet stores is typically inadequate when the animals are being used in research. Animals from pet stores may have undocumented diseases that can be transmitted to humans or even from animal to animal, thereby infecting the entire colony. Laboratory animals should be obtained from registered vendors, who routinely provide background information on the animals. In addition, laboratory animal suppliers also furnish researchers with quality control reports that certify that the animals received are disease free, and they list the names of tests conducted to warrant that certification. A certificate of disease free status is mandatory for all animals used in the Whitman Behavioral Science Laboratory.

Animals may also be acquired from a local college or university that maintains laboratory animal facilities. One advantage of using animals from a local college is that some colleges may be willing to take the animals back at the conclusion of a high school study either for reuse in one of their own studies, or they may help in euthanizing the animals. However, there may be liability issues for colleges wishing to provide animals to high school facilities; thus, colleges should consult with their IACUC and institutional official prior to establishing this type of relationship with a local high school animal research laboratory. Currently, animals for laboratory use at WWHS are obtained directly from a vendor and at the end of the academic term the animals are donated to a local college for use in its laboratories. It must be noted that as a rule colleges accept only animals that were originally obtained from a pathogen-free source. Two popular species options for use in a high school laboratory are Sprague-Dawley rats and invertebrates. Charles I. Abramson's (1990) *Invertebrate Learning, A Laboratory Manual and Source Book*, is a good reference for those who choose to work with invertebrates.

The multitude of rules and regulations that affect veterinary care and facilities apply only to federally funded programs. In other words, federal regulations do not technically apply to most high schools, especially when the animals involved in research are not covered by the regulations, such as laboratory rats, mice, and birds. Nevertheless, compliance with these standards, when possible, is good practice. Some facility standards may not be met because of financial or space constraints. However, institutional standards that adhere to federal regulations as closely as possible should be established. Once these standards have been established, it is necessary to maintain them regularly. There are numerous benefits to complying with federal standards. First, it is easier to demonstrate to the school administration, not only the advantages of such a program, but also show that every practical and reasonable precaution is being taken to safeguard the school, the animals, and the students. If school administrators are aware of all aspects of compliance and noncompliance, then they may be more willing to support the establishment of an animal laboratory. Second, laboratories that comply with federal or AAALAC standards are often eligible for funding or grants from many sources, including laboratory equipment manufacturers. And finally, one of the most important reasons for complying with federal standards is that compliance ensures a safe program for the students.

TEACHING WITH LIMITED RESOURCES

Obtaining resources and equipment may be the most difficult task in establishing a new laboratory, but with adequate knowledge and proper planning, it can be simpler. Again, an excellent source for testing and housing equipment is a local college or university that has research facilities. Colleges and universities are often the best source for almost all laboratory needs. Because colleges and universities are continually upgrading their facilities and purchasing new equipment, they often are willing to donate or lend their old equipment for use by high school students. Local colleges and universities can also help with animal acquisition, either by supplying animals directly or by providing a list of local suppliers that will deliver laboratory quality animals to a high school facility. Furthermore, large research companies may also be willing to donate old laboratory equipment to schools because such donations are often tax deductible. WWHS has been the beneficiary of donations from both the university and business communities.

Colleges are also excellent sources of ideas and information. Individual faculty members can assist in many ways, including helping with current research; aiding in the development of new protocols; training both high school faculty members and students in animal husbandry and laboratory techniques; and providing information on sources for obtaining laboratory equipment, animals, and so forth. College and university faculty members may also help with curricular support in many ways, including serving as a high school laboratory consultant or as a guest speaker in a high school class.

Perhaps the best way to secure the limited resources with which to run a laboratory is through the local Parent Teacher Association (PTA). Involving the PTA early and often can allow for and possibly lead to fiscal as well as other types of support. Parent–Teacher Associations are typically supportive of new and innovative programs that promote student involvement and foster hands-on learning. In this case, PTAs can be effective in soliciting equipment, supplies, and expertise from the local school community. In addition, some parents may be willing to lend their own expertise and become involved in the program as PIs, laboratory technicians, or general research scientists. Thus, parents may sometimes be able to provide knowledge, expertise, and supplies to an otherwise unsupported program. Sometimes PTAs may be skeptical of a program involving animals, but with careful planning and strong administrative support, PTAs can be one of the biggest supporters of a high school animal laboratory. PTAs can also help diffuse potentially controversial situations. For instance, having the PTA involved and informed about laboratory protocols and procedures can help eliminate some of the tensions that may be generated if faced with resistance from community groups that are opposed to the use of animals in research.

In some cases, parents (or even other members of the community) who are research scientists may be willing to serve as PIs on high school students' projects. Such an arrangement may sometimes involve the high school student working in the researcher's own laboratory. This system has been successfully implemented in the WWHS program, and it has helped forge links between the high school animal laboratory and a number of local institutions, such as the National Institutes of Health (NIH). There are also other agencies mentioned in Appendix M that may be of help to someone seeking resources, expertise, or any additional information about the use of animals in research.

STUDENT INVOLVEMENT

At WWHS, students pay a laboratory fee, which helps defray the cost of acquiring the animals required for experimentation, as well as for purchasing animal feed and laboratory equipment. Under the guidance of their instructor, students construct their own testing apparatus such as mazes and conditioned place preference chambers. This requirement has a number of benefits. First, students develop a sense of ownership in the lab and how it is run. Second, it is more economical. At WWHS, the estimated cost of running a typical behavioral experiment is $125. By having students create their own apparatus, it is possible to keep this figure low. Third, requiring students to plan the specific details of their apparatus makes them much more insightful about the nature and scope of their proposed study. And last, such a requirement helps increase the amount of apparatus available to students in subsequent years.

Students are also trained in basic animal care and are required to sign a contract for the care and use of animals (see Appendix K). This contract is more than just a parental release form for students to work in the laboratory. Although not legally binding, by signing the contract, the students assume personal responsibility for the care and well-being of the animals used in their studies. Working in a laboratory using animals is different from caring for a pet at home, and this difference is emphasized in the students' training. As part of the required training, students watch a video that was specifically designed and produced for WWHS in cooperation with a veterinarian, the American University psychology department, the local National Public Radio affiliate, and a musician. The video can be shown in its entirety (12 minutes), or in individual modules which mirror the laboratory manual. It covers the basics of animal care, handling, and lab maintenance. After watching the video, the students are required to take a quiz, followed by a tour of the lab, and finally sign an agreement form in their lab procedure booklets. Students are trained not only in the specific procedures that are required by their individual protocols but also in cleaning and animal care protocols, and they perform laboratory cleaning duties on a rotating basis. Students are also instructed on the rationale for using each of those procedures. Through classroom instruction, students are sensitized to the importance of the humane treatment and care of laboratory animals, and the instructor familiarizes them with prevailing guidelines and regulations that govern the conduct of research with animals.

A detailed laboratory manual that each student enrolled in the laboratory course receives supplements the instructions given in the classroom and laboratory. The manual for the Whitman Behavioral Science Laboratory was first developed with assistance from the Department of Psychology of American University in 1992. The manual has since been revised and updated by the WWHS IACUC and consulting veterinarians. The manual describes in detail procedures for (a) animal care and maintenance, (b) proper handling, (c) animal breeding, (d) cage cleaning, (e) preparation of solutions, (f) administering injections, and (g) emergency procedures and contacts.

Before initiating a research project, students are required to develop a specific research question. Through the conduct of an extensive literature review in their area of interest, students write a five- to seven-page review paper, with at least 15 references and a rationale for the proposed study. Students then develop a protocol for their proposed study and submit it to the IACUC for review and approval. Examples of projects undertaken by students at WWHS include (a) effects of caffeine and alcohol on learning tasks, (b) the role of caffeine in timed running tasks, (c) the effect of body mass on problem solving in rats, (d) the effect of prenatal exercise on learning tasks, (e) the effect of background noise on the concentration and learning process of lab rats, (f) effects of isolation on rats, (g) experimental investigation of approach–avoidance conflict, (h) altruistic behavior in rats, (i) effects of 100% normobaric oxygen on treatment with air following hypoxia on psychological processes involved in learning and performance, and (j) alcohol and memory.

By exposing students to, and involving them in research, the laboratory experience at WWHS is preparing tomorrow's researchers. A number of graduates of the Whitman Behavioral Science Laboratory report that the experience they gained at the high school level helped them understand the basis of psychological theories and proved to be an invaluable asset as they pursued careers in research-related fields. A research experience provides students with basic research skills that they can expand on at the college level. A number of graduates report that because of their high school research experience, they were able to take upper level research-based courses earlier in their college careers. This has to led to valuable experiences in terms of presenting research, as well as students being one step ahead of their peers when applying to graduate programs. As previously mentioned, although the operant laboratory at WWHS is by no means ideal, it is still an example of a successful attempt at using animals in research and teaching at the high school level. Involving students early and often allows them to become vested in the research process and see the true value of both basic and applied research.

REFERENCE

Abramson, C. I. (1990). *Invertebrate learning: A laboratory manual and source book*. Washington, DC: American Psychological Association.

IV

OVERVIEW OF REGULATIONS

9

LAWS, REGULATIONS, AND GUIDELINES

NELSON GARNETT

Regardless of the type and size of the academic institution where research with laboratory animals takes place, all federally funded research is required to comply with various federal, state, and local laws and regulations. Although the main intent of these laws, regulations, and policies is to ensure the humane care and treatment of the research animals, they also protect the investigator and the academic institution. Such research is also subject to oversight by various regulatory bodies. This chapter provides information about the agencies that enforce these laws, their structure, their regulations and policies, and their role in implementing requirements at the federal, state, and local levels.

BACKGROUND INFORMATION

Both the Department of Health and Human Services (DHHS; acting through the Public Health Service [PHS], National Institutes of Health [NIH]), and the U.S. Department of Agriculture (USDA) have regulatory or policy oversight responsibilities for the care and use of animals in research, teaching, and testing in the United States. Although differing somewhat in history, jurisdiction, and enforcement methods, the regulations and guidelines of both agencies have evolved in the same direction in recent years. Fundamental similarities include the following:

1. Primary accountability at the institutional level;
2. A heavy reliance on institutional self-regulation with federal monitoring, utilizing local Institutional Animal Care and Use Committees (IACUCs) for implementation;
3. A preference for performance-based or generally accepted professional standards where possible, with considerable allowances for flexibility and the exercise of professional judgment at the institutional level; and
4. A fundamental adherence to the "U.S. Government Principles for the Utilization and Care of Vertebrate Animals Used in Testing, Research, and Training" (U.S. Government Principles; see Appendix L).

The Health Research Extension Act (1985), Public Health Service Policy on Humane Care and Use of Laboratory Animals

The Health Research Extension Act of 1985 (Public Law [PL] 99-158) provided statutory authority for the already existing Public Health Service Policy on Humane Care and Use of Laboratory Animals (PHS Policy). It is widely believed that, by passing PL 99-158, Congress endorsed the PHS Policy and intended for any new USDA regulations promulgated under the amendments to the AWA to closely approximate the PHS Policy, with the addition of regulations to address some specific statutory mandates. PL 99-158 was passed some weeks before PL 99-198 (the corresponding 1985 amendment to the Animal Welfare Act [AWA]), and language was included in PL 99-198 requiring that the Secretary of Agriculture consult with the Secretary of Health and Human Services prior to promulgating specific standards for animal welfare.

The PHS Policy applies to all animal-related activities conducted or supported by the PHS. The term *activity* includes the care and use of animals involved in research as well as other forms of animal use such as teaching and testing, and the term *support* includes the traditional NIH grants and many other forms of support such as contracts, training grants, and collaborations. For PHS Policy purposes, "animal" is defined to mean all live vertebrate animals.

Incorporated into the PHS Policy by extensive reference is the *Guide for the Care and Use of Laboratory Animals* (hereinafter referred to as the *Guide*), produced by the National Academy of Sciences, Institute of Laboratory Animal Resources (ILAR, 1996). The *Guide* is a consensus document developed by the scientific community, and it represents the currently accepted professional standard in the field of laboratory animal science. Although deviations from the recommendations of the *Guide* may be acceptable under the PHS Policy, they must be justified for scientifically valid reasons and generally require approval by the IACUC.

The PHS Policy is administered by the Office of Laboratory Animal Welfare (OLAW), an office located in the Office of the Director, National Institutes of Health (NIH) within the Department of Health and Human Services, and having PHS-wide authority for implementation.

Prior to receiving an award from any component of the PHS (NIH, Centers for Disease Control [CDC], Food and Drug Administration [FDA], etc.) for activities involving animals, institutions must have on file with OLAW, an approved Assurance of Compliance (Assurance) that describes specific policies and procedures in place at the institution to ensure adherence to the PHS Policy. The Assurance is reviewed and approved by OLAW and provides the basis for a trust relationship between the institution and the government. It is this document, designed by the institution itself to meet its unique mission and circumstances, to which the institution will be held most directly accountable. For this reason, OLAW encourages all institutions to make available to its IACUC members, research administrators, research investigators and staff members, and other interested parties within the institution copies of the core contents of its Assurance (see Appendix C for a sample Assurance).

The OLAW implements the PHS Policy through a multifaceted approach to oversight. This includes review and approval of Assurances, reports from institutions certifying that the required internal semiannual inspections of animal facilities and evaluations of programs have been conducted, review of research protocols by IACUCs, requirements for prompt reporting of serious noncompliance, evaluation of allegations of noncompliance, the conduct of special reviews or site visits to selected institutions, and a nationwide education program.

Sanctions for noncompliance with the PHS Policy may range from acceptance of institutional corrective actions in cases of self-reported deficiencies, to OLAW negotiated resolution of deficiencies, to loss of institutional eligibility for PHS support for animal related activities. It is important for research investigators to be aware of the potential sanctions against their institutions resulting from individual transgressions, which may be seen by OLAW as a failure to have effective institutional policies and controls in place at the local level. This knowledge may help explain why IACUCs and research administrators generally find it in the institution's best interests to fully embrace the self-regulatory concept and impose institutional sanctions on individuals where necessary.

Also incorporated into the PHS Policy by reference is the Animal Welfare Act. Accordingly, confirmed violations of the USDA regulations are of direct concern to OLAW. Frequent interagency communications and cooperative actions serve to maintain consistency and supplement the effectiveness of both agencies.

U.S. Department of Agriculture Animal Welfare Act, Amendments, and Implementing Regulations

The original Laboratory Animal Welfare Act (AWA; PL-89-544), also known as the Pet Protection Act, was passed by Congress in 1966 and was intended to prevent the theft of pet dogs and cats, and their subsequent sale or use for research or experimentation. It also established limited standards for the humane treatment of dogs, cats, and several other species by animal dealers and medical research facilities. The current AWA includes the original law and the various amendments passed by Congress in 1970, 1976, and 1985, incorporating progressively increasing jurisdiction and specificity.

From a practical standpoint, the most important USDA document for institutions and investigators to be aware of is 9 CFR, Chapter 1, Subchapter A—Animal Welfare. This subchapter contains the current regulations, which implement the AWA and are enforced by USDA. The USDA office responsible for administering the AWA is Animal Care (AC) of the Animal Plant Health Inspection Service (APHIS). Similar to the PHS Policy, the USDA relies on the IACUC for day-to-day implementation of its standards. With a few exceptions, the USDA requirements for the IACUC are taken verbatim from the PHS Policy. Details of IACUC functions are described later in this chapter and in Appendix C.

The USDA regulations differ from, but generally do not contradict, the PHS Policy in the degree of specificity with which they deal with the issues such as the consideration of alternatives to painful procedures, avoidance of unintended duplication of research, exercise for dogs, and environmental enrichment for nonhuman primates.

In contrast to the PHS Policy, the USDA regulations are enforced by AC of the APHIS through a primarily inspection-based system. All registered research facilities must be inspected by representatives of AC, generally Veterinary Medical Officers (VMOs), on an annual basis. Sanctions for noncompliance are based on U.S. Administrative Law procedures and can result in civil or criminal penalties.

Role of Institutional Animal Care and Use Committees in Implementing Public Health Service Policy and U.S. Department of Agriculture Regulations

A description of the specific duties of the IACUC is included in chapter 10, this volume. However, it is important to emphasize that, for both PHS and USDA purposes, the IACUC serves as an agent of the institution.

In interactions between research investigators and the IACUC, it is important for both parties to recognize that the IACUC is carrying out institutional and federal policy on behalf of the institution. It is appointed by the chief executive officer of the institution and provides recommendations to the institutional official, an individual who is authorized to make commitments to the government on behalf of the institution. With the exception of an IACUC disapproval of a protocol (which cannot be overruled by the institution) or initial suspension of protocols, it is the institution that takes final action and is accountable to the government for compliance with the regulations and guidelines.

Although the federal regulations and policies are specific as to the duties required of IACUCs, they do not limit the institution from assigning other duties as it sees fit. For example, decisions regarding animal per diem rate setting or research space allocation are not covered by the regulations but frequently include IACUC involvement. Another area where interinstitutional variation may occur is in the degree of IACUC involvement in the evaluation of the scientific merit. Such evaluation has become a contentious issue at some institutions and OLAW has attempted to clarify PHS Policy expectations in this area. OLAW has divided the term *scientific merit* into two subcategories, peer review and scientific relevance, for the purposes of discussion. Peer review is that function normally conducted by NIH Initial Review Groups (IRGs) or study sections for the purpose of assigning priority scores, which assist in the making of funding decisions. These reviews are highly technical and involve in-depth review by nationally recognized peers in the specific scientific discipline involved. Although not prohibited from this type of review, IACUCs often lack the expertise to conduct true peer review of this type. Alternatively, the evaluation of scientific relevance involves a much more general judgment of the potential relevance of the research to human or animal health, the advancement of knowledge, or the good of society. It includes basic scientific issues such as the appropriateness of the species, quality, and number of animals required to obtain valid results. All IACUCs should be capable of and are expected to evaluate the scientific relevance of proposed research at this level.

State and Local Laws

In addition to federal laws and guidelines, state and local governments may impose rules, which affect the conduct of research. These most often take the form of general anticruelty laws, but they may also restrict access to animals from pounds and shelters. Also, states may affect research in a variety of other ways such as through enactment of occupational safety standards, hazardous waste disposal rules, and veterinary practice acts. A few state and local jurisdictions have entered directly into the regulation of research, including the development of regulations and establishment of enforcement mechanisms. The scope of this volume does not permit a detailed discussion of each state or municipality but an excellent reference on the subject is a publication by the National Association for Biomedical Research (NABR, 1991), *State Laws Concerning the Use of Animals in Research.*

Institutional Policies

Institutional policies can be divided into two broad categories: those that are regulation driven and those that are driven by other institutional interests. Many of the specifics of regulation-driven institutional policy are addressed in chapter 10. However, it is also important to mention some of the animal-related policies, which institutions may wish to put in place for nonregulatory reasons. Institutional policy manuals are commonly used to spell out the specific rules and procedures that apply to functions such as animal ordering, submission of protocols, and movement of animals. These manuals may also encompass areas such as public information and public relations policies, and policies designed to minimize institutional liability. Institutional mission statements are also useful communications tools for informing employees and the public regarding institutional goals and philosophy.

Professional Societies

Many professional societies have developed and adopted policy statements regarding the use of animals in research. Such policy statements serve several useful purposes. They serve as powerful tools for communicating to both the scientific community and to the public the high ethical standards that are demanded by the professional society of its members. These peer-developed and peer-enforced policies provide strong evidence that the self-regulatory approach can be highly effective in the biobehavioral research community. These policy statements generally include an endorsement of the various federal and international regulations and guiding principles, and they often detail more specific expectations. For example, the American Psychological Association issued in 1985 the *Guidelines for Ethical Conduct in the Care and Use of Animals.*[1] This document is described by the Office of Technology Assessment (1986) in its publication, *Alternatives to Animal Use in Research, Testing, and Education* as being "the most comprehensive of its type" (pp. 346–347).

Journals

Another powerful tool in promoting high standards for the care and use of animals involved in biobehavioral research is the use of editorial policy

---

[1]The most recent version of this document (APA, 1996) is available from the APA Order Department at (800) 374-2721 or order@apa.org.

and review. Many scientific journals refuse to consider for publication any animal-related research which does not adhere to certain basic guidelines. These editorial guidelines may be simply a restatement that all published materials must be conducted in accordance with the AWA and PHS Policy and they may include the specific policy statement of the professional society, which sponsors the particular journal. In many cases, reviewers may raise questions regarding the research conditions, methods, endpoints, and so forth, which, in their opinion, may not meet a particular ethical consideration.

CONCLUSION

It is useful for investigators to be aware that animal welfare oversight in the United States is provided by a patchwork of several different, usually complementary, mechanisms. Because of the different statutory authorities, not all of the regulations and policies are applicable to all of the animal research activities at a given institution. Most institutions have found it useful to integrate all of the commonly applicable requirements into a single institutional standard that satisfies the most stringent of the requirements for any given subject. This approach is much easier to implement and monitor than trying to gerrymander the program by applying standards selectively and only where absolutely required. For example, many institutions apply PHS Policy standards uniformly, without regard to whether PHS support is involved in a particular research study. Although this approach may cause some investigators to question the IACUC's authority to monitor non-PHS supported activities involving species not regulated by USDA, institutional interests usually dictate that a single standard be applied across the board.

In summary, all recipients of federal research grants from the PHS are subject to the laws and regulations for the care and use of animals in research that are overseen by the USDA, and to the PHS Policy that is implemented by OLAW. U.S. Department of Agriculture regulations differ from but do not generally contradict the PHS Policy. State and local governments may also impose rules for conducting research with animals. Finally, whether or not the research is federally funded, investigators and teachers using animals at an institution must comply with the institutional guidelines implemented by the IACUC, which is the local oversight entity that ensures compliance with all pertinent laws, regulations, and policies.

REFERENCES

American Psychological Association. (1985). *Guidelines for ethical conduct in the care and use of animals.* Washington, DC: Author.
American Psychological Association. (1996). *Guidelines for ethical conduct in the care and use of animals.* Washington, DC: Author.

Animal Welfare Act of 1985, Pub. L. No. 99-198, 7 U.S.C. § 2131 *et seq.*

Health Research Extension Act of 1985, Pub. L. No. 99-158, 42 U.S.C. § 289d (1985).

Institute of Laboratory Animal Resources, National Research Council. (1996). *Guide for the care and use of laboratory animals.* Washington, DC: National Academy Press.

Laboratory Animal Welfare Act, of 1966, Pub. L. No. 89-544, 7 U.S.C. § 2131 *et seq.*

National Association for Biomedical Research. (1991). *State laws concerning the use of animals in research* (3rd ed.). Washington, DC: Lowe, F. M. et al. (Eds.).

Office of Technology Assessment. (1986). *Alternatives to animal use in research, testing, and teaching.* Washington, DC: U.S. Government Printing Office.

U.S. Department of Agriculture Regulations Code of Federal Regulations (CFR, 1966), Title 9 (Animals and Animal products), Subchapter A (Animal Welfare). Washington, DC: U. S. Government Printing Office.

10

LOCAL INSTITUTIONAL POLICIES

JOHN D. STRANDBERG

As outlined in chapter 9, institutions that are the recipients of federal grants from the Public Health Service (PHS) are subject to the mandated policies for those projects, which receive this support. The question may arise as to whether other animal use within the institution should be governed by these policies as well. Most institutions have found it both practical and prudent to enforce uniform policies for all animal use regardless of its nature and the source of funding.

Similarly, although institutions without federal funding need not file an assurance of compliance with PHS Policy with the Office of Laboratory Animal Welfare (OLAW; see chap. 9), it is important to make sure that animal use by members of the institution is in accordance with societal standards. The most effective way of doing this is to have a formal review of animals used in research and teaching. This should be documented and be defensible in situations in which such animal use may come under scrutiny by the public, other scientists, or animal welfare advocates. State and local regulations also may mandate specific policies to be observed in the proposal and review of animal use in small institutions.

INSTITUTIONAL SUPPORT

As a starting point, it is an important administrative responsibility to have an institutional policy on such use; this policy should be clearly outlined in institutional circulars and catalogs. The lines of authority and oversight of animal use in research and teaching must be clear to all parties involved. For a program to be successful, the institution must support the humane use of animals. There may be philosophical or practical considerations, which will permit certain types of animal use and rule out others. For instance, the use of rodents in noninvasive studies or field observations of animals in their normal habitat may be institutionally acceptable, whereas projects using dogs, cats, or primates would be totally unacceptable from the institutional point of view. It is important for investigators and animal care committee members to know the institutional ground rules even before studies are proposed. The institution should also have a mechanism in place to deal with complaints and concerns raised by students, staff members, and the public concerning animal use in the institution, and means of communication with those responsible for the animal care and use program should be readily available.

It is also critical that senior institutional administrators are aware of the types of animal use that are proposed or in place to avoid potential embarrassment when they learn of them. This linkage is often well provided by having a representative of the institutional administration participate in animal care committee activities including laboratory site visits, which the committee members carry out.

INSTITUTIONAL ANIMAL CARE AND USE COMMITTEE

A formal Institutional Animal Care and Use Committee (IACUC) can be highly effective in advancing the appropriate instructional and research use of animals even if it is not required by law. The presence of such a committee helps to ensure that the use of animals is in accord with legal requirements and community standards. Inclusion of community representatives can be a positive asset in gaining wider support for projects within the institution and in furthering the appreciation of the role of animals in research.

Committee composition may vary from one setting to another depending on the institution's nature and size as well as geographic location. The U.S. Department of Agriculture (USDA) requirements for committee membership provide an important basis for the composition of such a committee. These rules stipulate that there must be at least three members on the committee and that these must include a veterinarian, a nonscientist, and a scientist familiar with the fields that use animals. At many small institutions, the veterinarian is frequently a local practitioner of small or large animal medicine; as such, he or she can also be the community representative. It is important to recognize that the veterinarian cannot act as the community representative if a fiduciary relationship exists. The role of nonscientist can be enlisted from administrative personnel from the institution as noted previously; equally there may be a desire to recruit an individual with a background in ethics such as a member of the local clergy.

Finding a committee member who represents the community provides an opportunity to recruit an individual who will be a valuable contributor to the committee and to the institution. Conversely, the community member can be a disruptive force. As can be seen by anyone who reads the newspapers, the use of animals in research and teaching is not universally supported. The range of individuals who can provide good community perspective includes members of the local clergy (who also have a background in ethics), a high school science teacher, or veterinarians or physicians maintaining local practices. There are also individuals who are in other walks of life but who have interest in animals and behavioral sciences and who can contribute to the committee's functions. Community representatives and all other committee members should be provided appropriate literature so that their decisions can be made on a factual basis rather than on uninformed personal opinions. (See Appendix C for a sample animal welfare assurance, which includes more details about IACUCs.)

In institutions in which there are projects focusing on wild animals and birds, personnel from the state or local natural resources units responsible for fish and game may be the most appropriate community members. These individuals will have the specialized knowledge about free-living species, which will be valuable in review of projects and programs. It might also be valuable to have someone with knowledge of environmental health and safety on the IACUC to ensure safety of humans who have contact with animals, in terms of protecting them from diseases that may be communicated from primates or wild animals and might be harmful or fatal to humans.

The animal welfare community is extremely diverse and includes the full spectrum of philosophical views of animal use. There are individuals who have animal welfare as a major concern but who also will support humane and conscientious use of animals in research and teaching. Such an individual may prove to be a valuable addition to the committee. Alternatively, there are animal rights activists who will not support the use of animals for these purposes in any way and whose presence on an IACUC would not be productive.

There is considerable diversity of opinion on whether the community representative should be paid for committee service. Some individuals feel that when an honorarium is provided, the participant cannot act as a true representative of the community. However, it may be difficult to entice an otherwise highly qualified individual to be a member of the committee, and a modest fee may alleviate this situation. Such an honorarium should not be tied to time devoted to the activity or of such magnitude that this individual could be considered an institutional employee.

Appointments on the committee should be of a fixed duration with some degree of continuity from one year to the next. At the same time, it is helpful to have some turnover in committee membership to get new perspectives in the review of projects. The committee may also turn out to be a valuable way to get more public and institutional support for animal studies in the institution and may provide good public relations for the work of the scientists.

With small research programs, there will also be a limited need to hold meetings. At the minimum, these should be conducted semiannually and coupled with a site visit or inspection of animal holding and research areas as well as a review of the institutional program of human care and use of animals. Support from the institution's administrators is essential to maintain records and file necessary reports.

INSTITUTIONAL ANIMAL CARE AND USE COMMITTEE REVIEW

Meetings of the IACUC can either be open to the public or held as closed sessions. Often there is no option in this regard because state-funded institutions frequently require that such meetings be open to the interested general public. At times this can prove challenging, but many potential problems can be prevented by avoiding potentially inflammatory language and by carefully ensuring the public of the necessary and humane nature of the work that is proposed. Private institutions often have no requirement that their meetings be held as public forums, and this question is less important in that instance.

In some cases, the use of institutional consortia for review of animal use at multiple institutions may be the most efficient and effective way of accomplishing the process. This is especially true in those instances in which only one or two projects are carried out at each of the units. Consortia allow efficiencies in record keeping and veterinary and other professional costs. At the same time they broaden the intellectual resources of the committee and may serve to improve the programs at each of the individual institutions.

One of the first questions to arise in the review of animal-based projects is determination of the scope of activities and range of species that are under the committee's purview. As a special case, does the committee consider only vertebrates as required by the animal welfare act or is work with invertebrates included as well? In many instances, this decision is made on an individual basis; species with highly developed nervous systems (e.g., cephalopods) usually gain more consideration than invertebrates, which exhibit less sophisticated behaviors. Vertebrate embryos also pose problems for committee reviews in biological sciences, but these are less frequently encountered in behavioral research. Although field studies are exempt from IACUC approval from the standpoint of USDA regulations, the committee may still choose to review them.

It is important that before animals are used in research and teaching, the IACUC has an opportunity to review and approve this use. Potential problems can be avoided, and the scientist can proceed with the knowledge that his or her work has institutional backing.

Similarly, the committee's oversight of ongoing projects helps to monitor animal use, which frequently changes as research projects evolve and as teaching programs undergo development. The continuing oversight is also important in being able to maintain institutional confidence in the behavioral research taking place with animals under its auspices.

Research uses of animals will vary from institution to institution as well as from region to region. Behavioral research in small institutions may or may not be invasive (i.e., involving surgical or other manipulations), which can result in pain and distress to the animals. When such research is performed, the IACUC must be composed of individuals who can assess such projects; when needed, outside experts should be brought in to help provide the background necessary for preliminary assessment and continuing oversight of the project.

However, research that does not include surgical procedures can also have effects on the research animals, which can cause significant pain and distress. Topics that require special attention by the IACUC include those that involve the inexact concept of stress. These include use of electrical shock and other noxious stimuli, swimming mazes, food and water restriction, temperature extremes, and other factors that can have a negative impact on the animals. In all cases it is important that the investigator, his or her staff members, and the committee be cognizant of the presence of these factors so that their necessity can be fully assessed and so that unnecessary discomfort can be avoided. On all these issues, it is important that empirical data, not personal opinion, should determine the guidelines established by the IACUC. Also a system to allow appeals by the proposing investigator should be established to provide clarification of issues and an opportunity to present additional information to the committee.

Teaching and demonstration are two of the most frequently employed uses of animals in psychology departments in small institutions. Here again, the use of noxious stimuli must be fully assessed. Of probably greater concern are the conditions under which these animals are kept from demonstration to demonstration and from year to year. In some cases, they may be kept in central animal colonies, but it is not unknown that a teacher will have an animal kept in the laboratory or even at home to bring in for such purposes. These situations should be reviewed by the committee. Health care and monitoring of these animals should be considered during such an assessment. Also, if the animals in this situation are covered by the Animal Welfare Act (i.e., mammals other than rats and mice), these sites could be considered as part of the site of the USDA registrant and inspected by this agency.

In contemporary society one frequently encounters students who are conscientious objectors concerning the use of animals in some or any educational settings. It is highly recommended that individuals with strongly held views against the use of animals in research and teaching not be forced to participate against their wishes. Occasionally, however, students make such assertions without much basis. Use of animals in the educational and research setting is an important topic, which should be clearly presented to students in advance so that questions can be answered and misconceptions clarified. For this reason as well, it is important that there be peer review of such activities by an IACUC. The committee can subsequently respond appropriately to student and institutional concerns. One frequently used mechanism to accomplish this is through the development of an alternate course. A term paper may be substituted for laboratory work, but students may elect such an alternative for reasons other than their concerns related to animal use.

VETERINARY CARE

Most small institutions will not have a staff veterinarian unless there is a relationship with a larger institution. Finding a consulting veterinarian may be relatively easy in a large urban area with other research facilities. Frequently, veterinarians with expertise in laboratory animal medicine on the staff of these institutions can be recruited as consultants on a fee-for-service basis. The need for a veterinarian will be twofold: to serve in the committee's review processes and to provide veterinary medical care to the research animals as the need arises. In both cases, the question of fee for such services arises. Certainly, it seems appropriate for the veterinarian to be paid for the medical care that he or she provides to animals with clinical problems. The veterinarian may also be paid on an hourly or other mutually agreed on mechanism for effort spent in committee review. The veterinarian must have authority in judgments that affect the health and well-being of the research animals and that are based on empirical data. This may be problematic at times when it is felt that an experimental subject should be euthanized for humane reasons. It is essential that this possibility is discussed at the outset of any study and that good communication is maintained between the veterinarian and the scientist to help ensure that mutually acceptable practices will assure humane treatment of the animals.

INVESTIGATOR AND STAFF TRAINING

Training is a critical element of any successful animal care and use program, no matter the size of the institution. The IACUC assesses whether the scientists and their staff members have appropriate training. Institutional training programs can be held on a regular or ad hoc basis. Such programs can use institutional staff members as faculty; alternatively there exists a large collection of training materials that are available from the National Agricultural Library, commercial sources, public and private libraries, and other scientific institutions as outlined elsewhere in this volume. All individuals who work with or are exposed to animals must be aware of potential hazards that accompany such exposure. These include inapparent infectious disease and traumatic injury that may occur during work with the animals. Special training to avoid infection from bacterial and viral agents from nonhuman primates is necessary because of their close phylogenetic relationship to humans and the sharing of susceptibility to such agents.

Investigators often have received extensive training during their formal education as well during the conduct of research. The incorporation of new procedures into studies may require further training, and encouragement should be given to scientists to gain such training either through formal programs or by working with qualified individuals.

Laboratory personnel are frequently trained by the scientists who supervise them. However, it may be valuable to supplement this training with annual reviews as well as through the use of the text and audiovisual materials noted previously.

Administrative and public affairs staff members are often completely unaware of the complexities of animal use in psychological research and teaching. Orientation of this group is important to prevent misinformation and to help support the academic programs. As noted earlier, education of administrative and public affairs staff members may also facilitate the scientific projects and prevent dissemination of incorrect information concerning scientific activities at the institution.

APPENDIX A: LIST OF ACRONYMS

AAALAC   Association for Assessment and Accreditation of Laboratory Animal Care, International
AALAS   American Association for Laboratory Animal Science
AC   Division of Animal Care (USDA)
ACLAM   American College of Laboratory Animal Medicine
APA   American Psychological Association
APHIS   Animal and Plant Health Inspection Service
ARENA   Applied Research Ethics National Association
ASLAP   American Society of Laboratory Animal Practitioners
ASPCA   American Society for the Prevention of Cruelty to Animals
AVMA   American Veterinary Medical Association
AWA   Animal Welfare Act
AWIC   Animal Welfare Information Center
CARE   Committee on Animal Research and Ethics (APA)
CDC   Centers for Disease Control and Prevention
CFR   Code of Federal Regulations
DEA   Drug Enforcement Administration
DHHS   Department of Health and Human Services
DVM   Doctorate in Veterinary Medicine
FDA   Food and Drug Administration
IACUC   Institutional Animal Care and Use Committee
ILAR   Institute of Laboratory Animal Resources
IRG   Initial Review Group (NIH)
ISEF   International Science and Engineering Fair
JCP   *Journal of Comparative Psychology*
JEP   *Journal of Experimental Psychology*
NABR   National Association for Biomedical Research
NASA   National Aeronautic and Space Administration
NIH   National Institutes of Health
NRC   National Research Council
NSF   National Science Foundation
OLAW   Office of Laboratory Animal Welfare
PHS   Public Health Service
PI   Principle Investigator
PL   Public Law
PTA   Parent Teacher Association
SWPA   Southwestern Psychological Association
USDA   United States Department of Agriculture
VMD   Doctorate in Veterinary Medicine
VMO   Veterinary Medical Officer

APPENDIX B: CASE STUDIES FOR CLASSROOM DISCUSSIONS OF INSTITUTIONAL ANIMAL CARE AND USE COMMITTEE FUNCTIONS

These exercises are designed to facilitate students' thinking on issues associated with the use of animals in research by asking them to make decisions about whether a series of hypothetical research and educational projects should be conducted. The 1985 amendments to the Animal Welfare Act required that institutions receiving federal research funds establish Institutional Animal Care and Use Committees (IACUCs) to inspect animal facilities on a regular basis and to review all uses of animals in education and research. In these exercises, students role-play serving as IACUC members.

One way to use the exercises is to divide the class into groups of between five and seven students. A group leader is chosen who is given a proposal to read to the IACUC members. The group must evaluate the project in terms of its costs and benefits, and either approve or reject the proposal. When the groups have made their decisions, the class reconvenes. The group leaders explain their proposal to the class as a whole and relate the IACUC's decision and its reasoning. The proposals are based on actual experiments or situations, and they were written to present a range of research and educational situations. The instructor should inform the students that the purpose of the exercises is to generate discussion and critical thinking; groups should be encouraged to try reach a consensus by discussing the proposals rather than simply taking a quick straw poll..

INSTRUCTIONS TO STUDENTS

Your group is the IACUC for your college. It is the committee's responsibility to evaluate and either approve or reject proposals submitted by faculty members who want to use animals for research or instructional purposes. The proposals describe the experiments, including their goals, potential benefits, and the costs of the research in terms of possible harm or discomfort to the animals. Your group must either approve or deny permission for the experiments. It is not your job to critique technical aspects of the projects such as the experimental design. You should make your decision on the basis of the information given in the proposal.

PROPOSALS

Case 1

Professor King is a psychobiologist working on transplantation of fetal stem cells, an exciting research area at the cutting edge of biological psychology. Previous studies have shown that stem cells tissue can be removed from a monkey embryo and implanted into the brains of monkeys that have suffered brain damage. The stem cells develop into neurons that can make the proper connections and are sometimes effective in improving performance in the brain-damaged animals. It is clear that this line of research is an important animal model for human degenerative diseases such as Parkinson's disease and Alzheimer's disease. Dr. King wants to conduct an experiment in which he will transplant tissue from monkey embryos into the entorhinal cortex, an area that appears to be associated with Alzheimer's disease.

The experiment will involve 20 adult rhesus monkeys as subjects. First, all the monkeys will be subjected to ablation surgery. This procedure will involve anesthetizing the animals, opening their skulls, and making lesions in the entorhinal cortex. After they recover, the monkeys will be given a learning task to make sure their memory is impaired. Three months later, the experimental group consisting of 10 of the animals will be given transplant surgery. Embryonic stem cells will be implanted into the area of the brain damage in the experimental subjects. The 10 control animals will be subjected to sham surgery. All of the monkeys will then be allowed to recover for 2 months. Finally, the animals will be given a learning task to test the hypothesis that the animals having brain grafts will show better memories than the control group.

According to Dr. King, this research is in the exploratory stages and can only be done using animals. He states that nearly 1 in every 10 Americans over the age of 65 suffer from Alzheimer's disease. He feels that this research will be a significant step toward developing a treatment for the devastating memory loss that afflicts individuals with Alzheimer's disease.

Case 2

The question of instinct has been hotly debated in psychology for many years. Some psychologists have argued that the plans for some complex behaviors in animals are essentially hard wired into the brain at birth. Other psychologists, however, believe that all behavior is the result of learning. Dr. Fine is a developmental psychobiologist whose research concerns the genetic basis of behavior. One of the major debates in his field concerns how behavior develops when an animal has no opportunity to learn a response. He notices that the grooming behavior of mice is a complex behavior that occurs in virtually identical form in all mice. He hypothesizes that this behavioral sequence might be a good example of a behavior pattern that is built into the brain at birth, although it is not expressed until the animals are several weeks old.

To investigate whether the motor patterns involved in grooming are acquired or innate, he proposes to raise a small group of mice who have no opportunity to learn the behavior. Rearing animals in social isolation is not sufficient; the mice could teach themselves the response. Certain random movements could accidentally result in the removal of debris. These movements would then be reinforced and repeated, and they could eventually be coordinated into a complex sequence that would appear to be instinctive but would actually be learned. To show that the behaviors are truly innate, he needs to demonstrate that animals raised with absolutely no opportunity to perform any groominglike behaviors would make the proper movements when they are old enough.

Dr. Fine proposes to conduct the experiment on 10 newborn mice. As soon at the animals are born, they will be anesthetized and their front limbs painlessly amputated. This procedure will ensure that they will not be self-reinforced for making random grooming movements that remove debris from their bodies. The mice will then be returned to their mothers. The animals will be observed on a regular schedule using standard observation techniques. Their limb movements will be filmed and analyzed. If grooming is a learned behavior, the mice should not make grooming movements with their stumps as the movements will not remove dirt. If, however, grooming movements are genetically encoded, the animals will show groominglike movement with the stumps of their forelimbs.

In his proposal, Dr. Fine notes that the experimental results cannot be directly applied to human behavior. He argues, however, that the experiment will be very important in shedding light on one of the central debates in the field of developmental psychobiology. He also stresses that the amputations will be painless and that the animals will be well treated after the operation.

Case 3

Your university includes a college of veterinary medicine. In the past, the veterinary students have practiced surgical techniques on dogs procured from a local animal shelter. Recently, however, there have been some objections to this practice and the veterinary school wants the approval of your committee to continue this practice. They make the following points:

1. Almost all of these animals will eventually be killed at the animal shelter. It is wasteful to breed animals for practice surgery when there is an ample supply of animals that are going to be killed anyway.

2. It costs at least 10 times as much to raise purebred animals for research purposes. This money could be better used to fund research that would benefit many animals.
3. Research with dogs from animal shelters and the practice surgeries will, in the long run, aid the lives of animals by training veterinarians and producing treatments for diseases that afflict animals.

A local group of animal welfare activists has urged your committee to deny the veterinary school's request. They argue that the majority of these animals are lost or stolen pets. No one likes to think that his or her lost pet may wind up on a surgical table or in an experiment. They claim that as people become aware that animals taken to shelters may end up in research laboratories, they will stop using the shelters. Finally, the activists point out that in countries such as England, veterinary students do not perform practice surgery; they learn surgical techniques in an extensive apprenticeship.

Case 4

The psychology department is requesting permission from your committee to use 10 rats per semester for use in Psychology 431: Learning and Memory. Dr. Henderson, the instructor, feels that it is important that students get firsthand experience in working with the phenomena that they read about in their textbooks. He wants each student to be given a rat to train. The students will be assigned to teach their rats a series of tasks in a standard operant chamber. They will first practice shaping behavior so that their animal learns to press a bar for food reinforcement. They will then go on to a series of exercises to illustrate learning phenomena such as extinction, discrimination learning, and response chaining. As is standard practice, each animal will be deprived of food for 23 hours prior to each session so that it will be motivated to work for food.

Dr. Henderson admits that no new information will be discovered as a result of the laboratory exercise. He feels strongly, however, that students learn best when they are putting what they learn from lectures into practice.

NOTES TO THE INSTRUCTOR

Case 1 forces students to consider whether injury to another species that is fairly closely related to humans is justified if the results will be applicable to human beings. Case 2 asks students to think about the use of animals in pure research in which there is no direct connection to future human application. Based on a study by Fentress (1973),[1] this case offers an excel-

---

[1]Fentress, J. C. (1973). Development of grooming in mice with amputated forelimbs. *Science, 179,* 704–705.

lent opportunity for the instructor to discuss the importance of pure research in the progress of science. Incidentally, in the Fentress experiment, amputated mice exhibited "remarkably normal" grooming movements with their stumps, demonstrating that the movements were innate. Case 3 involves the use of pound animals and is one of the more controversial issues in biomedical and veterinary research. Several state legislatures have passed laws banning the use of pound-seizure animals for biomedical research or student surgeries in veterinary schools. The use of animals in student laboratories (Case 4) has been singled out by animal welfare groups as particularly unnecessary. They argue that videotapes and computer simulations are adequate substitutes for live animals in classroom behavioral studies and dissections.

Modifications can be made with these scenarios to tailor them to the needs of particular topics or courses. For example, Case 1 could be changed so that some groups are given the case using monkeys as subjects and some are given the same case using rats. This would lead to a discussion of factors that come into play in making ethical decisions (e.g., why might it be acceptable to use rodents in the study but not primates?). Other cases could be added for different courses. Thus, a proposal in which an ethologist wants to confront mice with snakes to study antipredator behavior could be included for a course in animal behavior.

Your students will probably have considerable disagreements in their evaluations of the scenarios. This is to be expected; in reality, IACUC members often disagree about the relative merits of an animal research project. In one recent study (Plous & Herzog, 2001[2]), IACUC members were asked to evaluate a series of proposals that had already gone through the IACUC process at a different institution. There was a surprising lack of agreement in how the members rated the proposals in areas such as scientific merit, applied value, and quality of the experimental design.

---

[2]Plous, S., & Herzog, H. (2001). Animal research: Reliability of protocol reviews of animal research. *Science, 293,* 608–609.

APPENDIX C: SAMPLE ANIMAL WELFARE ASSURANCE INSTITUTIONAL LETTERHEAD

(Name of Institution)

Assurance of Compliance With Public Health Service Policy on
Humane Care and Use of Laboratory Animals

(Name of institution), hereinafter referred to as institution, hereby gives assurance that it will comply with the Public Health Service (PHS) Policy on Humane Care and Use of Laboratory Animals, hereinafter referred to as PHS Policy.

I. **Applicability**

This Assurance is applicable to all research, research training, experimentation, and biological testing and related activities, hereinafter referred to as activities, involving live vertebrate animals supported by the PHS and conducted at this institution, or at another institution as a consequence of the subgranting or subcontracting of a PHS-conducted or supported activity by this institution. "Institution" includes the following branches and major components of (name of institution; list every branch and major component covered by this Assurance). (If applicable), "Institution" also includes the following branches and major components of (name[s] of any other institution[s] to be included under this Assurance; list every branch and major component of other institution[s] to be covered by this Assurance).

II. **Institutional Policy**

A. This institution will comply with all applicable provisions of the Animal Welfare Act and other federal statutes and regulations relating to animals.

B. This institution is guided by the "U.S. Government Principles for the Utilization and Care of Vertebrate Animals Used in Testing, Research, and Training."

C. This institution acknowledges and accepts responsibility for the care and use of animals involved in activities covered by this Assurance. As partial fulfillment of this responsibility, this institution will make a reasonable effort to ensure that all individuals involved in the care and use of laboratory animals understand their individual and collective responsibilities for compliance with this

Assurance as well as all other applicable laws and regulations pertaining to animal care and use.

D. This institution has established and will maintain a program for activities involving animals in accordance with the *Guide for the Care and Use of Laboratory Animals (Guide)*.

III. **Institutional Program for Animal Care and Use**

A. The lines of authority and responsibility for administering the program and ensuring compliance with this Policy are as follows: (Describe or diagram the organization of the administration and staff, including the Institutional Animal Care and Use Committee [IACUC], the institutional official, and the veterinarian.)

B. The qualifications, authority, and percentage of time contributed by veterinarian(s) who will participate in the program are: (Indicate professional or academic degrees and the number of years of pertinent training or experience in laboratory animal medicine. Describe the veterinarians' functions, percentage of time contribution, and responsibilities insofar as they relate to implementation of this Policy and the recommendations in the *Guide for the Care and Use of Laboratory Animals*.)

C. This institution has established an IACUC, which is qualified through the experience and expertise of its members to oversee the institution's animal program, facilities, and procedures. The IACUC consists of at least five members, and its membership meets the compositional requirements set forth in the PHS Policy at IV.A.3.b. Attached is a list of the names, position titles, earned degrees, and other credentials of the IACUC chairperson and members.

D. The IACUC will do the following:

1. Review at least once every 6 months the institution's program for humane care and use of animals, using the *Guide* as a basis for evaluation.

2. Inspect at least once every 6 months all of the institution's animal facilities (including satellite facilities) using the *Guide* as a basis for evaluation.

3. Prepare reports of the IACUC evaluations as set forth in the PHS Policy at IV.B.3. and submit the reports to (insert name or title of the institutional official signing the Assurance).

4. Review concerns involving the care and use of animals at the institution.

5. Make written recommendations to (insert name or title of the institutional official signing the Assurance) regarding any aspect of the institution's animal program, facilities, or personnel training.

6. Review and approve, require modifications in (to secure approval) or withhold approval of those activities related to the care and use of animals as set forth in the PHS Policy at IV.C.

7. Review and approve, require modifications in (to secure approval), or withhold approval of proposed significant changes regarding the use of animals in ongoing activities as set forth in the PHS Policy at IV.C.

8. Notify investigators and the institution in writing of its decision to approve or withhold approval of those activities related to the care and use of animals, or of modifications required to secure IACUC approval as set forth in the PHS Policy at IV.C.4.

9. Be authorized to suspend an activity involving animals as set forth in the PHS Policy at IV.C.6.

E. The procedures that the IACUC will follow to fulfill the requirements set forth in the PHS Policy at IV.B. are as follows:

   (Describe how the IACUC will fulfill each of the functions set forth in the PHS Policy at IV.B. Include how often the IACUC will meet, how often it will inspect facilities, and how the inspections will take place. Describe the procedures the IACUC will follow to address any concerns, and how recommendations will be developed and forwarded to the institutional official. The channels for receiving proposed activities and for reporting the results of IACUC review of applications and proposals should be addressed.)

F. The individual(s) authorized by this institution to verify IACUC approval of those sections of applications and proposals related to the care and use of animals is (insert name of individual).

G. The health program for personnel who work in laboratory animal facilities or have frequent contact with animals is:

   (Describe the institution's occupational health program, including the frequency of tuberculosis tests, if any, requirements for medical examinations, etc. The institution may submit a memorandum or pamphlet [if one exists] that informs animal care and use staff of institutional policies regarding health screening or tests.)

H. The total gross number of square feet in each animal facility (including each satellite facility), the species of animals housed therein, and the average daily inventory, by species, of animals in each facility. (This information may be provided in an attached chart.)

I. The training or instruction available to scientists, animal technicians, and other personnel involved in animal care, treatment, or use are as follows:

   (Provide a synopsis of the training or instruction available in the humane practice of animal care and use, as well as training or instruction in research and testing methods that minimize the number of animals required to obtain valid results and minimize animal distress.)

IV. Institutional Status

As specified in the PHS Policy at IV.A.2., as Category 1, all of this institution's programs and facilities (including satellite facilities) for activities involving animals have been evaluated and accredited by the American Association for Accreditation of Laboratory Animal Care. All of this institution's programs and facilities (including satellite facilities) for activities involving animals have also been evaluated by the IACUC and will be reevaluated by the IACUC at least once every 6 months.

OR

As specified in the PHS Policy at IV.A.2, as Category 2, all of this institution's programs and facilities (including satellite facilities) for activities involving animals have been evaluated by the IACUC and will be reevaluated by the IACUC at least once every six months. The report of the IACUC evaluation has been submitted to (insert name or title of the institutional official signing the Assurance) and a copy of the report is attached. The report contains a description of the nature and extent of this institution's adherence to the *Guide*. Any departures from the *Guide* are identified specifically and reasons for each departure are stated. Where program or facility deficiencies are noted, the report contains a reasonable and specific plan and schedule for correcting each deficiency. The report distinguishes significant deficiencies from minor deficiencies. Semiannual reports of the IACUC evaluation submitted to the institutional official (insert name or title of the institutional official signing the Assurance) will also contain a reasonable and specific plan and schedule for correcting each deficiency and distinguish significant deficiencies from minor deficiencies. Semiannual reports of IACUC evaluations will be maintained by this institution and made available to OLAW on request.

V. Record-Keeping Requirements

A. This institution will maintain for at least 3 years:
  1. A copy of this Assurance and any modifications thereto, as approved by PHS.
  2. Minutes of IACUC meetings, including records of attendance, activities of the committee, and committee deliberations.
  3. Records of applications, proposals, proposed significant changes in the care and use of animals, and whether IACUC approval was given or withheld.
  4. Records of semiannual IACUC reports and recommendations as forwarded to (insert name or title of the institutional official signing the Assurance).

5. Records of accrediting body determinations.

B. This institution will maintain records that relate directly to applications, proposals, and proposed changes in ongoing activities reviewed and approved by the IACUC for the duration of the activity and for an additional 3 years after completion of the activity.

C. All records shall be accessible for inspection and copying by authorized Office of Laboratory Animal Welfare (OLAW) or other PHS representatives at reasonable times and in a reasonable manner.

VI. **Reporting Requirements**

A. At least once every 12 months, the IACUC, through the institutional official, will report in writing to the Office for Protection from Research Risks (OLAW):

1. Any change in the status of the institution (e.g., if the institution becomes accredited by the Association for Assessment and Accreditation of Laboratory Animal Care, International (AAALAC) or if AAALAC accreditation is revoked), any change in the description of the institution's program for animal care and use as described in this Assurance, or any changes in IACUC membership. If there are no changes to report, this institution will submit a letter to OLAW stating that there are no changes.

2. Notification of the date that the IACUC conducted its semiannual evaluations of the institution's program and facilities (including satellite facilities) and submitted the evaluations to (insert name or title of the institutional official signing the Assurance).

B. The IACUC, through the institutional official, will provide the OLAW promptly with a full explanation of the circumstances and actions taken with respect to the following:

1. Any serious or continuing noncompliance with the PHS Policy;

2. Any serious deviations from the provisions of the *Guide*; and

3. Any suspension of an activity by the IACUC.

C. Reports filed under VI.A.2. and VI.B. above shall include any minority views filed by members of the IACUC.

VII. **Institutional Endorsement and Public Health Service Approval**

A. Authorized Institutional Official

Name: _____

Title: _____

Address: _____

_____

_____

_____

Telephone: _____

Signature: _____ Date: _____

B. PHS Approving Official

Name: _____

Title: _____

Address: _____

_____

_____

_____

Telephone: _____

Signature: _____ Date: _____

C. Effective date of Assurance: _____

D. Expiration date of Assurance: _____

APPENDIX D: ASSOCIATION FOR ASSESSMENT AND ACCREDITATION OF LABORATORY ANIMAL CARE INTERNATIONAL ACCREDITATION PROGRAM

The following is adapted from materials provided by Association for Assessment and Accreditation of Laboratory Animal Care International (AAALAC), with permission:

The scientific community actively and voluntarily participates in a program of accreditation for organizations using animals in research, testing, and education. Prompted by the growing number of issues related to the well-being of laboratory animals, pioneering scientific organizations founded the AAALAC International in 1965. A unique organization, AAALAC's mission is to promote high standards of animal care, use, and well-being, and enhance life sciences research and education through the accreditation process. As a voluntary, nonregulatory, nonprofit corporation, AAALAC is guided by a Board of Trustees comprised of representatives from more than 60 scientific, professional, and educational member societies.

Council on Accreditation

The 32-member Council on Accreditation serves as the core of the AAALAC accreditation process. These individuals are knowledgeable about laboratory animal programs and management issues. Council members and specialists are appointed by the AAALAC Board of Trustees and may serve up to four 3-year terms. Ad hoc consultants and specialists assist council members with the site visits. Consultants have diverse backgrounds; they are recommended by the scientific community and appointed by the council to 3-year, renewable terms.

The Value of AAALAC Accreditation

Accreditation by the AAALAC is widely accepted by the scientific community, and the Association is highly respected as an independent organization that evaluates the quality of laboratory animal care and use. An accredited facility achieves standards beyond the minimum required by law. Achieving and maintaining accreditation is a voluntary step in demonstrating accountability and responsibility for the use of animals in research, testing, and education.

An important function of the accreditation process is to provide a self-assessment of the animal program. This nonbiased, independent peer review is valuable to any size program. The findings highlight program strengths and identify potential weaknesses. Program managers maintaining accreditation demonstrate a high degree of accountability and program excellence. For researchers, participating in an accredited program ensures the highest quality care for the animals involved in their activities.

The AAALAC accredits facilities all over the world, and currently there are more than 650 research units in 18 countries that are accredited. Accredited organizations include leading biomedical research centers in the United States. Accreditation is an excellent means to assure federal funding agencies that an organization meets and exceeds the guidelines established by the Public Health Service and the National Institutes of Health. The Department of Veterans Affairs requires its active laboratory animal research facilities to achieve AAALAC accreditation or demonstrate an equivalent level of standards. All Department of Defense facilities must be accredited by the AAALAC. Private biomedical organizations, for example, the Cystic Fibrosis Foundation and the American Heart Association, strongly recommend that all grantees be supported at institutions accredited by the AAALAC. Certification that a program is accredited by the AAALAC assures funding organizations that the animal care and use program meets the highest standards. The value of AAALAC accreditation has become synonymous with a gold standard.

An Important Resource

The AAALAC is a resource for information on laboratory animal issues and emerging trends in animal care and use. The Association provides assistance to accredited units—interpreting the *Guide*, apprising of changes to federal regulations, and informing about modifications in AAALAC procedures.

Applying for Accreditation

Any private or public institution, organization, or agency maintaining, importing, breeding, or using animals in research, testing, or education may apply for accreditation. An active animal care and use program must be operational prior to applying for accreditation. Accredited units vary in size and complexity. The AAALAC accredits units from small laboratories to large multisite programs using farm animals and exotic and traditional laboratory species. (An AAALAC application packet is available online at the AAALAC International Web site: http://www.aaalac.org or upon request from the AAALAC office.)

The Site Visit

Site visits are conducted to all approved applicants; revisits are scheduled within a 3-year period. A member of the council and an ad hoc consultant conduct the site visit at a mutually convenient time established with the unit. The length of time required for a site visit depends on the size and complexity of the unit.

Site visitors rely on the *Guide for the Care and Use of Laboratory Animals* (1996), as the primary source of guidelines for evaluating a program. Other published sources are consulted for the most current information and accepted practices. A list of select "Reference Resources" is provided by AAALAC.

The Exit Briefing

The site visitors conduct an exit briefing to present their preliminary findings and impressions to the management, research, and animal program staff. This provides immediate feedback, affords time for clarification of concerns, discussion of issues, and, where possible, correction of deficiencies in advance of the written report being submitted to the council.

Following the Site Visit

The site visitors prepare a written evaluation of each site visit for submission to the Council on Accreditation. The council meets three times per year to formally review reports. The site visitor from the council represents the unit during the meeting. Following full review, the unit is notified in writing of its accreditation status, usually within 2 months of the council meeting. Accredited units must submit an annual report. Throughout the year, AAALAC expects to be kept informed of any significant programmatic changes. All reports and communications with the unit are kept confidential.

Accreditation Status

The accreditation process affords the opportunity to both achieve and maintain a quality animal care and use program. Categories of accreditation allow for maintaining accreditation while responsibly addressing deficiencies. Recognizably, programmatic deficiencies range from minor to major; most are correctable in reasonably short time periods. Failure to satisfactorily address deficiencies can result in revocation of accreditation. (For more information on the AAALAC process on accreditation, contact AAALAC at 11300 Rockville Pike, Suite 1211, Rockville, Maryland, 20852-3035; telephone: 301-231-5353; e-mail: accredit@aaalac.org; Web site: http://www.aaalac.org.)

APPENDIX E: RESEARCH PROJECTS FOR ANIMAL BEHAVIOR COURSES

ZEBRA FINCH STUDY

From September 11 through September 22, study groups will be observing zebra finch aggression. The title of this research project is "Male and Female Levels of Aggression in a Zebra Finch Colony: A Comparison." In preparation for this research, read the resources on the behavior of zebra finches listed at the end of this section. The classification of this research design is Laboratory Investigation—Naturalistic Observation.

Study groups will be assigned a time period for observations. During the week of September 11 through September 15, you will simply watch the birds. During this time you will familiarize yourself with the phenotypic differences between male and female birds, and identify aggressive behaviors.

During the week of September 11 through September 22, you will be collecting data. Data collection forms are attached to this package of information. You will be using all-occurrences sampling method (page 46 of manual) for aggressive behavior in all of the adult birds. The following aggressive behavior should be recorded: beak fencing, supplanting, chasing, pecking, and the aggressive "whsst" call (see Case, 1986).[1] Each instance of these behaviors should be recorded using a single hatch mark on the data form under the corresponding behavior for the bird performing the behavior. What scale of measurement would this be? What are the dependent and independent variables?

During the first half hour of the assigned observation period, two observers from the group should watch the behavior and make independent recordings. One individual should record the behavior of the male birds and one should record the behavior of the female birds. The remaining two group members should collect the data during the last half-hour period. At the end of the week, you will have 5 hours of observation.

After completing data collection, calculate means and standard deviations of the various aggressive behaviors for males and for females per half hour observation period. Plot the data on a graph with observation days on the horizontal axis and the average number of beak fencing, and so forth on the vertical axis. A t test (Ambrose & Ambrose, 1987, p. 85)[2] and a Mann-Whitney U test should then be performed on the data. A summary of the

---

[1]Case, V. M. (1986). Breeding cycle aggression in domesticated zebra finches (*Poephila guttata*). *Aggressive Behavior, 12,* 337–348.
[2]Ambrose, H. W., & Ambrose, K. P. (1987). *A handbook of biological investigation* (4th ed.). Winston-Salem, NC: Hunter Textbooks.

results will be presented to the class on September 27. Each group will write a Results section for a scientific paper based on this study. This should include data tables and/or graphs. The paper will be due on October 4.

RESOURCES

Adkins-Regan, E., & Robinson, T. M. (1993). Sex differences in aggressive behavior in zebra finches (*Poephila guttata*). *Journal of Comparative Psychology, 107*, 223–229.

Caryl, P. G. (1975). Aggressive behavior in the zebra finch (*Taeniopygia guttata*). Fighting provoked by male and female social partners. *Behaviour, 52*(3–4), 226–252.

Evans, S. M. (1970). Aggressive and territorial behavior in captive zebra finches. *Bird Study, 17*(1), 28–35.

Data Collection Form: Zebra Finch Study

Observer name: Date: Time of observation:

Animal	Beak fencing	Supplanting	Pecking	Whsst Call

MOCKINGBIRD STUDY

From September 25 through October 20, study groups will be observing mockingbird territorial defense behavior. The title of this research project is "Mockingbird Territorial Defense in Response to a Conspecific 'Model'". In preparation for this research, read the attached resources at the end of this section. The classification of this research design is Field Investigation— Experimentation: Manipulation of the Environment.

Resident mockingbirds are found all around town and campus. Prior to fall break, groups should identify six territorial mockingbirds for study. The groups should then observe these birds to identify territorial defense behavior and to delineate the boundaries of each bird's territory. The experimental manipulation for this study will involve the introduction of a mockingbird "model" into the territories of the subject birds. During the time before fall break, the group should determine how they will use the model mockingbird (e.g., the location where they will place the model), as well as the amount of time birds will be observed, the behaviors that will be recorded, and so forth. The groups will also design their own data collection form. Specific details of the study will be reviewed with the instructor prior to data collection. You will use focal-animal sampling in this study and determine the time spent in specific territorial defense behavior. What is the scale of measurement? What are the dependent and independent variables?

Data collected will be analyzed with a Friedman two-way analysis of variance (Ambrose & Ambrose, 1987, p. 58).[3] Your presentations will be made on October 25. Each group will turn in Results and Discussion sections for a scientific paper based on this study on the date of the presentation.

RESOURCES

Derrickson, K. C., & Breitwisch, R. (1992). Northern mockingbird. *The Birds of North America, 7,* 1–24.

Logan, C. A. (1985). Mockingbird use of chatbursts with neighbors versus strangers. *Journal of Field Ornithology, 56,* 69–71.

Logan, C. A. (1987). Fluctuations in fall and winter territory size in the Northern mockingbird (*Mimus polyglottos*). *Journal of Field Ornithology, 58*(3), 297–305.

Michener, J. R. (1951). Territorial behavior and age composition in a population of mockingbirds at a feeding station. *Condor, 53,* 276–283.

Safina, C., & Utter, J. M. (1989). Food and winter territories of northern mockingbirds. *Wilson Bulletin, 101*(1), 97–101.

Stokes, D. W., & Lansdown, J. F. (1983). *A guide to bird behavior. Vol. 1.* (Reprint ed.). Boston: Little, Brown.

GRAY SQUIRREL STUDY

From October 23 through November 3, study groups will be observing either alert/pause behavior or agnostic behavior in gray squirrels on campus. Each group will choose one or the other general category of behavior to study. In preparation for this research, read the resources listed at the end of this section. The classification of this research design is Field Investigation—Naturalistic Observation.

After choosing the dependent variable for the research project (alert/pause behavior or agnostic behavior), study groups will decide on an independent variable (e.g., size of squirrel group, type of location, etc.) and other aspects of the experimental design. The scale of measure should be at least ordinal and the statistical analysis should be one of the following: Kruskal-Wallis one way analysis of variance (ANOVA), or Spearman's rho or chi square (Ambrose & Ambrose, 1987).[4] Consultation with the instructor will occur during the design phase of the study.

---

[3]Ambrose, H. W., & Ambrose, K. P. (1987). *A handbook of biological investigation* (4th ed.). Winston-Salem, NC: Hunter Textbooks.

[4]Ambrose, H. W., & Ambrose, K. P. (1987). *A handbook of biological investigation* (4th ed.). Winston-Salem, NC: Hunter Textbooks.

During the week of October 30 through November 3, you will collect data and perform the data analysis. Presentation summaries will be made on November 8. Each group must turn in a written Methods and Materials section and a Results section for a scientific paper based on this study, including data tables and/or graphs.

RESOURCES

Allen, D. S., & Aspey, W. P. (1986). Determinants of social dominance in eastern gray squirrels (*Sciurus carolinensis*): A quantitative assessment. *Animal Behavior, 34,* 81–89.

Bakken, A. (1959). *Behavior of gray squirrels.* Proceedings of the Southeast Game Fish Commissioners, 13, 393–406.

Lima, S. L., & Valone, T. J. (1986). Influence of predation risk on diet selection: A simple example in the grey squirrel. *Animal Behavior, 34,* 536–44.

Lima, S. L., Valone, T. J., & Caraco, T. (1985). Foraging-efficiency predation-risk trade off in the gray squirrel. *Animal Behavior, 33,* 155–165.

Pack, J. C., Mosby, H. S., & Siegel, P. B. (1967). Influence of social hierarchy on gray squirrel behavior. *Journal of Wildlife Management, 31,* 720–728.

Taylor, J. C. (1966). Home range and agonistic behaviour in the grey squirrel. *Symposium of the Zoological Society of London, 18,* 229–235.

GERBIL STUDY

From November 6 through December 6, study groups will be observing either gerbil hoarding behavior or gerbil nesting behavior. In preparation for this research, read the resources at the end of this section. The classification of this research design is Laboratory Investigation—Experimentation: Manipulation of the Environment.

This study will be designed from beginning to end by the study group in consultation with the instructor. The scale of measurement should be interval or ratio. On December 13, projects will be presented in class and a complete scientific paper (Abstract, Introduction, Methods, Results, and Discussion) is due at that time.

RESOURCES

Agren, G., Zhou, Q., & Zhong, W. (1989). Ecology and social behaviour of Mongolian gerbils, *Meriones uguiculatus,* at Xilinhot, Inner Mongolia, China. *Animal Behavior, 37,* 11–27.

Agren, G., Zhou, Q., & Zhong, W. (1989). Territoriality, cooperation and resource priority: Hoarding in the Mongolian gerbil, *Meriones uguiculatus*. *Animal Behavior*, *37*, 28–32.

Ambrose, H. W., & Ambrose, K. P. (1987). *A handbook of biological investigation* (4th ed.). Winston-Salem, NC: Hunter Textbooks.

Nyby, J., & Thiessen, D. D. (1980). Food hoarding in the Mongolian gerbil (*Meriones uguiculatus*): Effects of food deprivation. *Behavioral and Neural Biology*, *30*, 39–48.

Wong, R. (1984). Hoarding versus the immediate consumption of food among hamsters and gerbils. *Behavioural Processes*, *9*, 3–11.

Wong, R., & Jones, C. H. (1985). A comparative analysis of feeding and hoarding in hamsters and gerbils. *Behavioural Processes*, *11*, 301–308.

APPENDIX F: SAMPLE INSTITUTIONAL ANIMAL CARE AND USE COMMITTEE PROTOCOL FOR A BEHAVIORAL PROJECT IN A ZOOLOGY COURSE

Course title: Mammology Laboratory, Zoology

Academic level of students: Undergraduate students in zoology

Project title: Behavioral Responses of *Peromyscus* to Sounds

Species: Deer mice (*Peromyscus*)

Estimated number per year (and per student): XX

Summary: As part of their research projects in the course, these students will live trap *Peromyscus* mice with Sherman traps, place them in cages, and observe their behavior under normal conditions and when various natural (e.g., predator sounds) and unnatural (e.g., music and automobile sounds) are played on a tape recorder. Mice will be housed with food and water for 2 days during the testing and then released at the sites where they were originally trapped. These are the most abundant of wild rodents in the Nearctic area. This study will enable these students to develop and test a hypothesis while learning techniques of behavioral observation of mammals.

Method and duration of fasting animals if used: None.

Surgical procedures used if any (indicate terminal, survival, multiple survival): None.

Anesthetics, analgesics, or tranquilizers used: None.

Neuromuscular blocking agent used: None.

Approach to alternative exercise for students judged to have valid objections: Students not wishing to participate will prepare and present an oral report of effects of urban development on animal habitat. This will be presented during the last 20 minutes of the lab.

APPENDIX G: SAMPLE INSTITUTIONAL ANIMAL CARE AND USE COMMITTEE PROTOCOL FOR A LIVE ANIMAL PROJECT

Course title: Laboratory Research in Psychology

Academic level of students: Undergraduate students, junior and senior psychology majors (required as part of courses for the major)

Project title: Exploring Learning Principles in a Laboratory Course

Species: Rat

Estimated number per year (and per student): 60 (approximately one rat per six students)

Abstract (including pedagogical value of the project, justification of animal use rather than alternatives): The students train a rat to press a lever to receive a water reward (reinforcer), alter this behavior systematically by varying the schedule of reinforcement, and restrict the behavior to one stimulus condition by delivering the reinforcer only in this stimulus. These experiences provide an irreplaceable contact with principles of learning. Students often report that these principles come alive for them when they see the world "in their own hands." Their understanding of the details and importance of the considerable research that uses and builds further knowledge of the processes revealed by these procedures is deepened in a way that no "book learning" or simulation allows. The characterization and explicit application of these principles during the past 40 years has dramatically improved the lives of developmentally disabled and psychiatrically impaired individuals, allowing many to return to their community and engage in more normal living rather than be warehoused in institutions. Further, this methodology is critical to developing an understanding of the biological bases of normal and abnormal behavior.

Our "experiment" in this project is therefore the direct contact our students have with principles of reinforcement. This direct contact with the application of these principles provides an education that no other experience provides. We consider this educational experience to be of great importance in training the next generation of individuals who will improve health care. The project is designed to ensure that all students in the course have the potential for this experience.

Further, the project is designed to ensure and to train good animal care and provide a vehicle for direct consideration of the ethical principles involved in research with animal subjects. If a student is personally against participating in the project, then alternative experiences are developed for him or her by the principle investigator.

As animal research is a primary source of knowledge of psychological principles, a student's training in psychology is deficient until they have had exposure to this approach. The laboratory project is designed to provide this exposure in a manner that is effective in training the student and is noninvasive to the animal. We have selected the rat for this project because this species is used so frequently in the research the students need to evaluate. We include this exercise with real animals because simulations demonstrate only sketches of these principles. There is no alternative to this exercise that engages and trains the students as effectively. Whenever possible, we have students complete a simulation as preliminary training for the present project. The difference in effect of the two experiences is dramatic—students consider the simulation as "a game," but they see the importance and meaning of the work with much greater clarity after shaping the rat.

Summary (including how students are prepared and supervised): Appetitive conditioning is used. Animals press a lever to produce drops of water. They are first trained (shaped) to press the lever by delivering drops for closer and closer approximations to this behavior. Once lever pressing is well established (i.e., the animal will consistently display lever-pressing behavior), the schedule of reinforcement is changed to demonstrate that performance shifts in such a way that the number of drops received is maximized. As the number of presses required to obtain a drop is gradually increased, then the rate of pressing generally increases as well. When presses no longer produce water, the pressing ceases. When presses produce water only in one stimulus condition, the presses continue in this condition but decrease in other conditions.

Pairs or triads of students work with a rat in each half hour training session. These subgroups are drawn from the team of eight students working with the particular rat. The team works with the rat on 5 days of each week of the project, with team members rotating throughout each week. The ratio of one rat per eight students provides a good educational opportunity for the students and ensures that students who are more readily trained in appropriate animal handling and care can be distributed to teams and subgroups.

Rats are adapted to a watering regimen of half-hour access per day during the week prior to the start of the project. Rats are then trained in one half-hour session per weekday and are given their half-hour access to water in their home cages immediately following this session. They are given half-hour access to water on each weekend day as well. They are, therefore, never severely deprived of water and have an assured period of drinking each day. The project is complete in a 5-week period.

Veterinary care provided by: XX

Nonsurgical invasive manipulations performed if any: None.

Method and duration of restraint if used: None.

Method and duration of fasting animals if used: Access to water restricted for 23 hours per day for 4 weeks.

Surgical procedures used if any (indicate terminal, survival, multiple survival): None.

Anesthetics, analgesics, or tranquilizers used: None.

Neuromuscular blocking agents used: None.

Approach to alternative exercise for students judged to have valid objections: A human operant conditioning exercise (dynamically adjusting concurrent reinforcement schedules) is being developed.

APPENDIX H: INSTRUCTIONS ON THE CARE OF PIGEONS FOR PSYCHOLOGY STUDENTS

1. You are responsible for the well-being of the pigeon that is assigned to you. If your bird is not properly cared for, your privilege to perform animal experiments will be revoked. Also, you will not get good results in your experiment if your animal is not in perfect health and well maintained.

2. The animal caretaker will clean the cage and provide water for your bird.

3. YOU HAVE THE RESPONSIBILITY OF FEEDING YOUR BIRD. A BIRD THAT IS NOT FED CAN STARVE TO DEATH WITHIN 24–48 HOURS. PLEASE REMEMBER THAT YOU ARE RESPONSIBLE FOR THE LIFE OF THIS ANIMAL. THERE IS NO EXCUSE FOR PERMITTING AN ANIMAL TO GO WITHOUT FOOD BEYOND THE TIME NECESSARY FOR PROPER EXPERIMENTAL MOTIVATION.

4. Normally, the animal caretaker will feed the bird on the weekend. If you do not want your bird to be fed on the weekend because you will be coming in to train it, please put a DO NOT FEED sign on its cage. IMPORTANT: If you put a DO NOT FEED sign on a cage, YOU WILL BE RESPONSIBLE FOR THAT BIRD'S FEEDING FOR THE WEEKEND.

5. If a feed dish has stool in it, the dish must be cleaned before placing food in it.

6. Be sure that your bird always has grit available. Be sure that all trash cans and feed cans are TIGHTLY CLOSED. These cans must always have a plastic bag liner inside before feed or trash is put in them.

7. The animal's test chamber must be cleaned after each use. Clean the dropping pans and remove any accumulated feed.

8. Please do not leave trash lying about the laboratory or vivarium. Trash should always be placed in the trashcan and the lid tightly closed.

9. If your bird (or any other bird) shows signs of illness (see handout on Signs of Illness in birds), immediately notify the Animal Caretaker or Supervisor, or the Teaching Assistant (TA), or the Director of Laboratory Animal Care.

SECTION 1: IS SOMETHING WRONG WITH MY PIGEON? SIGNS OF ILLNESS

The following symptoms may indicate a serious health problem, and veterinary assistance should be sought at once.

1. Change in character of the droppings. The sick bird may exhibit the following:
   - decrease in the total number or volume of droppings;
   - change in the color of the URATES or URINE;
   - increase in the water content of the FECES (diarrhea);
   - decrease in the FECES volume with increased URATES; and
   - increase in the URINE portion (polyuria).
2. Decreased or excessive food or water consumption.
3. Change in attitude, personality, or behavior. Decreased activity, decreased talking and singing, increased sleeping, no response to stimuli, sudden taming of normally "wild" bird.
4. Change in appearance or posture. Ruffled feathers, weakness, inability to stand, staying on bottom of the cage, sitting low on the perch, drooping wings, convulsions.
5. Change in character of respiration. Any noticeable breathing movement (e.g., tail bobbing) while resting, heavy breathing after exertion, change in quality of voice, respiratory sounds such as sneezing, wheezing, or clicking.
6. Change in weight or general body condition as determined by a gram scale or by handling. A prominent breastbone due to loss of breast muscle tissue is serious!
7. Enlargement or swelling on the body.
8. Injury or bleeding.
9. Vomiting or regurgitation.
10. Discharge from nostrils, eyes, or mouth.

SECTION 2: CARE OF THE PIGEON

At the first laboratory session, you and your lab partners will be assigned a White Carneaux pigeon (*Columba livia*). It is your responsibility for the duration of the semester to ensure the well-being of your pigeon: This entails feeding and watering your bird, keeping a constant supply of grit at the bottom of the food container, and changing its droppings pan. The pigeons are housed in individual cages in a temperature and humidity controlled vivarium, with a 12-hour light/dark cycle.

Your lab instructor and animal laboratory technician will demonstrate proper handling of the pigeon, that is, how to catch, hold, and carry it. Several points should be kept in mind when handling a pigeon: (a) avoid loud noises and sudden movements; (b) when holding a pigeon, be sure to provide firm support for the bird and to keep its wings folded; (c) it is generally preferable to slowly approach the bird from above so as to intercept or inhibit flight responses. Every bird develops its own strategies for eluding you—presumably, you are clever enough to outwit it. Please remember that pigeons have hollow bones and are fragile animals. Be firm but not rough.

Your pigeon should be maintained at its running weight (RW), typically calculated as 80% to 85% of its free-feeding weight (FFW). These values (RW and FFW) have been previously ascertained and will be provided by your instructor. The bird will be given to you at or near its running weight.

Weigh the pigeon at the beginning and end of each experimental session and record these values on its weight chart. Minor fluctuations in weight are to be expected. Be sure the scale starts at zero before you weigh your bird, and that the 500-gram counterweight is set in the right notch (if it is needed). Also, be sure to subtract the weight of the holder from the weight shown on the scale.

There are two sources of food available to your bird: that which it receives from the magazine during a session, usually about 2 grams, and that which it receives from the feeder located outside its cage. As a general rule, feed your pigeon up to its RW every day (feed the bird after the session). After several days you should be able to determine the amount of food (i.e., maintenance food) needed to maintain the bird at its RW: Usually this ranges from 10 grams to15 grams per day. If you bird is under its RW, feed it the difference between its present weight and its RW. If this difference is greater than 20 grams, check with your lab instructor about the proper feeding amount. Calculate weekend feeding amount, which will be fed by the TAs, as described in class. If you bird is consistently over or under its RW on Monday, check with your TA.

SPECIAL REMINDERS:

- Never feed your bird more than 20 grams on a day before an experimental session unless approved by your TA.
- Make sure your bird always has clean, fresh water and grit in its food container (grit is essential to the pigeon's digestion and mineral intake).
- There are three variables, besides the experimental procedures, that can affect the performance of your bird. These must be carefully monitored in order to maintain the pigeon in its proper state: body weight, number of hours of food deprivation, and the amount of food given the bird the day before.

- Feed your bird at approximately the same time every day.
- If you notice anything unusual concerning the physical condition of your pigeon, see your lab instructor or the professor immediately!

APPENDIX I: SAMPLE INSTITUTIONAL ANIMAL CARE AND USE COMMITTEE PROTOCOLS FOR LEARNING COURSES

SAMPLE PROTOCOL 1:

SECTION 1

Title: Spatial and Nonspatial Working Memory in Long-Evans Rats

STARTING DATE: _____
PROJECTED COMPLETION DATE: _____
PRINCIPAL INVESTIGATOR:
DEPARTMENT:
ADDRESS:
TELEPHONE:
RESEARCH ASSISTANTS (students or technicians):
1.
2.

I. CATEGORY OF RESEARCH (Check appropriate category):
    _____A. Animals covered by the Animal Welfare Regulations. (Category A is to be completed by Institutional Animal Care and Use Committee [IACUC] and Research Assistant only.)
    _____B. Animals being bred, conditioned, or held for use in teaching, testing, experiments, research, or surgery but not yet used for such purposes.
    _____C. Animals upon which teaching, research, experiments, or tests are conducted involving no pain, distress, or use of pain-relieving drugs.
    _____D. Animals upon which experiments, teaching, research, surgery, or tests are conducted involving accompanying pain or distress to the animals and for which appropriate anesthetic, analgesic, or tranquilizing drugs are used.
    _____E. Animals upon which experiments, teaching, research, surgery, or tests are conducted involving accompanying pain or distress to the animals and for which the use of appropriate anesthetic, analgesic, or tranquilizing drugs will adversely affect the procedures, results, or interpretation of the teaching, research, experiments, surgery, or tests.

II. ANIMAL CHARACTERISTICS AND HOUSING NEEDS
    SPECIES: *Rattus rattus*.

STRAIN/BREED: Long-Evans.

SEX: Male.

WEIGHT: 200–500 g.

VENDOR: Hilltop Laboratories C.

OTHER CHARACTERISTICS (e.g., diabetic, immunosuppressed, etc.): None.

TOTAL NUMBER: 16.

AVERAGE DAILY INVENTORY: 16.

CAGING OR HOUSING: One rat per polycarbonate cage.

DESIRED FEED (State standard or specific type): Standard rat chow.

LIGHTING CYCLE (State standard or specific cycle): Standard.

ROOM TEMPERATURE (State standard or specific temperature): Standard.

III.   BIOHAZARDOUS MATERIAL

If the animal use involves biohazardous materials, then the appropriate category should be checked. Attach a detailed list of safety procedures and a copy of your approval letter(s) or permit(s). Mark all pertinent categories:

Not applicable: X

SECTION 2

INSTRUCTIONS: The following information is requested by the Committee pursuant to its charge by the Public Health Service (PHS) Policy on Humane Care and Use of Laboratory Animals. Answer each section completely. If the question is not appropriate to your protocol, answer NA. Answers must be provided on these sheets and not simply provided in an attachment (e.g., grant proposal).

I.   PURPOSE OF THE STUDY

A.   State: (a) specific scientific objectives and goals, and (b) value of the study to biomedical research. Does this project have a primary purpose of teaching or research?

1.   This study will explore the existence of mnemonic capabilities required to successfully complete spatial and nonspatial working-memory tasks in Long-Evans rats.

2.   The value of this study to biomedical research lies in the innovation of an improved methodology to study working memory in rats.

3.   If rats can indeed perform (a) the nonmatching-to-sample task and (b) the radial-arm maze analog problem, then this model may prove to be a valuable tool in studying brain-damage-produced amnesia in a viable rat model. This study's primary purpose is research.

B. Give a general outline of the experimental protocol to include timing of all procedures, drugs, treatments, treatment groups, and so forth.

Subjects. Subjects will be 12 Long-Evans rats, about 8 weeks old at the start of the study. The rats will first be placed on a free-feeding regimen. When their free-feeding weights are stable, they will be placed on a restricted food regimen by limiting their daily intake to 15 grams per day. The restriction will be arranged to maintain the rats at 80% of ad lib weight. On a daily basis, limited numbers of food pellets will be available as reinforcement during sessions lasting approximately 1 hour, and free food will be available after sessions to maintain their 80% ad lib weight. Food deprivation is a standard and widely accepted research practice with Long-Evans rats, ensuring that food will be an effective reinforcer during experimental sessions. It is not anticipated that the rats will suffer significant discomfort because of this operation. Throughout procedures the rats will have constant access to water at their home cage.

Experiment 1. The purpose of this experiment is to ascertain whether an oddity performance can be established with a nose-poke response. Four rats will learn to perform nose pokes through openings in an aluminum plate placed in front of an infrared touch screen and computer monitor. The nose poke will not require touching a surface, but rather only extend far enough to break the infrared beams projected in front of the monitor surface. An image will appear on the monitor screen, and nose pokes toward the image will be reinforced. Reinforcers will be 1 gram Noyes pellets. During this and remaining parts of the study, rats will receive postsession feeding to maintain 85% ad lib weight. (Anticipated duration of this condition is two sessions). Once the rats reliably poke through the plate at the image, they will be switched onto a trial-based nonmatching-to-sample task. During this procedure, a sample image will appear at a central position on the screen. The rat is then required to nose poke this image to produce a novel nonmatching image and the sample image. A nose poke to the nonmatching image will produce a food pellet. Training will occur 6 days a week during the light phase of the rats' 12:12 light/dark cycle. Sessions will last about 1 hour each day.

Experiment 2. The purpose of this experiment is to build a rat chamber analog of the radial-arm maze using nose-poke responses rather than locomotion. Four rats will learn to perform nose pokes through openings in an aluminum plate placed in front of an infrared touch screen and computer monitor. As in Experiment 1, the nose poke will only extend far enough to break the infrared beams. An image will appear on the monitor screen, and nose pokes toward the image will be reinforced. Reinforcers will consist of 1 gram Noyes pellets. During this and remaining parts of the study, rats will receive postsession feeding to maintain 85% ad lib weight. (Anticipated duration of this condition is two sessions). Once the rats reliably poke at the image, they will be switched onto a trial-based radial-arm maze analog. During this procedure, six images (analogous to the six arms of a radial maze) will appear at different positions on the screen. The rat is then required to nose poke at the images. Once an image is poked, a pellet is dispensed, followed by a 20-second time out during which the screen will be darkened. The rat can then similarly earn pellets by poking at the remaining five images. Every poke to an already visited stimulus, however, will produce a 20-second time out. Once all six stimuli have been visited, a 2-minute intertrial interval will be followed by a new trial. Training will occur 6 days a week during the light phase of the rats' 12:12 light/dark cycle. Sessions will last about 1 hour each day.

II. RATIONALE FOR THE USE OF LIVING VERTEBRATE ANIMALS

A. Are methods available whereby the scientific or teaching goals of this project can be as effectively achieved without the use of live animals? Why or why not?

No. The scientific goals of this project cannot be met without the use of live animals. Knowledge of the particular condition that gives rise to nonspatial working memory is lacking. Moreover, the rigor required to answer the question could not be achieved with human subjects.

B. Justify the appropriateness of species or strain to be used in this study.

Long-Evans rats have been used in the very limited number of attempts to study nonmatching-to-sample procedures. They have been chosen for this study because they represent a species that has moderate difficulty in acquiring matching-to-sample behavior and because of their longevity.

C. Justify the number of animals requested.

Previous studies find high intersubject reliability with few animals. The usual number of animals in such studies is about four per group.

III. PREVIOUS APPROVAL: Has this protocol or any part been previously approved by the IACUC? If yes, when?

Yes, I was approved in 1995.

IV. ANIMAL PROCEDURES

A. Injections, immunizations, medications, or other drugs used in the study separate from anesthetics, analgesics, or agents used for euthanasia:
None.

B. Tissue collection procedures (include tissue removed and method):
Not applicable.

C. Blood collection (include method, amount, and frequency):
Not applicable.

D. Surgical procedures: List specific operation(s) and note if animals will have multiple survival operations. In cases of survival surgery, describe specific aseptic techniques that will be used.
Not applicable.

E. Postoperative care and monitoring (frequency and method):
Not applicable.

F. Analgesics, hypnotics, sedatives and tranquilizers, anesthesia, euthanasia:
Medications: None.
Anesthesia: None.
Euthanasia:
Drug name: Pentobarbital sodium.
Dose: 1/1000 ml/gram.
Route: Intraperitoneal.
Concentration: 6 grains/ml.

G. Use of restraints (device, duration, frequency of use, adaptation method):
Not applicable.

H. Other procedures (e.g., irradiation, tumor inoculation, chemical exposure, behavioral testing, etc.):
Not applicable.

I. Painful or distressful procedures:
1. Will any procedures be done that produce pain or distress without the use of appropriate analgesics or anesthetics?
Food deprivation will be arranged to reduce rat's ad lib weight to 80%.
If so, how will the animal be monitored for pain and distress?
We will monitor activity levels and general health.

2. What methods will be used to reduce the time period of pain and distress?
Not applicable.

3. What is the scientific justification for all procedures that cause more than slight or momentary pain or discomfort that are performed without sedation, analgesia, or anesthesia?
Food deprivation is a standard procedure required to establish food pellets as reinforcers.

V. ASSURANCES

A. Assurance is provided, as required by federal regulations, that alternative procedures have been considered for any procedure likely to produce pain or distress in an experimental animal and no other procedures are suitable. The following alternative procedures were considered (and rejected) related to this assurance:

Water deprivation was considered but rejected because it increases the risk of urinary tract infections.

The experiment does not unnecessarily duplicate previous experiments. The following reference sources confirm this assurance:

(Twenty-four references follow)

The following techniques will be used to minimize pain and discomfort to the animals:

No techniques will be used to minimize the discomfort of food deprivation.

B. The Principal Investigator provides assurance that he or she is familiar with the animal care and use requirements of the Public Health Service (NIH *Guide for Grants and Contracts*, vol. 143, no. 8, June 25, 1985, or the PHS *Guide for the Care and Use of Laboratory Animals*), the Code of Federal Regulations (Title 9), and Davidson College policies for animal care and use, and that this investigation will be conducted in accordance with those guidelines and regulations.

C. The Principal Investigator certifies that he or she is qualified to conduct or direct the animal research outlined in this protocol and accepts responsibility for maintaining standards of animal care required by the Animal Welfare Act.

Signature of Principal Investigator	Date
Signature of Department Chair	Date
Signature of IACUC Chair	Date

Date of full approval: _____
Date of approval termination: _____
Date of addendum approval(s): _____
Date of audit: _____
Deficiencies: _____ Yes _____ No

SAMPLE PROTOCOL 2:

SECTION 1

Title: Foraging in Pigeons

STARTING DATE: _____
PROJECTED COMPLETION DATE: _____
PRINCIPAL INVESTIGATOR:
DEPARTMENT:
ADDRESS:
TELEPHONE:
RESEARCH ASSISTANTS (students or technicians):
1.
2.
I. CATEGORY OF RESEARCH (Check appropriate category):
    _____ A. Animals covered by the Animal Welfare Regulations. (Category A is to be completed by IACUC and Research Assistant only.)
    _____ B. Animals being bred, conditioned, or held for use in teaching, testing, experiments, research, or surgery but not yet used for such purposes.
    _____ C. Animals upon which teaching, research, experiments, or tests are conducted involving no pain, distress, or use of pain-relieving drugs.
    _____ D. Animals upon which experiments, teaching, research, surgery, or tests are conducted involving accompanying pain or distress to the animals and for which appropriate anesthetic, analgesic, or tranquilizing drugs are used.
    _____ E. Animals upon which experiments, teaching, research, surgery, or tests are conducted involving accompanying pain or distress to the animals and for which the use of appropriate anesthetic, analgesic, or tranquilizing drugs will adversely affect the procedures, results, or interpretation of the teaching, research, experiments, surgery, or tests.
III. ANIMAL CHARACTERISTICS AND HOUSING NEEDS
    SPECIES: *Columba livia.*
    STRAIN/BREED: Homer.
    SEX: Male and Female.
    WEIGHT: 200-400 g.
    VENDOR: Local breeders.
    OTHER CHARACTERISTICS (e.g., diabetic, immunosuppressed, etc.):
    None.
    TOTAL NUMBER: 12.
    AVERAGE DAILY INVENTORY: 12.

CAGING OR HOUSING: One pigeon per stainless steel cage.

DESIRED FEED (State standard or specific type): Purina racing pigeon checkers.

LIGHTING CYCLE (State standard or specific cycle): Standard.

ROOM TEMPERATURE (State standard or specific temperature): Standard.

IV. BIOHAZARDOUS MATERIAL

If the animal use involves biohazardous materials, then the appropriate category should be checked. Attach a detailed list of safety procedures and a copy of your approval letter(s) or permit(s). Mark all pertinent categories:

Not applicable: X

SECTION 2

INSTRUCTIONS: The following information is requested by the Committee pursuant to its charge by the Public Health Service (PHS) Policy on Humane Care and Use of Laboratory Animals. Answer each section completely. If the question is not appropriate to your protocol, answer NA. Answers must be provided on these sheets and not simply provided in an attachment (e.g., grant proposal).

I. PURPOSE OF THE STUDY

A. State: (a) specific scientific objectives and goals, and (b) value of the study to biomedical research. Does this project have a primary purpose of teaching or research?

1. This study will examine properties of foraging behavior in pigeons: (a) what pigeons learn about the locations of scattered food, (b) factors that affect memory for the location of food, (c) the role of finding food in the recognition that a food site has been visited, and (d) the structure of foraging behavior over time.

2. This study makes no direct contribution to biomedical research, but it will help to understand basic processes of learning.

3. This study's primary purpose is research, but parts of it will be conducted during the course of an undergraduate laboratory in learning and cognition.

B. Give a general outline of the experimental protocol to include timing of all procedures, drugs, treatments, treatment groups, and so forth.

Subjects. Subjects will be 8 Homer pigeons, about 3 years old at the start of the study. The pigeons will first be placed on a free-feeding regimen. When their free-feeding weights are stable, they will be placed on a restricted food regimen by limiting their daily intake to 5 grams per day. The restriction will be arranged to maintain the pigeons at 80% of ad lib weight. On a daily basis, a limited amount of food will be available as reinforcement during sessions, and free food will be available after sessions to maintain their 80% ad lib weight. Food deprivation is a standard and widely accepted research practice with pigeons, ensuring that food will be an effective reinforcer during experimental sessions. It is not anticipated that the pigeons will suffer significant discomfort because of this operation. Throughout procedures, the pigeons will have constant access to water at their home cage.

General procedure. Pigeons will serve in daily experimental sessions lasting approximately 1 hour. Pigeons will learn to peck at stimuli presented on a computer monitor. Pecks will be recorded by an infrared touch screen placed over the monitor. The pigeon's pecks will occasionally produce Purina pigeon checkers (commercial pigeon food) reinforcers. Each procedure will use three pigeons.

Experiment 1. Maze learning. This procedure will arrange a virtual analog of the radial-arm maze frequently studied with rats. During this procedure, six images (analogous to the six arms of a radial maze) will appear at different positions on the screen. The pigeon is then required to peck at the images. Once an image is pecked, food is dispensed, followed by a 16-second time out during which the screen will be darkened. The pigeon can then similarly earn food by pecking at the remaining five images. Pecks to already visited stimuli, however, will produce a 16-second time out. Once pigeons show stable and accurate performances, tests will be conducted to explore what the pigeons have learned about the maze problem. For these tests, trials will be arranged in which the positions and appearances of stimuli will be altered, or food will be withheld for choosing particular stimuli. These tests will attempt to ascertain what pigeons have learned about the task, that is, whether they learn about stimulus appearances or positions.

Experiment 2. Spatial versus nonspatial mazes. This study will examine whether they can learn to forage in situations that force them to learn about stimulus appearance versus mazes that force them to learn about stimulus positions. Thus, in the first case, we will arrange a task in which the stimuli signaling food are distinctive colors, but their positions on the touch screen are highly variable. The performance of pigeons in this condition will be compared to that of pigeons that are exposed to identical stimuli with fixed positions on the touch screen.

Experiment 3. Short-term memory in mazes. Studies in the foraging literature (e.g., Zentall et al., 1990) suggest that pigeons in tasks like that in Experiment 1 use different memory strategies to solve such a problem depending on where they are in the problem. For example, if they have just begun a foraging task, they use a prospective memory strategy, remembering places that have not yet been visited. If instead they are finishing a task, they use a retrospective memory strategy, remembering places that have already been visited. These inferences about memory strategies have been made by interrupting closely spaced foraging problems and seeing what pigeons remember about the interrupted problem. This study will examine whether such findings are better explained by an interference effect between problems. This will be explored by manipulating the time between foraging problems. For example, evidence for an interference effect would be provided if such effects are obtained when the time between foraging problems is short, but not when it is long.

Experiment 4. Stimulus properties of behavior in a running memory task. This study seeks to determine whether remembering a previous choice shows characteristics of visual short-term memory (STM). A typical STM experiment with pigeons is carried out in a chamber with three responses. For example, an upper response area is first illuminated with a red or green light. The pigeon is then required to peck at this stimulus sample, thus making an observing response to the to-be-remembered stimulus. The peck darkens the light for a retention interval of a few seconds. Following the retention interval, two lower response areas are illuminated, one with red and the other with green. If the top light was red, then pecks to the red light are reinforced; if the top light was green, then pecks to the green light are reinforced. In such tasks, the strength of a visual short-term memory is directly related to how it signals a delay to reinforcement. Thus, if T is the time between reinforcers, d is the time between the onset of a sample and a reinforcer, and t is a retention interval, then the strength of memory is directly related to the quantity $(T - d)/t$. This experiment proposes to examine whether running memory shows this STM relation. The running-memory task we are exploring is an analog of the alternation problem frequently studied with rats. In the problem we will study with pigeons, at the start of a trial, the subject will be presented with left and right response boxes. The pigeon will be forced to choose one of the boxes on the first trial (i.e., only pecks to one will be reinforced), on the next trial, selection of the other box will be reinforced, and so on. Thus, the pigeon is required to alternate from trial to trial. Once pigeons acquire the alternation problem, we will systematically vary the T and d parameters of the task (we will assume that t is a constant). If pigeons are more accurate with larger T – d values, then we may assume that running memory is functionally analogous to visual STM.

II. RATIONALE FOR THE USE OF LIVING VERTEBRATE ANIMALS

   A. Are methods available whereby the scientific or teaching goals of this project can be as effectively achieved without the use of live animals? Why or why not?

     No. The scientific goals of this project cannot be met without the use of live animals. Knowledge of the particular condition that gives rise to nonspatial working memory is lacking. Moreover, the rigor required to answer the question could not be achieved with human subjects.

   B. Justify the appropriateness of species or strain to be used in this study.

     Pigeons have been used in the very limited number of attempts to study maze-learning procedures. They have been chosen for this study because they represent a species that has moderate difficulty in acquiring matching-to-sample behavior and because of their longevity.

   C. Justify the number of animals requested.

     Previous studies find high intersubject reliability with few animals. The usual number of animals in such studies is about four per group.

III. PREVIOUS APPROVAL: Has this protocol or any part been previously approved by the IACUC? If yes, when?

   No.

IV. ANIMAL PROCEDURES

   A. Injections, immunizations, medications, or other drugs used in the study separate from anesthetics, analgesics, or agents used for euthanasia:

     Not applicable.

   B. Tissue collection procedures (include tissue removed and method):

     Not applicable.

   C. Blood collection (include method, amount and frequency):

     Not applicable.

   D. Surgical procedures: List specific operation(s) and note whether animals will have multiple survival operations. In cases of survival surgery, describe specific aseptic techniques that will be used.

     Not applicable.

   E. Postoperative care and monitoring (frequency and method):

     Not applicable.

   F. Analgesics, hypnotics, sedatives and tranquilizers, anesthesia, euthanasia:

     Medications: Not applicable.

Anesthesia: Not applicable.

Euthanasia:

Drug name: Pentobarbital sodium.

Dose: 1/1000 ml/gram.

Route: Intraperitoneal.

Concentration: 6 grains/ml.

G. Use of restraints (device, duration, frequency of use, adaptation method):

Not applicable.

H. Other procedures (e.g., irradiation, tumor inoculation, chemical exposure, behavioral testing, etc.):

Not applicable.

I. Painful or Distressful Procedures

1. Will any procedures be done that produce pain or distress without the use of appropriate analgesics or anesthetics?

Food deprivation will be arranged to reduce pigeon's ad lib weight to 80%.

If so, how will the animal be monitored for pain and distress?

We will monitor activity levels and general health.

2. What methods will be used to reduce the time period of pain and/or distress?

Not applicable.

3. What is the scientific justification for all procedures that cause more than slight or momentary pain or discomfort that are performed without sedation, analgesia, or anesthesia?

Food deprivation is a standard procedure required to establish food pellets as reinforcers.

V. ASSURANCES

A. Assurance is provided, as required by federal regulations, that:

Alternative procedures have been considered for any procedure likely to produce pain or distress in an experimental animal and no other procedures are suitable. The following alternative procedures were considered (and rejected) related to this assurance:

Water deprivation was considered but rejected because it increases the risk of urinary tract infections.

The experiment does not unnecessarily duplicate previous experiments. The following reference sources confirm this assurance:

(Ninety-seven references follow:)

The following techniques will be used to minimize pain and discomfort to the animals:

No techniques will be used to minimize the discomfort of food deprivation.

B. The Principal Investigator provides assurance that he or she is familiar with the animal care and use requirements of the Public

Health Service (NIH *Guide for Grants and Contracts*, vol. 143, no. 8, June 25, 1985, or the PHS *Guide for the Care and Use of Laboratory Animals*), the Code of Federal Regulations (Title 9), and Davidson College policies for animal care and use, and that this investigation will be conducted in accordance with those guidelines and regulations.

C. The Principal Investigator certifies that he or she is qualified to conduct or direct the animal research outlined in this protocol and accepts responsibility for maintaining standards of animal care required by the Animal Welfare Act.

_____   _____
Signature of Principal Investigator   Date

_____   _____
Signature of Department Chair   Date

_____   _____
Signature of IACUC Chair   Date
Date of full approval: _____
Date of approval termination: _____
Date of addendum approval(s): _____
Date of audit: _____
Deficiencies: _____ Yes _____ No

SAMPLE PROTOCOL 3:

Title: Learning and Cognition Laboratory Experimental Project: Equivalence in Pigeons

General Guidelines for the Experiment

This experiment requires running pigeons for the purpose of generating an American Psychological Association (APA)-style poster and brief report at the end of the semester. You are responsible for data collection, analysis, and writing. After reading this handout, you should begin to familiarize yourself with the research question by examining background papers and assembling an annotated bibliography (see Catania, 1980, for an example). You should also begin to write the Method section of your report.

You will only have an opportunity to collect a few data by the quit time. This experiment, like most single-subject projects with nonhuman animal subjects, may take years to complete. Your results section will describe all previous data you and others have collected up to November 21, the last day you will be required to run your pigeon.

Your discussion will speak to the data you collected and previously collected data. You should provide closure by summarizing findings in APA-style figures and tables. How do your anticipated findings relate to the existing literature; what are their theoretical implications? Possibilities and rationale for future research, and possible practical applications should also be discussed.

The end result of this experiment will be an APA-style poster (based on a partial data set because the study will not be completed when the report is due), and an accompanying APA-style manuscript handout, about 10 pages in length. The poster will present an encapsulated report stressing the research question and major findings, while your handout should contain the same in greater detail (e.g., including summary data tables). This report represents 20%, or 40 points, of your final grade. Evaluation of this report will stress the visual presentation of data: how creative you are in discovering and economically portraying meaningful relations between variables. This report will be based on five primary readings. The handout will contain APA-style report sections including a brief introduction, a complete method section and results, figures and tables, and a brief discussion. Visual analysis and corresponding interpretation are 40% of the project, the text and presentation will account for 20%, and the handout will account for the final 40% of the assignment.

Method for Equivalence in Pigeons

Subjects. Subjects are two Homer pigeons (*Columba livia*) of mixed genders, about 1 year old at the start of the study. Prior to beginning the research, pigeons were maintained for 3 weeks under free-feeding conditions to determine their ad lib weights. They were reduced to 80% of their ad lib weights by reducing their grain intake to 5 grams per day. Feeding after that time was adjusted to maintain them at 80% of ad lib weight. Throughout procedures, the pigeons have constant access to fresh water at their home cage.

Apparatus. Experiment control was accomplished with a 386DX 40 mhz computer. Stimuli were presented to pigeons on a 15-inch VGA color monitor displaying 16,000,000 colors on a 320×200 pixel array. Pigeons' responses were recorded on a 12-inch Carrol-Touch infrared touch screen placed in front of the monitor. The resolution of the touch screen was 78×58. Pigeons ran in a $24 \times 24 \times 18$ inch box juxtaposed to the monitor. A pigeon feeder with a 2×2 inch opening was located, perpendicular and to the right of the monitor display, approximately 2 inches from the chamber floor. The feeder was white illuminated during operation.

Pretraining. Pigeons first learned to peck at a three-centimeter white disk projected on a computer monitor by reinforcing successive approximations to the peck. Reinforcer durations were adjusted to maintain pigeons at approximately 80% ad lib weight.

Matching-to-sample pretraining. Once the pigeons reliably pecked at the disk, they were switched onto a trial-based task approximating symbolic matching to sample. During this procedure, a sample colored square appeared at 1 of 12 locations on the computer screen. The first observing response to the sample after a 4-second fixed interval (FI 4 s) caused the sample to disappear and a single, different colored square comparison to appear at another location on the screen. The first response to the comparison after an FI 4 s operated the feeder. Trials in this and the remaining conditions were separated by a 40-second intertrial-interval (40 s ITI). Stimuli in this and remaining conditions will be 58 millimeters wide by 55 millimeters high.

Matching to sample. The pigeons were then exposed to the same set of five pairs of symbolically related stimuli. The sample stimuli comprised colored geometric patterns and the comparison stimuli were digitized colored images (an experimental chamber, a dog, a pigeon's head, a human hand, a bonobo, and B. F. Skinner). During a trial, a sample stimulus appeared (e.g., a triangle), and a peck produced four comparisons, including the symbolically related comparison. A correction procedure was arranged for incorrect responses; with error trials repeated after a 50-second time out.

Testing. Tests will be arranged with new sample and comparison pairs to examine whether exclusion responding will be shown (given a new sample, choosing a new comparison), symmetry (correct responding given a reversal in the roles of sample and comparison stimuli), identity (correct responding given identical sample and comparison stimuli) and to examine the nature of the pigeons' performance. For example, one test will examine the role of the correction procedure in the pigeons' choices. Thus, if we repeat error trials in the correction procedure, but scramble stimulus positions, how will we affect the pigeons' accuracy?

Potential Questions

Do we have evidence of symmetry or identity in any of the pigeons? Have the pigeons adopted a strategy to maximize reinforcement? If so, what strategy?

General Instructions for Running Pigeons in the Experiment: Pigeon Care

Handling. Pigeons must be handled with care. There are a few basic rules for handling pigeons: (a) When capturing a pigeon from a chamber or its home cage, do not hesitate—you must reach in and quickly trap the bird; (b) always fold the wings against their body; (c) hold them with two hands, or pressed against your body with one hand; (d) release them slowly so that they walk out of your hands; (e) always close the door in the room you are handling the bird so that it cannot escape far. Birds are injured when they are held by a single wing or foot—never grab a bird in flight. If a bird should escape, move it toward a corner and throw a lab coat over it. Report any rough handling to the instructor.

Feeding. Pigeons are maintained at a body weight, which approximates that of a wild bird. Their weight is maintained at 80% of their free-feeding weight to ensure that food will be reinforcing during sessions. Pigeons must receive food every day and fresh water every day. Fresh water must be provided every day after its session. If a pigeon has run in an experiment and it is more than 80% ad lib weight, then it receives water only. If a pigeon has run in an experiment and it is under 80% ad lib weight, then it receives food and water.

Housing. The pigeon cages should be clean at all times. Report dirty cages or food and water cups to the instructor.

Health. It is not unusual to see small abrasions on pigeons, particularly on their beaks. Drooping wings or fluffed up feathers usually mean something serious. Report cuts, abrasions, or unusual behavior to the instructor.

Laboratory Guidelines

The laboratory is a quiet place when research is in progress: Do not talk loudly, never talk in the experimental chamber area when birds are running, and be very quiet when handling equipment in the chamber area. Everyone must do their part in keep the laboratory clean. Please contribute to the cleaning every day. Do not take food or drink in the chamber area, and do not place food or drink on the computer tables. Always leave lab lights on during research times. Always wear a lab coat in the animal-housing areas.

Running a Session

1–7. Turn on the power switch . . . (how to turn on the equipment and start a session).

8. Retrieve your pigeon from its home cage, check to make sure you have the right bird by looking at its band number, and get its weight to within 1 gram. Put the pigeon in the chamber that corresponds to the computer. Make sure the Rubbermaid box aligns with the computer screen.

8. Type <the pigeon's weight> and press <ENTER>.

9–10. If you are ready to begin, press <y>, and . . . (how to end the session).

11. Retrieve your pigeon from the chamber, check to make sure you have the right chamber by looking at its number, and get the pigeon's weight to within 1 gram. Put the pigeon back in its home cage, making sure the pigeon's band number corresponds to the number on the home cage.

12–14. Type <the pigeon's weight> and press <ENTER> then . . . (how to end the day).

REFERENCE

Catania, A. C. (1980). Operant theory: Skinner. In G. M. Gazda & R. Corsini (Eds.), *Comparative theories of learning* (pp. 135–177). Itasca, IL: F. E. Peacock.

APPENDIX J: SAMPLE INSTITUTIONAL ANIMAL CARE AND USE COMMITTEE PROTOCOLS FOR COURSES IN PHYSIOLOGICAL PSYCHOLOGY

SAMPLE PROTOCOL 1:

SECTION 1

Title: Effects of Entorhinal Cortex Lesions on Differential Reinforcement of Low Rate Response Performance in Rats

STARTING DATE: _____
PROJECTED COMPLETION DATE: _____
PRINCIPAL INVESTIGATOR:
DEPARTMENT:
ADDRESS:
TELEPHONE:
RESEARCH ASSISTANTS (students or technicians):
1.
2.
I. CATEGORY OF RESEARCH (Check appropriate category)
    _____ A. Animals covered by the Animal Welfare Regulations. (Category A is to be completed by Institutional Animal Care and Use Committee [IACUC] and research assistant only.)
    _____ B. Animals being bred, conditioned, or held for use in teaching, testing, experiments, research, or surgery but not yet used for such purposes.
    _____ C. Animals upon which teaching, research, experiments, or tests are conducted involving no pain, distress, or use of pain-relieving drugs.
    _____ D. Animals upon which experiments, teaching, research, surgery, or tests are conducted involving accompanying pain or distress to the animals and for which appropriate anesthetic, analgesic, or tranquilizing drugs are used.
    _____ E. Animals upon which experiments, teaching, research, surgery, or tests are conducted involving accompanying pain or distress to the animals and for which the use of appropriate anesthetic, analgesic, or tranquilizing drugs will adversely affect the procedures, results, or interpretation of the teaching, research, experiments, surgery, or tests.

II. ANIMAL CHARACTERISTICS AND HOUSING NEEDS
SPECIES: *Rattus norvegicus*.
STRAIN/BREED: Sprague-Dawley.
SEX: Male.
WEIGHT: 400 grams.
VENDOR: Hilltop.
OTHER CHARACTERISTICS (e.g., diabetic, immunosuppressed, etc.):
TOTAL NUMBER: 200.
AVERAGE DAILY INVENTORY: 20.
CAGING OR HOUSING: Individually.
DESIRED FEED (State standard? or specific type): Standard.
LIGHTING CYCLE (State standard? or specific cycle): Standard room.
TEMPERATURE (State "standard? or specific temperature): Standard.

III. BIOHAZARDOUS MATERIAL
If the animal use involves biohazardous materials, then the appropriate category should be checked. Attach a detailed list of safety procedures and a copy of your approval letter(s) or permit(s). Mark all pertinent categories:
Infectious agents ___; Carcinogens ___; Radioisotopes ___; Recombinant DNA ___; Other biohazards (list):
Not applicable: X

SECTION 2

INSTRUCTIONS: The following information is requested by the committee pursuant to its charge by the Public Health Service (PHS) Policy on Humane Care and Use of Laboratory Animals. Answer each section completely. If the question is not appropriate to your protocol, answer NA. Answers must be provided on these sheets and not simply provided in an attachment (e.g., grant proposal).

I. PURPOSE OF THE STUDY
A. State: (a) specific scientific objectives and goals, and (b) value of the study to biomedical research. Does this project have a primary purpose of teaching or research?

To determine whether the entorhinal cortex, fimbria-fornix, or the hippocampal formation of rats is involved in differential reinforcement of low rate response (DRL) performance. The project has relevance to understanding the role of hippocampal connectivity in the brains of individuals with Alzheimer's disease. It is unclear whether the neural changes going on in the hippocampus of patients with Alzheimer's disease are debilitative, compensatory, or insignificant. We hope to get at this question by manipulating the connectivity in the hippocampus of rats as a model preparation for the events that occur in the brains of individuals with Alzheimer's.

B. Give a general outline of the experimental protocol to include timing of all procedures, drugs, treatments, treatment groups, and so forth.

Design. 200 male Sprague-Dawley rats will be purchased from Hilltop Labs. The rats will be 2.5 months old on arrival to the laboratory, will be housed individually, and will be maintained on a 14h:10h day–night cycle. After the rats have had 1 week to adapt to their home cages, the amount of food given to them will be gradually reduced until they reach 90% of their normal weight. The animals will be randomly assigned to one of six conditions: (a) Sham Group (S); (b) Total Entorhinal Group (TE); (c) Unilateral Entorhinal Group (LE); (d) Unilateral Entorhinal Group and TRANS; (e) Fimbria-fornix Lesions (FFX); or (f) Hippocampal Commissure Transection (TRANS). Compared with last year's request, we are requesting an additional 100 rats for this experiment to ensure an adequate yield for performing our statistical analyses. Properly placed lesions in all the animals done to date has been elusive; we therefore need additional animals to improve our yields.

Apparatus. All behavioral testing will be conducted in four Lafayette Rat Operant Chambers housed in sound-attenuating enclosures. One wall of each operant chamber has a centrally located response lever flanked on the right by a trough containing a food well. Microcomputers located in the lab will control the operant chambers and collect all behavioral data.

Behavioral testing. The rats will be preoperatively trained to bar-press on a CRF operant schedule for 2 days in 50-minute sessions. Subsequently, the rats will be switched to a fixed ratio (FR) requiring two bar presses for a reinforcement (FR 2) for 1 day and then trained on a DRL 20 schedule. Each session will be terminated when 50 reinforcements are obtained, or at the end of a 50-minute period. Preoperative training on DRL 20 will continue until the rats exhibit a daily efficiency score (number of reinforced lever presses/total number of lever presses in that session x 100 [cf. Johnson, et al., 1977]) of at least 20% for 5 consecutive days. On reaching criterion performance, the rats will sustain surgery and will be retested beginning 2 days later. Postoperative DRL 20 testing will continue for 30 consecutive days.

II. RATIONALE FOR THE USE OF LIVING VERTEBRATE ANIMALS
  A. Are methods available whereby the scientific or teaching goals of this project can be achieved without the use of live animals? Why or why not?

  To determine how the entorhinal cortex (EC) is involved in DRL performance, researchers must use living animals with lesions. There is at present no computer model that will provide us with this information.

B. Justify the appropriateness of species or strain to be used in this study.

Rats are the species that have traditionally been used for this kind of study.

C. Justify the number of animals requested.

This number is the minimum necessary to make statistically meaningful statements about the role of the entorhinal area in DRL performance.

III. PREVIOUS APPROVAL: Has this protocol or any part been previously approved by the IACUC? If yes, when?

Yes, 1992.

IV. ANIMAL PROCEDURES

A. Injections, immunizations, medications, or other drugs used in the study separate from anesthetics, analgesics or agents used for euthanasia:

Material: ATROPINE.

Frequency: BEFORE SURGERY.

Dose: 0.1 cc/400 gm.

Route: I.P.

Concentration: 1%.

B. Tissue collection procedures (include tissue removed and method): *Histology*. At the termination of testing, the rats will be given an overdose of Nembutal and perfused transcardially with physiological saline (0.9%) followed by 10% buffered formalin. Every sixth section will be stained with cresyl violet acetate to determine lesion placement and extent, and every seventh section will be processed with AChE histochemistry and qualitatively analyzed to confirm sprouting by the septodentate and C/A inputs to the dentate gyrus.

C. Blood collection (include method, amount, and frequency):

D. Surgical procedures: List specific operation(s) and note if animals will have multiple survival operations. In cases of survival surgery, describe specific aseptic used in the study separate from anesthetics, analgesics, or agents used for euthanasia:

The rats receive lesions of the entorhinal cortex, fimbria-fornix, or hippocampal commissure. All surgical tools are chemically sterilized before each use. The surgical area is wiped down with 70% ethanol before surgery. The surgeons wear latex gloves and lab coats throughout the procedures.

E. Postoperative care and monitoring (frequency and method):

My research team and my students look in on the animal regularly after surgery. The animal's weights are regularly taken.

F. Analgesics, hypnotics, sedatives and tranquilizers, anesthesia, euthanasia:

Anesthesia: Nembutal.

>   Drug name: Sodium pentobarbital.
>
>   Frequency: At surgery.
>
>   Dose: 50 mg/kg I.P.
>
>   Route: I.P.
>
>   Concentration: 50 mg/cc.

Euthanasia: Nembutal.

>   Drug name: Sodium pentobarbital.
>
>   Dose: At surgery.
>
>   Route: I.P.
>
>   Concentration: 50 mg/cc.

G. Use of restraints (device, duration, frequency of use, adaptation method):

Not applicable.

H. Other procedures (e.g., irradiation, tumor inoculation, chemical exposure, behavioral testing, etc.):

Not applicable.

I. Painful or distressful procedures:

1. Will any procedures be done that produce pain or distress without the use of appropriate analgesics or anesthetics?

    No.

    If so, how will the animal be monitored for pain and distress?

    Not applicable.

2. What methods will be used to reduce the time period of pain or distress?

    Not applicable.

3. What is the scientific justification for all procedures that cause more than slight or momentary pain or discomfort that are performed without sedation, analgesia, or anesthesia?

    Not applicable.

V. ASSURANCES

A. Assurance is provided, as required by federal regulations, that alternative procedures have been considered for any procedure likely to produce pain or distress in an experimental animal and no other procedures are suitable. The following alternative procedures were considered (and rejected) related to this assurance:

The experiment does not unnecessarily duplicate previous experiments. The following reference sources confirm this assurance:

>   See 1992 National Institute for Mental Health grant application for details.

The following techniques will be used to minimize pain and discomfort to the animals:

Anesthetics are given prior to surgery.

B. The Principal Investigator provides assurance that he or she is familiar with the animal care and use requirements of the Public Health Service (National Institutes of Health *Guide for Grants and Contracts*, 143[8], June 25, 1985, or the PHS *Guide for the Care and Use of Laboratory Animals*), the Code of Federal Regulations (Title 9), and Davidson College policies for animal care and use, and that this investigation will be conducted in accordance with those guidelines and regulations.

C. The Principal Investigator certifies that he or she is qualified to conduct or direct the animal research outlined in this protocol and accepts responsibility for maintaining standards of animal care required by the Animal Welfare Act.

_____   _____
Signature of Principal Investigator   Date

_____   _____
Signature of Department Chair   Date

_____   _____
Signature of IACUC Chair   Date
Date of full approval: _____
Date of approval termination: _____
Date of addendum approval(s): _____
Date of audit: _____
Deficiencies: _____ Yes _____ No

SAMPLE PROTOCOL 2:

SECTION 1

Title: Methods in Behavioral Neurobiology

Surgery, procedures using live animals, dietary manipulations:

Procedures are limited to those described in section V of the protocol unless prior approval of the IACUC has been obtained. Students will not be required to perform procedures that they find objectionable and refusal to perform such procedures will not result in any penalty. Enrollment procedures will select for students with a need for direct experience in research procedures.

Housing rat pups in the laboratory for greater than 12 hours must be justified and requires specific IACUC approval after site inspection.

During deprivation, it is necessary to maintain pups in containers inside warm, humid incubators. Pups at the ages tested have limited thermoregulatory capacities, and a warm incubator is essential to ensure their comfort and survival. During this deprivation period, pups are kept with their litter-mates but isolated from the mother and left undisturbed until the time of testing. Because the focus of our behavioral studies is an understanding of the controls of ingestive behavior, deprivation of food and water are essential independent variables. Thus, during the deprivation period, the animals are subjects in an experiment. Placing the animals in incubators in the labora-tory allows the experimenter to maintain control over the pups in an en-closed environment that readily permits visual observation during the ex-perimental manipulation, but which isolates from any potential disturbances.

Animals are euthanized by an overdose of CO_2. CO_2 is the method of choice because it is easily administered to young rat pups and causes rapid loss of consciousness with little distress, and it is nontoxic to laboratory per-sonnel. This method is consistent with the recommendations of the Panel on Euthanasia of the American Veterinary Medical Association. Adult ani-mals are picked up by the institutional animal care group for euthanizing.

I. PURPOSE OF THE STUDY

This laboratory course, Methods in Behavioral Neurobiology, is spe-cifically designed to meet the needs of a small number of undergradu-ate science and premedical majors. The enrollment procedures select for students with a need for direct experience and desire for hands-on training in research procedures. The course will be taught by Professor XXX, who has extensive experience and is well qualified (see below). The course attracts undergraduate science majors or premedical stu-dents who wish to obtain practical experience in design and imple-mentation of research experiments in preparation for their careers. The experiments in the course will be conducted in the context of ongoing research by Professor XXX. Students in the course are not required to perform procedures that they find objectionable and refusal to perform such procedures will not result in any penalty.

II. POTENTIAL SCIENTIFIC BENEFITS

This class represents one of the few opportunities offered to under-graduate students by the university to obtain experience in research design and procedures. Under the direct guidance and supervision of Professor XXX, these students will also independently design experi-ments that have not previously been conducted, thereby generating novel and meaningful data for analysis. Procedures for these indepen-dent projects will be limited to those described in section V of this protocol unless specific prior approval of the IACUC has been ob-tained.

III. ALTERNATIVES TO ANIMAL USE

On the basis of information obtained from professional meetings, con-sultation with colleagues, and current literature, the principal investi-gator is aware of no alternatives to the use of live animals in behavioral and neural studies of the development of feeding. Our interest is in the changes in the complex control of mammalian feeding and in identifying the actual origins of these controls in early development. There are no alternatives that successfully mimic the intricate relationships of neurological, physiological, and anatomical growth and development in the growing animal.

IV. SPECIES JUSTIFICATION

Rats are extremely well-suited to this laboratory course for several reasons. The focus of this behavioral neurobiology course will be the understanding of the neural controls of feeding behavior. The experiments that will be carried out in this course will explore the characteristics of a simple ingestive control, oral habituation, in response to a number of physiological manipulations. The majority of previous work in this area has been done in the rat species, specifically in young rat pups. Therefore, opportunities are available to the students for relevant and informative research experience as well as to extend previous knowledge in the study of these behaviors and their neural control. A total of approximately 8 litters of pups and 6 adult Sprague-Dawley CD strain rats will be used during the entire semester.

V.   PROCEDURES

A. *Surgical procedures* in rat pups include implantation of oral and gastric cannulas, implantation of electrodes, and decerebration. Surgical procedures in adult rats include implantation of oral cannulas. See attached IACUC Animal Use Involving Surgical Procedures form.

B. *Nonsurgical procedures.* The experiments of this course are designed to examine the behavioral and neural control of simple ingestive behaviors in rat pups and adults. During behavioral testing, pups are housed in containers inside warm (32° C), humid incubators and adult animals are housed in clear plastic cages. Animals receive brief (3-second) infusions of a saccharin or sucrose solution through indwelling oral cannulas (cannula implantation is described in surgical procedures). During testing, the mouthing behavior of animals will be observed. Individual experiments are designed to examine the specific effects of physiological and pharmacological manipulations on the mouthing responses of adults and pups to these brief oral infusions of sucrose or saccharin. Only one manipulation will be performed on each animal prior to testing. Physiological and pharmacological manipulations to be tested are as follows:

1. Deprivation of food and water for 0, 6, or 24 hours occurs by removing pups from the mother and suckling or by removing food and water from adult rats for 0, 6, or 24 hours. During

deprivation, pups will be housed in containers inside warm, humid incubators; adult rats will be housed in their home cages from which food and water have been removed.

2.   Acute dehydration is produced by a single subcutaneous injection of 2ml NaCl solution (volume of injection = 2% of pup's body weight).

3.   The effects of dopamine Dl and D2 antagonists will be examined using intraperitoneal injections of Raclopride (0-200, ug/kg in a volume of 0.1 ml) or Schering 23390 (0-250, ug/kg in a volume of 0.1 ml).

4.   Gastric fill will be provided by a gastric load of a glucose or sucrose solution delivered through an indwelling gastric cannula (cannula implantation is described in surgical procedures).

5.   The effects of decerebration (decerebration is described in surgical procedures) will be examined in pups with midcollicular transections.

6.   Electrophysiological measurements will be collected from subcutaneous electrodes or electrodes implanted in jaw muscles or nerves (electrode implantation is described in surgical procedures).

C.   Pups will be housed in warm, humid incubators in the laboratory for periods of 6 to 24 hours. This laboratory has been inspected and approved by the IACUC according to PHS Policy on 12/2/92.

D.   No hazardous substances will be administered.

E.   No specimens will be collected from live animals.

F.   Carcasses are frozen and picked up for disposal by DLAR.

G.   Alternatives to painful procedures. N/A.

VI.   PAIN CONTROL DURING NONSURGICAL PROCEDURES. Not expected.

During testing, pups will be housed in plastic containers inside warm, humid incubators so that the pups' behavior may be observed for periods of 30 minutes to 1 hour.

VII.   QUALIFICATIONS/EXPERIENCE

Professor XXX, the principal investigator on this project, has worked with rats since beginning his research career in 19XX. Professor XXX studied at YYY where he learned many of the general experimental techniques and procedures used in these studies. He frequently visits other labs to observe and learn new techniques. He has maintained a breeding colony room in his laboratory since coming to ZZZ in 19XX. Dr. AAA, DVM, has been working with rats since 1986. Prior to that, she was a practicing small animal clinician for 10 years. Dr. AAA is responsible for the general operation of the animal colony, directing breeding and attending to animal health matters, and provides instruction and supervision in lab animal care.

SURGICAL PROCEDURES

A. Oral and gastric cannulas of PE-10 tubing are installed in pups using a fine wire guide while the animal is under CO_2 or methoxyflurane anesthesia.

B. Oral cannulas of PE-50 tubing are installed in adults using a 23-gauge syringe tubing guide. The open end of the tubing is run dorsally subcutaneously to exit through the top of the neck where it is anchored in place with sutures and marlex mesh while the animal is under Ketamine and Xylazine anesthesia. Atropine is administered preoperatively.

C. To install electrodes, a skin incision along the ventral surface of the jaw while the pup is under methoxyflurane anesthesia. Bipolar, fine wire electrodes are inserted into various jaw muscles or nerves, and the incision is closed with a surgical adhesive.

D. Decerebrations in pups are performed under methoxyflurane anesthesia. Through a small skin incision on the dorsal surface of the cranium, two adjacent burr holes are drilled through the skull. Through this opening, decerebrations are performed with a microknife. The incision is closed with liquid surgical adhesive.

Postoperative pain or distress: None anticipated.

APPENDIX K: SAMPLE HIGH SCHOOL RELEASE/PARENTAL PERMISSION FORM

WALT WHITMAN HIGH SCHOOL
7100 WHITTIER BLVD.
BETHESDA, MD 20817

———

(301) 320-6600
AP PSYCHOLOGY PROGRAM

RELEASE

For Parent/Guardian:

I understand my son/daughter: _____
will be involved in a Psychology research project. I understand the project involves the use of laboratory animals. I agree to not hold Montgomery County Public Schools or its agents liable for injuries or accidents that may occur.

In the event of an accident, I release an agent of Montgomery County Public Schools to seek medical attention if necessary.

Date of last tetanus shot: _____
Insurance Co.: _____ Policy No. _____
Signed: _____
Please print name: _____

To the Student:

I agree I will care for the animals involved in my experiment by providing adequate food and drink, keeping the cage(s) clean, and performing general laboratory maintenance. When handling animals I will wear a lab coat, protective glasses, and gloves.

Signed: _____
Please print name: _____

APPENDIX L: U.S. GOVERNMENT PRINCIPLES FOR THE UTILIZATION AND CARE OF VERTEBRATE ANIMALS USED IN TESTING, RESEARCH, AND TRAINING

The development of knowledge necessary for the improvement of the health and well-being of humans as well as other animals requires in vivo experimentation with a wide variety of animal species. Whenever U.S. government agencies develop requirements for testing, research, or training procedures involving the use of vertebrate animals, the following principles shall be considered; and whenever these agencies actually perform or sponsor such procedures, the responsible institutional official shall ensure that these principles are adhered to:

I.   The transportation, care, and use of animals should be in accordance with the Animal Welfare Act (7 U.S.C. 2131 et. seq.) and other applicable federal laws, guidelines, and policies.[1]

II. Procedures involving animals should be designed and performed with due consideration of their relevance to human or animal health, the advancement of knowledge, or the good of society.

III. The animals selected for a procedure should be of an appropriate species and quality, and the minimum number required to obtain valid results. Methods such as mathematical models, computer simulation, and in vitro biological systems should be considered.

IV. Proper use of animals, including the avoidance or minimization of discomfort, distress, and pain when consistent with sound scientific practices, is imperative. Unless the contrary is established, investigators should consider that procedures that cause pain or distress in human beings may cause pain or distress in other animals.

V.   Procedures with animals that may cause more than momentary or slight pain or distress should be performed with appropriate sedation, analgesia, or anesthesia. Surgical or other painful procedures should not be performed on unanesthetized animals paralyzed by chemical agents.

VI. Animals that would otherwise suffer severe or chronic pain or distress that cannot be relieved should be painlessly killed at the end of the procedure or, if appropriate, during the procedure.

---

[1]For guidance throughout these Principles, refer to the *Guide for the Care and Use of Laboratory Animals* (Institute of Laboratory Animal Resources, National Research Council, 1996).

VII. The living conditions of animals should be appropriate for their species and contribute to their health and comfort. Normally, the housing, feeding, and care of all animals used for biomedical purposes must be directed by a veterinarian or other scientist trained and experienced in the proper care, handling, and use of the species being maintained or studied. In any case, veterinary care shall be provided as indicated.

VIII. Investigators and other personnel shall be appropriately qualified and experienced for conducting procedures on living animals. Adequate arrangements shall be made for their in-service training, including the proper and humane care and use of laboratory animals.

IX. Where exceptions are required in relation to the provisions of these Principles, the decisions should not rest with the investigators directly concerned but should be made, with due regard to Principle II, by an appropriate review group such as an institutional animal care and use committee. Such exceptions should not be made solely for the purposes of teaching or demonstration.

APPENDIX M: OTHER RESOURCES FOR RESEARCH INVOLVING LABORATORY ANIMALS

I. Selected Organizations

American Association for Laboratory Animal Science (AALAS) is a professional, nonprofit organization engaged in the dissemination of knowledge about the responsible care and use of laboratory animals for the benefit of human and animal health. AALAS sponsors an annual meeting at which original papers are presented and workshops and seminars on laboratory animal science are held. AALAS also conducts certification programs for laboratory animal technicians. Documents and catalogs may be obtained using an automated Fax response system, Fax on Demand (FOD), by calling (901) 754-2546. For more information contact AALAS:

> **American Association for Laboratory Animal Science**
> 9190 Crestwyn Hills Drive
> Memphis, TN 38125
> Tel.: (901) 754-8620
> Fax: (901) 753-0046
> E-mail: info@aalas.org
> URL: http//www.aalas.org

American College of Laboratory Animal Medicine (ACLAM) is an organization of veterinary specialists in laboratory animal medicine. It is also a good source for position statements on laboratory animal issues.

> **American College of Laboratory Animal Medicine**
> Dr. Melvin Balk
> Executive Director
> 96 Chester Street
> Chester, NH 03036
> Tel.: (603) 887-2467
> Fax: (603) 887-0096
> E-mail: mwbaclam@gsinet.net
> URL: http://www.aclam.org

American Society of Laboratory Animal Practitioners (ASLAP) provides education and training in laboratory animal medicine. It is also a good source for small organizations to identify veterinarians with an interest in laboratory animals.

> **American Society of Laboratory Animal Practitioners**
> ASLAP Coordinator
> 11300 Rockville Pike
> Suite 1211

Rockville, MD 20852
Tel.: (301) 231-6349
Fax: (301) 231-6071
E-mail: aslap@aaalac.org
URL: http://www.aslap.org

Association for Assessment and Accreditation of Laboratory Animal Care, International (AAALAC) is a private nonprofit organization that promotes high-quality and humane animal care and use in research and education, through a voluntary accreditation program. Any institution, private or public, that is engaged in research using animals is eligible to apply for AAALAC accreditation. Accreditation by AAALAC is viewed as proof that the institution's animal care facilities are in compliance of federal codes applicable to animal research.

> **Association for the Assessment and Accreditation of Laboratory Animal Care International**
> 11300 Rockville Pike
> Suite 1211
> Rockville, MD 20852-3035
> Tel.: (301) 231-5353
> Fax: (301) 231-8282
> E-mail: accredit@aaalac.org
> URL: http://www.aaalac.org/

Animal Welfare Information Center (AWIC) was established by congressional mandate and provides a variety of information related to animal welfare issues. Included are Quick Bibliographies, which are frequently updated; Special Reference Briefs; Annotated Bibliographies; Fact Sheets; and many miscellaneous items such as information on animal welfare legislation. Contact AWIC at the following address for a complete list of available documents:

> **Animal Welfare Information Center**
> National Agricultural Library
> 10301 Baltimore Avenue, 4th Floor
> Beltsville, MD 20705-2351
> Tel.: (301) 504-6212
> Fax: (301) 504-7125
> E-mail: awic@nal.usda.gov
> URL: http://www.nalusda.gov/awic

Foundation for Biomedical Research (FBR) has available (for a nominal charge) brochures, posters, videos, and monographs on the use of animals in biomedical research. Contact FBR:

> **Foundation for Biomedical Research**
> 818 Connecticut Avenue, NW
> Suite 200
> Washington, DC 20006

Tel.: (202) 457-0654
Fax: (202) 457-0659
E-mail: info@fbresearch.org
URL: http://www.fbresearch.org

Institute of Laboratory Animal Resources (ILAR) develops guidelines and disseminates information on the humane care and use of laboratory animals and also provides information on the use of alternatives to the use of animals in research. A number of publications developed by ILAR are available either free of charge or for a nominal charge. Contact ILAR:

Institute of Laboratory Animal Resources
The Keck Center of The National Academies
500 Fifth St., NW
Washington, DC 20001
Tel.: (202) 334-2590
Fax: (202) 334-1687
E-mail: ilar@nas.edu
URL: http://dels.nas.edu/ilar

Office of Laboratory Animal Welfare (OLAW) has available copies of federal and state laws and regulations as well as other well-accepted codes and regulations regarding animal research. For more information, call or write to the address here:

Office of Laboratory Animal Welfare
National Institutes of Health
RKL1; Suite 360, MSC 7982
6705 Rockledge Drive
Bethesda, MD 20892-7982
Tel.: (301) 496-7163
Fax: (301) 402-2803
E-mail: OLAW@od.nih.gov
URL: http://www.nih.gov/grants/OLAW/OLAW.htm

Scientists Center for Animal Welfare (SCAW) publishes a variety of information related to animal welfare, such as well-being of agricultural animals, rodents, and nonhuman primates used in research. SCAW also organizes conferences on issues dealing with the care and humane treatment of animals in research.

Scientists Center for Animal Welfare
7833 Walker Drive, Suite 410
Greenbelt, MD 20770-3229
Tel.: (301) 345-3500
Fax: (301) 345-3503
E-mail: info@scaw.com
URL: http://www.scaw.com

U.S. Department of Agriculture (USDA), Animal and Plant Health Inspection Service (APHIS), Regulatory Enforcement of Animal Care

(REAC). One of the missions of the USDA-APHIS is the establishment of acceptable standards of humane care and treatment of animals used in research, exhibition, and the wholesale pet trade. APHIS also administers the Animal Welfare Act and monitors compliance with the act through regular inspections and educational efforts. Copies of various regulatory codes as well as the Animal Welfare Act and Animal Care Regulations may be obtained from the USDA-APHIS:

> **USDA/APHIS/Animal Care**
> 4700 River Road
> Unit 84
> Riverdale, MD 20737-1232
> Tel.: (301) 734-7833
> Fax: (301) 734-4978
> E-mail: ace@aphis.usda.gov
> URL: http://www.aphis.usda.gov/ac/

II. Associations

In addition to the previously mentioned organizations, many professional and scientific associations have information on the use of animals in research. These organizations include the following:

> **Association of American Medical Colleges (AAMC)**
> Division of Biomedical & Health Sciences Research
> 2450 N Street, NW
> Washington, DC 20037-1126
> Tel.: (202) 828-0400
> Fax: (202) 828-1125
> E-mail: webmaster@aamc.org
> URL: http://www.aamc.org/
> **Americans for Medical Progress Educational Foundation (AMPEF)**
> 908 King Street, Suite 301
> Alexandria, VA 22314-3121
> Tel.: (703) 836-9595
> Fax: (703) 836-9594
> E-mail: info@amprogress.org
> URL: http://www.ampef.org
> **American Psychological Association (APA)**
> Science Directorate
> 750 First Street, NE
> Washington, DC 20002-4242
> Tel.: (202) 336-6000
> Fax: (202) 336-5953
> E-mail: science@apa.org
> URL: http://www.apa.org/science

American Veterinary Medical Association (AVMA)
1931 North Meacham Road, Suite 100
Schaumburg, IL 60173-4360
Tel.: (847) 925-8070
Fax: (847) 925-1329
E-mail: AVMAINFO@avma.org
URL: http://www.avma.org
Association for Research in Vision and Ophthalmology (ARVO)
12300 Twinbrook Parkway, Suite 250
Rockville, MD 20852-1606
Tel.: (240) 221-2900
Fax: (240) 221-0370
URL: http://www.arvo.org
California Biomedical Research Association (CBRA)
1008 Tenth Street, Suite 328
Sacramento, CA 95814
Tel.: (916) 558-1515
Fax: (916) 558-1523
E-mail: info@ca-biomed.org
URL: http://www.ca-biomed.org
incurably ill For Animal Research (iiFAR)
P. O. Box 27454
Lansing, MI 48909
Tel.: (517) 887-1141
Fax: (517) 887-1710
E-mail: info@iifar.org
URL: http://www.iifar.org
Massachusetts Society for Medical Research (MSMR)
73 Princeton Street, Suite 311
North Chelmsford, MA 01863
Tel.: (978) 251-1556
Fax: (978) 251-7683
E-mail: msmr@att.net
URL: http://www.msmr.org/
National Association for Biomedical Research (NABR)
818 Connecticut Avenue, NW
Suite 200
Washington, DC 20006
Tel.: (202) 857-0540
Fax: (202) 659-1902
E-mail: info@nabr.org
URL: http://www.nabr.org
Society for Neuroscience (SFN)
11 Dupont Circle, NW

Suite 500
Washington, DC 20036
Tel.: (202) 462-6688
Fax: (202) 462-9740
E-mail: info@sfn.org
URL: http://www.sfn.org
Society of Toxicology (SOT)
1821 Michael Faraday Drive
Suite 300
Reston, VA 20190
Tel.: (703) 438-3115
Fax: (703) 438-3113
E-mail: sothq@toxicology.org
URL: http://www.toxicology.org

III. Selected Regulations and Guidelines

Animal Welfare Laws, Regulations, and Guidelines

Animal Behavior Society. (1997). Guidelines for the treatment of animals in behavioural research and teaching. *Animal Behaviour, 53*(1), 229.

Applied Research Ethics National Association Office of Laboratory Animal Research. (2002). *Institutional animal care and use committee guidebook.* Rockville, MD: National Institutes of Health.

Institute of Laboratory Animal Resources, National Research Council. (1996). *Guide for the care and use of laboratory animals* (7th ed.). Washington, DC: National Academies Press.

National Association for Biomedical Research. (1998). *State laws concerning the use of animals in research.* Washington, DC: Author.

National Research Council. (1989). *Principles and guidelines for the use of animals in pre-college education.* Washington, DC: National Academies Press.

National Research Council. (2003). *Guidelines for the care and use of mammals in neuroscience and behavioral research.* Washington, DC: National Academies Press.

U.S. Department of Agriculture. (2001). *Code of Federal Regulations (CFR), Title 9 (Animals and Animal products), Subchapter A (Animal Welfare).* Washington, DC: U.S. Government Printing Office.

U.S. Department of Health and Human Services. (1996). *Public Health Services Policy on Humane Use and Care of Laboratory Animals.* Washington, DC: Author.

Professional Guidelines for Use of Animals in Research

ABS Animal Care Guidelines
Animal Behavior Society
2611 East 10th Street, #170

Indiana University
Bloomington, IN 47408-2603,
Tel.: (812) 856-5541
Fax: (812) 856-5542
E-mail: aboffice@indiana.edu
http://www.animalbehavior.org/ABS/Handbook/abspolicy99.html#treatment

Ethical Guidelines for Investigations of Experimental Pain in Conscious Animals
International Association for the Study of Pain
909 NE 43rd Street, Suite 306
Seattle, WA 98105-6020
Tel.: (206) 547-6409
Fax: (206) 547-1703
E-mail: iaspdesk@juno.com
URL: http://www.iasp-pain.org

Guidelines for Ethical Conduct in the Care and Use of Animals

Guidelines for the Use of Animals in Behavioral Projects in Schools (K–12)
American Psychological Association
Science Directorate
750 First Street, NE
Washington, DC 20002-4242
Tel.: (202) 336-6000
Fax: (202) 336-5953
E-mail: science@apa.org
URL: http//www.apa.org/science/anguide.html
http://www.apa.org/science/AniResbro03.pdf

Guidelines for the Use of Animals in Neuroscience Research
Society for Neuroscience
11 Dupont Circle, NW
Suite 500
Washington, DC 20036
Tel.: (202) 462-6688
E-mail: info@sfn.org
URL: http://web.sfn.org/content/Publications/HandbookfortheUseof
AnimalsinNeuroscienceResearch/Policy.htm

Guiding Principles in the Care and Use of Animals
The American Physiological Society
9650 Rockville Pike
Bethesda, MD 20814
Tel.: (301) 634-7164
Fax: (301) 634-7241
E-mail: webmaster@the-aps.org
URL: http://www.the-aps.org/pa/humane/pa%5faps%5fguiding.htm

International Guiding Principles for Biomedical Research Involving Animals

World Health Organization
Avenue Appia 20
CH-1211 Genève 27
Switzerland
Tel.: 41-22-791 34 06
Fax: 41-22-791 07 46
E-mail: cioms@who.int
URL: http://www.cioms.ch/frame_1985_texts_of_guidelines.htm

Principles for Use of Animals in Research
Dr. Nellie Laughlin
Historian, International Society for Developmental Psychobiology
Harlow Center for Biological Psychology
University of Wisconsin—Madison
Madison, WI 53715
Tel.: (608) 263-3553
Fax: (608) 262-6020
E-mail: nklaughl@wisc.edu
URL: http://www.oswego.edu/isdp/Subject%20Protection.htm

Professional Guidelines: Education

The Use of Animals in Biology Education
National Association of Biology Teachers
12030 Sunrise Valley, Suite 110
Reston, VA 20191
Tel.: (703) 264-9696 or (800) 406-0775
Fax: (703) 435-5582
E-mail: education@nabt.org
URL: http://www.nabt.org/sub/position_statements/animals.asp

NSTA Guidelines for Responsible Use of Animals in the Classroom
National Science Teachers Association
1840 Wilson Boulevard
Arlington, VA 22201-3000
Tel.: (703) 243-7100
Fax: (703) 243-7177
E-mail: handbook@nsta.org
URL: http://www.nsta.org/positionstatement&psid=2

Principles and Guidelines for the Use of Animals in Precollege Education
Institute of Laboratory Animal Research
The Keck Center of The National Academies
500 Fifth Street, NW
Washington, DC 20001
Tel.: (202) 334-2590
Fax: (202) 334-1687
E-mail: ilar@nas.edu

URL: http://dels.nas.edu/ilar/prin_guide.asp

IV. Alternatives to the Use of Animals in Research and Education

Alternatives to Animal Use in Research, Testing, and Education
Office of Technology Assessment
Superintendent of Documents
P.O. Box 371954
Pittsburgh, PA 15250-7974
Tel.: (202) 512-1800
Fax: (202) 512-2250
E-mail: ota@princeton.edu
URL: http://www.wws.princeton.edu/~ota/ns20/alpha_f.html
For a list of software programs that may possibly augment the use of live animals in classrooms, see the following:
Stoloff, M. L., & Couch, J. V. (1992). *Computer use in psychology: A directory of software* (3rd ed.). Washington, DC: American Psychological Association.

Information Resources for Animal Alternatives: Bibliographies, Education, Recommended Journals, and Training Materials on Animal Care and Handling
Center for Alternatives to Animal Testing (CAAT)
Johns Hopkins University, School of Public Health
111 Market Place, Suite 840
Baltimore, MD 21202-6709
Tel.: (410) 223-1692
Fax: (410) 223-1603
E-mail: caat@jhsph.edu
URL: http://caat.jhsph.edu

University of California Center for Animal Alternatives
School of Veterinary Medicine
University of California, Davis
Davis, CA 95616-8684
Tel.: (530) 757-8448
E-mail: animalalternatives@ucdavis.edu
URL: http://www.vetmed.ucdavis.edu/Animal_Alternatives/main.htm
Educational Program in Ethics and Value in Veterinary Medicine (Includes Animal Research Ethics Issues)
Center for Animals and Public Policy
Tufts University
School of Veterinary Medicine
200 Westboro Road
North Grafton, MA 01536
URL: http://www.tufts.edu/vet/cfa/

V. Educational Materials

Animals in Education and Science Information Materials
　Foundation for Biomedical Research
　818 Connecticut Avenue, NW
　Suite 200
　Washington, DC 20006
　Tel.: (202) 457-0654
　Fax: (202) 457-0659
　E-mail: info@fbresearch.org
　URL: http://www.fbresearch.org
CARE Video Series—Importance of Lab Animal Research in Psychology
Segment 1: Perception & Action; Segment 2: Psychopharmacology
American Psychological Association
Order Department
750 First Street, NE
Washington, DC 2002-4242
Tel.: 1-800-374-2721
Fax: (202) 336-5502
E-mail: order@apa.org
URL: http://www.apa.org/books

VI. Selected Bibliography

Laboratory Animal Welfare

Allen, T., & Clingerman, K. (1992). *Animal care and use committees* (Special Reference Briefs: 92-16; Updates SRB 90-06). Beltsville, MD: Animal Welfare Information Center, National Agricultural Library.

Bennett, B. J., Brown, M. J., & Schofield, J. C. (Eds.). (1990). *Essentials for animal research: A primer for research personnel.* Beltsville, MD: National Agriculture Library. (Also available at http://www.uiowa.edu/~vpr/research/animal/ess_idex.htm).

Committee on Educational Programs in Laboratory Animal Science, Institute of Laboratory Animal Resources Commission on Life Sciences, National Research Council. (1991). *Education and training in the care and use of laboratory animals: A guide for developing institutional programs.* Washington, DC: National Academies Press.

Committee on the Use of Animals in Biomedical and Behavioral Research, Commission on Life Sciences, National Research Council and Institute of Medicine. (1988). *Use of laboratory animals in biomedical and behavioral research.* Washington, DC: National Academies Press.

Demarest, J. (1989). The impact of federal regulations on science and education in small colleges. In J. W. Driscoll (Ed.), *Animal care and use in behavioral research: Regulations, issues, and applications* (pp. 30–36).

Beltsville, MD: Animal Welfare Information Center, National Agricultural Library.

Driscoll, J. W., & Rambo T. C. (1989). Forming an IACUC at a small institution. In J. W. Driscoll (Ed.), *Animal care and use in behavioral research: Regulations, issues, and applications* (pp. 23–28). Beltsville, MD: Animal Welfare Information Center, National Agricultural Library.

Mench, J. A. (1989). Institutional Animal Care and Use Committees: Making them responsible and responsive. In J. W. Driscoll (Ed.), *Animal care and use in behavioral research: Regulations, issues, and applications* (pp. 15–22). Beltsville, MD: Animal Welfare Information Center, National Agricultural Library.

Stephens, M. L. (1989). Oversight of the care and use of animals in animal behavior research in the United States. In J. W. Driscoll (Ed.), *Animal care and use in behavioral research: Regulations, issues, and applications* (pp. 2–8). Beltsville, MD: Animal Welfare Information Center, National Agricultural Library.

Animal Research Ethics

Caplan, A. L. (1978). Rights, language and the ethical treatment of animals. In L. McCullough & J. P. Morris (Eds.), *Implications of history and ethics to medicine—Veterinary and human* (pp. 126–135). College Station: Texas A & M University Press.

Caplan, A. L. (1983). Beastly conduct: Ethical issues in animal experimentation. In J. A. Sechzer (Ed.), *Annals of the New York Academy of Sciences: Vol. 406. The role of animals in biomedical research* (pp. 159–169). New York: New York Academy of Sciences.

Cohen, C. (1986). The case for the use of animals in biomedical research. *New England Journal of Medicine, 315,* 865–870.

Cooper, T., & Stucki, J. C. (1983). Commentary on "Animal research—For and against: A philosophical, social and historical perspective." *Perspectives in Biological Medicine, 27,* 18–21.

Dawkins, M. (1980). *Animal suffering.* New York: Chapman Hall.

Diamond, C. (1981). Experimenting on animals: A problem in ethics. In D. Sperlinger (Ed.), *Animals in research* (pp. 337–362). New York: Wiley.

Fraser, A. (1975). Ethology and ethics. *Applied Animal Ethology, 1,* 211–212.

Glenn, S. S. (1986). On Rollin: Rational ethics? *American Psychologist, 41,* 841–842.

Hodos, W. (1983). Animal welfare considerations in neuroscience research. In J. A. Sechzer (Ed.), *Annals of the New York Academy of Sciences: Vol. 406. The role of animals in biomedical research* (pp. 119–127). New York: New York Academy of Sciences.

Hoff, C. (1980). Immoral and moral uses of animals. *New England Journal of Medicine, 302,* 115–118.

Lansdell, H. (1986). Rollin's article may condone immorality. *American Psychologist, 41*, 842–843.

Midgley, M. (1981). Why knowledge matters. In D. Sperlinger (Ed.), *Animals in research* (pp. 319–336). New York: Wiley.

Miller, N. E. (1985). The value of behavioral research on animals. *American Psychologist, 40*, 423–440.

Moriarty, D. D., & Allen, J. L. (1986). Researcher responsibilities, not animal rights: A comment on Rollin. *American Psychologist, 41*, 842.

Moss, T. H. (1984). The modern politics of animal use. *Bioscience, 34*, 621–626.

Orlans, F. B. (1993). *In the name of science: Issues in responsible animal experimentation.* New York: Oxford University Press.

Petrinovich, L. F. (1999). *Darwinian dominion: Animal welfare and human interests.* Cambridge, MA: MIT Press.

Philip, R. B. (1986). Comment on Rollin. *American Psychologist, 41*, 841.

Porter, D. (1992). Ethical scores for animal procedures. *Nature, 356*, 101–102.

Rollin, B. E. (1981). *Animal rights and human morality.* Buffalo, NY: Prometheus Books.

Rollin, B. E. (1985). The moral status of research animals in psychology. *American Psychologist, 40*, 920–926.

Rollin, B. E. (1986). Reply to Lansdell. *American Psychologist, 41*, 843.

Rollin, B. E., & Kesel, M. L. (Eds.). (1990). *The experimental animal in biomedical research: Vol. I. A survey of scientific and ethical issues for investigators.* Boca Raton, FL: CRC Press.

Rowan, A. N. (1984). *Of mice, models, and men: A critical evaluation of animal research.* Albany, NY: SUNY Press.

Rowan, A. N., & Rollin, B. E. (1983). Animal research—for and against: A philosophical, social, and historical perspective. *Perspectives in Biological Medicine, 27*, 1–17.

Rudacille, D. (2000). *The scalpel and the butterfly: A war between animal research and animal protection.* New York: Farrar, Straus & Giroux.

Russel, J. C., & Secord, D. C. (1985). Holy dogs and the laboratory: Some Canadian experiences with animal research. *Perspectives in Biological Medicine, 28*, 374–381.

Sechzer, J. A. (1983). The ethical dilemma of some classical animal experiments. In J. A. Sechzer (Ed.), *Annals of the New York Academy of Sciences: Vol. 406. The role of animals in biomedical research*, (pp. 5–12). New York: New York Academy of Sciences.

Short, R. V. (1986). Primate ethics. In K. Benirschke (Ed.), *Primates: The road to self-sustaining populations* (pp. 1–13). New York: Springer Verlag.

Smith, J. A., & Boyd, K. (Eds.). (1991). *Lives in the balance: The ethics of using animals in biomedical research.* London: Oxford University Press.

Sperlinger, D. (1981). Natural relations: Contemporary views of the relationship between humans and other animals. In D. Sperlinger (Ed.), *Animals in research* (pp. 79–104). New York: Wiley.

Uvarov, O. (1984). Research with animals: Requirement, responsibility, welfare. *Laboratory Animals, 19,* 51–75.

Visscher, M. B. (1975). *Ethical constraints and imperatives in medical research.* Springfield, IL: Charles C Thomas.

Wall, P. D. (Ed.). (1982). Editor's note to readers and authors on the ethics of animal experiments. *Pain, 12,* 199.

White, R. J. (1971). Anti-vivisection: The reluctant hydra. *American Scholar, 40,* 503–507.

Animal Research in Psychology

Anderson, B. (1994). Role for animal research in the investigation of human mental retardation. *American Journal on Mental Retardation, 99*(1), 50–59.

Bannister, D. (1981). The fallacy of animal experimentation in psychology. In D. Sperlinger (Ed.), *Animals in research* (pp. 307–318). New York: Wiley.

Becker, H. C., Randall, C. L., Salo, A. L., Saulnier, J. L., & Weathersby, R. T. (1994). Animal research: Charting the course for FAS. *Alcohol Health & Research World, 18*(1), 10–16.

Bowd, A. D. (1980). Ethical reservations about psychological research with animals. *Psychological Records, 30,* 201–210.

Branch, M. N., & Hackenberg, T. D. (1998). Humans are animals too: Connecting animal research to human behavior and cognition. In W. T. O'Donohue, (Ed.), *Learning and behavior therapy* (pp. 15–35). Boston: Allyn & Bacon.

Burghardt, G. M. (1985). Animal awareness: Current perceptions and historical perspective. *American Psychologist, 40,* 905–919.

Carroll, M. E., & Overmier, J. B. (Eds.). (2001). *Animal research and human health: Advancing human welfare through behavioral science.* Washington, DC: American Psychological Association.

Domjan, M., & Purdy, J. E. (1995). Animal research in psychology: More than meets the eye of the general psychology student. *American Psychologist, 50,* 496–503.

Domjan, M., & Purdy, J. E. (1996). Teaching about animal research in psychology. *American Psychologist, 51,* 736–737.

Domjan, M., & Purdy, J. E. (1996). Teaching about animal research in psychology: Erratum. *American Psychologist, 51,* 979–980.

Gallup, G. G., & Suarez, S. D. (1980). On the use of animals in psychological research. *Psychological Records, 30,* 211–218.

Haug, M., & Whalen, R. E. (Eds.). (1999). *Animal models of human emotion and cognition.* Washington, DC: American Psychological Association.

Keehn, J. D. (1977). In defense of experiments with animals. *Bulletin of the British Psychological Society, 30,* 404–405.

King, F. A. (1984). Animals in research: The case for experimentation. *Psychology Today, 18,* 56–58.

McMimm, M. R., Beins, B. C., Rosnow, R. L., Strohmetz, D. B., Skleder, A. A., Kallgren, C. A., et al. (1999). Teaching ethics. In M. E. Ware & C. L. Brewer (Eds.), *Handbook for teaching statistics and research methods* (2nd ed., pp. 132–153). Mahwah, NJ: Erlbaum.

National Institute of Mental Health. (2002). Methods and welfare considerations in behavioral research with animals. In A. R. Morrison, H. L. Evans, N. A. Ator, & R. K. Nakamura (Eds.), *Report of a National Institutes of Health workshop.* (NIH Publication No. 02-5083). Washington, DC: U.S. Government Printing Office.

Sevcik, R. A., & Romski, M. A. (1995). Additional support for the role of animal research in the study of human mental retardation. *American Journal on Mental Retardation, 100*(1), 95–97.

Alternatives to the Use of Animals in Research and Education

Russell, W. M. S., & Burch, R. L. (1996). *The principles of humane experimental technique.* Hertfordshire, England: Universities Federation for Animal Welfare.

Zurlo, J., Rudacile, D., & Goldberg, A. M. (1994). *Animals and alternatives in testing: History, science and ethics.* New York: Mary Ann Liebert Publishers.

Zurlo, J., Rudacile, D., & Goldberg, A. M. (1996). The three Rs: The way forward. *Environmental Health Perspectives, 108,* 878.

INDEX

ARVO (Association for Research in Vision and Ophthalmology), 247
ASEE. *See* American Society for Engineering Education
Aseptic techniques, 79
ASLAP. *See* American Society of Laboratory Animal Practitioners
Assessment of Student Achievement in Undergraduate Education (CCLI–ASA), 95, 96
Association for Assessment and Accreditation of Laboratory Animal Care, International (AAALAC), 70, 81, 82, 154, 193–195, 244
Association for Psychological and Educational Research in Kansas, 104, 105
Association for Research in Vision and Ophthalmology (ARVO), 247
Association for the Assessment and Accreditation of Laboratory Animal Care International, 244
Association of American Medical Colleges (AAMC), 246
Assurance of Compliance, 165, 171, 187–192
Assured institutions, 44
Attacks by animal activists, 14, 23
Attitudes
    toward animals, 133
    toward research with animals, 10–11
Audiovisuals, 147
Aversive situations, 54
Aversive stimuli, 54, 58–61, 136
AVMA. *See* American Veterinary Medical Association
Avoidance procedures, 60
AWA. *See* Animal Welfare Act
AWIC (U.S. Government Animal Welfare Information Center), 59
AWR. *See* Animal Welfare Regulations

Baboons, 49
Bacterial infections, 78
Bamfield Center for Marine Science, 98
Bartlett, R. Wayne, 148
Baseline performance, 59
Bats, 88
Bedding, 73
"Behavioral Observation" demonstration, 117–118
Behavioral pharmacology, 62, 144
Behavioral research, 43–65
    and animal rights, 13

apparatus used in, 53–54
appetitive stimuli used in, 55–58
aversive stimuli used in, 58–61
contributions of, 25
disposition of animals at end of, 64, 121
and drugs/toxicants, 61–63
educating the public about, 3–4
experimental design of, 46–47
experimental procedures used in, 54–55
and IACUCs, 45
importance of, 19
obstacles to, 4
personnel used in, 51–52
rationale for using animals in, 45
regulations/policy for, 44–45
societal benefits derived from, 149
subjects used in, 47–51
and surgical procedures, 63–64
undergraduate. *See* Undergraduate behavioral research
Behavioral toxicology experiments, 62
Behaviorism, 10
Behavior on a Disk (computer simulation), 148
Bekesy Laboratory of Neurobiology, 92
Bentham, Jeremy, 16
Bihm, Elson M., 148
Biological model concept, 133
Birds, 82
    and AWR, 44
    procurement of, 48
    psychology department use of, 47
    sample protocols for, 197–199
Bite kits, 72
Bites, 72
Bitterman, M. E., 91–92
Bleach, 116
The Box (computer simulation), 148
Brain-behavior interactions, 139

CAAT (Center for Alternatives to Animal Testing), 251
Caffeine, 62
Cage cards, 74
Caged-Bird Club of America, 114–115
Cages/caging, 73
    considerations for, 115
    microisolator, 78
    sanitation of, 74
California Biomedical Research Association (CBRA), 247
Canadian Council on Animal Care, 137
Cannula, 53

Infectious agents, 72

Infectious disease, 177

Information Resources for Animal Alternatives (CAAT), 251

"Inherent value," 17

In-house grants, 120, 126

Initial Review Groups (IRGs), 167

Inspections, 81, 166

Instinct, 182–183

Institute of Laboratory Animal Resources (ILAR), 50, 58, 72, 164, 245, 248

Institutional Administrator's Manual for Laboratory Animal Care and Use (U.S. Department of Health and Human Services), 83

Institutional animal care and use committees (IACUCs)
    and alternative exercises, 138
    and anesthesia training/monitoring, 78–79
    and animal activists, 128
    and animal environment/housing/management, 73
    animal welfare advocates on, 13
    annual reports of, 82
    and attacks by animal activists, 23
    case studies of, 181–185
    educational use of animals approved by, 134
    establishing, 114
    and euthanasia, 64, 136
    and euthanasia training, 79
    and experimental design, 46–47
    faculty on, 22
    for high school programs, 152–154
    and housing of animals, 80
    and laboratories/housing arrangements, 81
    letters for grants approved by, 82
    meetings of, 174
    members of, 172–173
    minutes of, 82
    oversight by, 26
    and painful procedures, 58, 59
    and PHS Policy/USDA regulations, 166–167
    policies/responsibilities of, 70
    and rationale for using animals, 45
    release of animals approved by, 127
    restraints approved by, 54
    review/approval of, 174–176
    role of, 45
    self-regulation by, 164
    semiannual program and facility evaluations of, 82
    SOP manuals required by some, 52
    and species selection, 47
    and student involvement, 20
    and surgical procedures, 79
    terms of service for, 173–174
    and training, 176–177

Institutional policies, 168, 171–177
    and administrative support, 171–172
    and IACUCs, 172–174
    on sample Assurance of Compliance, 187–188
    on training, 176–177
    on veterinary care, 176

Institutional review boards (IRBs), 32–33

Institutional status, 190

Instructional Scientific Equipment Program (ISEP), 89, 90, 92

Instructional use of animals, 135–136

International Association for the Study of Pain, 249

International Guiding Principles for Biomedical Research Involving Animals (World Health Organization), 250

International Journal of Comparative Psychology, 103

International Science and Engineering Fair (ISEF), 151

Internet, 50, 54

Interstate health certificates, 75

Intracranial catheters, 62

Introductory psychology, 140–141

Invertebrate Learning (Charles I. Abramson), 155

Invertebrates, 20, 47, 155, 174

IRBs. *See* Institutional review boards

IRGs (Initial Review Groups), 167

ISEF (International Science and Engineering Fair), 151

ISEP. *See* Instructional Scientific Equipment Program

Isolation, 77

James, William, 113

Journal of Comparative Psychology (JCP), 103–104

Journal of Experimental Psychology (JEP), 102, 103

Journal of Fish Biology, 103

Journal of Psychological Inquiry, 104

ABOUT THE EDITORS

Chana K. Akins, PhD, is an associate professor of psychology at the University of Kentucky. She is also chair of the American Psychological Association Committee on Animal Research and Ethics. She earned her bachelor's and master's degrees from Texas Tech University in the field of animal science in 1987 and 1989, respectively. She later received her doctorate from the University of Texas at Austin in experimental psychology in 1994, where she conducted research on sexual behavior under the tutelage of Dr. Michael Domjan. Dr. Akins's current research interests focus on what motivates drug-taking behavior and on the overlap between risky sexual behavior and drug-taking behavior. Her research has been supported by the National Science Foundation, the National Institute of Mental Health, and the National Institute on Drug Abuse. She has also been honored as a Top Ten Arts and Sciences Teacher and a Great Teacher at the University of Kentucky and for the Commonwealth of Kentucky.

Sangeeta Panicker, PhD, is director of research ethics in the American Psychological Association (APA) Science Directorate. Dr. Panicker earned a bachelor's degree and a master's degree in clinical psychology from the University of Bombay, a master's degree in experimental psychology (psychopharmacology) from the University of Cincinnati, and a doctoral degree in applied experimental psychology (cognitive neuroscience) from the Catholic University of America. Her research experience includes research with both humans and other animals. She has been at the APA Office of Research Ethics for the past eight years focusing on regulatory and ethical issues pertaining to research with humans and laboratory animals.

Christopher L. Cunningham, PhD, is a professor of behavioral neuroscience at the Oregon Health and Science University (OHSU). He also serves as the associate dean for Graduate Studies in the School of Medicine. He has published over 100 scientific papers on animal learning, behavioral pharmacology, and behavioral genetics. His research program is currently focused on behavioral, genetic, and neurobiological processes that are thought to contribute to alcoholism and drug addiction. Dr. Cunningham earned a bachelor's degree from the University of Notre Dame, a master's degree from the University of Iowa, and a doctorate in experimental psychology from the University of Oregon Medical School. After teaching for a year at Indiana University and completing postdoctoral work in Pavlovian conditioning at Yale University, Dr. Cunningham returned to Oregon to assume a faculty position at OHSU. He is a fellow of the American Psychological Association (APA) Divisions 3 (Experimental Psychology) and 28 (Psychopharmacology and Substance Abuse) and previously served as chair of the APA Committee on Animal Research and Ethics. His research is funded by a MERIT award and other research grants from the National Institute on Alcohol Abuse and Alcoholism.